Ten Years of New Labour

Ten Years of New Labour

Edited by

Matt Beech
Lecturer in Politics, University of Hull, UK

and

Simon Lee
Senior Lecturer in Politics, University of Hull, UK

Foreword by Anthony Giddens

palgrave
macmillan

First published 2008 by
PALGRAVE MACMILLAN
Houndmills, Basingstoke, Hampshire RG21 6XS and
175 Fifth Avenue, New York, N.Y. 10010
Companies and representatives throughout the world

PALGRAVE MACMILLAN is the global academic imprint of the Palgrave
Macmillan division of St. Martin's Press, LLC and of Palgrave Macmillan Ltd.
Macmillan® is a registered trademark in the United States, United Kingdom
and other countries. Palgrave is a registered trademark in the European
Union and other countries.

ISBN-13: 978–0–230–57442–7 hardback
ISBN-10: 0–230–57442–4   hardback
ISBN-13: 978–0–230–57443–4 paperback
ISBN-10: 0–230–57443–2   paperback

This book is printed on paper suitable for recycling and made from fully
managed and sustained forest sources. Logging, pulping and manufacturing
processes are expected to conform to the environmental regulations of the
country of origin.

A catalogue record for this book is available from the British Library.

A catalog record for this book is available from the Library of Congress.

10 9 8 7 6 5 4 3 2 1
17 16 15 14 13 12 11 10 09 08

Printed and bound in Great Britain by
CPI Antony Rowe Ltd, Chippenham and Eastbourne

Contents

Notes on Contributors

Matt Beech is Lecturer in Politics and Director of the Centre for British Politics at the University of Hull. He has published widely on New Labour and social democracy. His most recent monograph is *Labour's Thinkers: The Intellectual Roots of Labour from Tawney to Gordon Brown* with Kevin Hickson (2007).

Jim Buller is Lecturer in Politics at the University of York. He has written widely on the subject of Britain's relations with the European Union, including recent articles in the *British Journal of Politics and International Relations*, *West European Politics* and *British Politics*. He is currently completing a book entitled *The International Sources of British Politics*.

Philip Cowley is Professor of Parliamentary Government at the University of Nottingham. He is the author of *The Rebels: How Blair Mislaid His Majority* (2005) and co-editor of *Developments in British Politics* (2006). He also runs the website www.revolts.co.uk.

Stephen Driver is Principal Lecturer in the School of Business & Social Sciences at Roehampton University. He has co-written two studies of New Labour with Luke Martell, *New Labour: Politics after Thatcherism* (1998) and *Blair's Britain* (2002). Stephen completed a second edition of *New Labour* in 2006. Stephen is also the Director of the Social Research Centre at Roehampton, which is currently working with Amnesty International UK on a project on political activism.

Mark Evans is Professor of Politics at the University of York. He is Director of York's MPA and professional training programmes; editor of the international journal *Policy Studies* (since 2003); and Deputy Director of the Post-war Reconstruction and Development Unit. He publishes research in three broad areas: party politics and reform, comparative public administration, and post-war reconstruction and development. His most recent monograph is *Constitution-making and the Labour Party* (2003).

Anthony Giddens [Lord Giddens] is Professor Emeritus at the London School of Economics. He was Director of the London School of Economics from 1997 to 2003 and is a fellow of King's College, University of Cambridge. He is a Fellow of the American Academy of Arts and Sciences. His many books include *Capitalism and Modern Social Theory* (1971), *Beyond Left and Right* (1994) and *The Third Way* (1998). His most recent monograph is *Over to You, Mr. Brown* (2007).

Simon Lee is Senior Lecturer in Politics at the University of Hull. His teaching and research interests are principally in the field of political economy, with a particular emphasis upon the politics of globalization and governance and the political economy and national identity of contemporary England. His most recent monograph is *Best for Britain? The Politics and Legacy of Gordon Brown* (2007).

David Lonsdale is Lecturer in Strategic Studies at the University of Hull. Prior to his current appointment he worked at King's College London, based at the Joint Services Command & Staff College and the University of Reading. His publications include *The Nature of War in the Information Age: Clausewitzian Future* (2004) and *Alexander the Great: Lessons in Strategy* (2007).

Maurice Mullard is Reader in Social and Public Policy at the University of Hull. His research interests include the politics of public expenditure, citizenship, globalization, poverty and the War on Terror. He has written monographs on New Labour and on globalization. His most recent book is an edited volume with B. Cole, *Globalisation, Citizenship and the War on Terror* (2007).

Philip Norton [Lord Norton of Louth] is Professor of Government and Director of the Centre for Legislative Studies at the University of Hull. He is the author or editor of 27 books covering British politics, the constitution, the Conservative Party, parliament and legislatures in comparative perspective. He was elevated to the peerage in 1998. He chaired the Conservative Party's Commission to strengthen parliament and has served as chairman of the House of Lords Select Committee on the Constitution.

Raymond Plant [Lord Plant of Highfield] is Professor of Jurisprudence and Political Philosophy at King's College London and was Master of St Catherine's College, University of Oxford. He was Chairman of the Labour Party Commission on Electoral Reform (the 'Plant Report') and of the Fabian Commission on Taxation and Citizenship. He was awarded the

PSA Lifetime Achievement Award in 2003. He is currently the Vincent Wright Professor at Sciences Po and is writing a book on the Neo-liberal State and the Rule of Law.

Eric Shaw is Senior Lecturer in the Politics Department, University of Stirling. Formerly a Labour Party researcher he has written extensively on Labour, including four books and numerous articles and book chapters. His most recent work is the recently published *Losing Labour's Soul? New Labour and the Blair Government 1997–2007* (2008).

Mark Stuart is a researcher in the School of Politics at the University of Nottingham, where he helps run a long-running project on backbench voting behaviour. He is also a political biographer, having published *John Smith. A Life* (2005) and *Douglas Hurd. The Public Servant* (1998). He writes a regular political column in the *Yorkshire Post*.

Raymond Swaray is Lecturer in Economics at the University of Hull. He is a specialist on international macroeconomics and finance and has written widely on UK public expenditure, primary commodity price movements and the economics of crime and criminal justice. His articles have been published in, amongst others, *The Annals*, *Social Indicators Research*, *Criminal Justice Policy Review*, *Applied Economics* and *Policy and Politics*.

Foreword

Anthony Giddens

Every left of centre party that gets into power is doomed to disappoint – more so, probably, than governments of the right, since the left aspires more definitively to reshape society. It is a phenomenon found around the world in democratic countries. Once into the grind of day to day government, the left's erstwhile supporters will be quick to say that the party lacks direction, or it has betrayed its values, or that its policies are not radical enough, or all three together. The 1945 Attlee government is fondly remembered by many activists as the most radical and accomplished of all Labour regimes. Yet at the time it was vociferously denounced for its timidity and its lack of purpose.

Having deserted the academy for an active involvement in politics, and having witnessed the unfolding of the New Labour story to some extent from the inside, I have a full appreciation (I think) of the pressures and difficulties of political life. As a previous Director of the LSE, I found it hard enough to secure substantial change in a single institution, let alone a whole society. The institution runs you far more than you run it, and the same is true on a much larger stage for any national political leader. Many held quite unrealistic hopes of a new dawn when Labour was elected in 1997. It is a virtue of this volume that most of the contributors take a realistic view of what the party under the leadership of Tony Blair managed to achieve in ten years of government.

I first got involved directly in Labour politics in the early 1990s, partly as a result of just having written a book called *Beyond Left and Right*. At that time it was difficult to get anyone in the Labour hierarchy to take new ideas seriously. I had started writing about globalization, the new economy and the rise of a more reflexive citizenry in the 1980s, but struggled to get a hearing in the political arena. Talk of globalization met with uncomprehending stares, as I remember only too well from several seminars held just after Neil Kinnock's defeat in 1992. Much of this had changed by the time I got involved in Blair–Clinton dialogues that began in 1997 and subsequently became regular events. I talked to many other political leaders around that period. Blair (and Clinton) was far more ready than most others at that point to take on board the thesis that globalization and attendant changes were completely changing the nature of the political field.

As I would see it, the whole point of New Labour – and other forms of social democratic revisionism elsewhere – was (and is) to respond to three linked sets of changes, beginning with globalization. The scope and pace of globalization continues to intensify. For me (and I believe also for Blair) globalization is a concept that stretches far beyond the intensifying of world economic competition, important though that is. It covers many other forms of intensifying interdependence, political and cultural. For example, the rise of new-style terrorism (foreseen in some of the writings of the New Democrats in the US well before 9/11) is an expression of it. New-style terrorism (networked, existing in many countries and geopolitical in its aims) is quite different in scope and aims from the more limited forms of local nationalist terrorism with which we were previously familiar.

In the early 1990s it was still unusual to speak of the emergence of the knowledge economy and many were sceptical. As with globalization the idea has now become part of conventional wisdom. Blair and Brown were convinced early on, and much of Labour's economic and social policy follows from this conviction. The pronounced decline in the role of manufacture in the economy is not solely, or even primarily, the result of the transfer of industry to China and other developing countries; it is mainly the result of technological change, which has sharply reduced the need for labour-power, especially unskilled labour power. The knowledge economy is not just about the increasing numbers of people who work in technical jobs and education. It refers to something much more pervasive: the transformation of work by the introduction of new modes of competition driven by IT. Agriculture, for example, has become as much a part of the new economy as any other sector.

The increasing reflexivity of citizens is the other big change, marked as it is by a proliferation of life-styles, some quite consciously 'chosen', others not. In some part it expresses the rise of consumerism, stimulated in the UK by Mrs Thatcher's policies and by the privatizing of major areas previously within the purview of the state. But in my view consumerism is only one part of the story. The most important source of growing reflexivity is the shrinking role of tradition and custom in structuring our activities. We live increasingly in an information society, where all of us have to make sense, in some way or another, of a swirl of information in deciding how to act. 'Life-style' should not be seen as a consumerist term, but as one reflecting quite profound changes in our everyday lives. Reflexivity preceded the appearance of the internet and other new communications technologies, which give it a more refined and global form.

It is plain that the advent of a more reflexive population requires a new contract between the individual and the state. People become more accustomed to making choices in the various areas of life; at the same time, and as part of the same process, they become more sceptical of authority and less deferential towards pre-established symbols of such authority – an attitude very noticeable in the political field, but certainly not confined to it.

I am not suggesting that Labour's leaders would ever themselves have deployed such arcane terminology as 'reflexivity' (although the financial guru George Soros does). But I do believe they accepted the need to respond to these three sets of influences, and that this acceptance helps one understand much about the New Labour project. New Labour has been widely condemned as all smoke and mirrors, with no real substance, and of course the party did give a great deal of attention to presentation. However, one can't understand much about why Labour managed to win three elections on the trot without recognizing that there was a great deal of ideological transformation – and much effective policy innovation too.

I think this view is shared by those who have written chapters in this book, which provides the reader with an admirable exposition of the core areas of New Labour thinking. I would take the key dimensions of New Labour's policy orientation to be the following. First, as discussed by Matt Beech, a stress on controlling the centre-ground of politics as essential to gaining and holding onto political power. With the decline in manufacture, Labour can never again be a class party in the same sense as it was (or was often seen as being) in the past. It has to appeal to a much broader coalition than once was the case: indeed, it aspires to be a one-nation party, appealing to a large majority. To aim to control the political centre is not at all the same as foregoing radicalism. Rather, the purpose is to shift the political centre to the left – put more grandly, to shift the country decisively in the direction of social democracy. It is an aim, as Maurice Mullard and Raymond Swaray note, that has been in some considerable degree reached. There is a consensus among the political parties today, shared by most of the public, upon effective investment in health-care, education and welfare and that poverty must be tackled in a direct way through government intervention.

Holding the political centre, New Labour's leaders recognized, also means ensuring that all policy areas must be tackled. In other words, no policy fields should be abandoned to the right. This was a position

– like many of the others mentioned above – influenced by the thinking of the American New Democrats. The right has always been strong (or perceived to be so by voters) in areas such as the management of the economy, the protection of the national interest, maintaining law and order and the control of migration. Labour sought to make inroads into traditional Conservative dominance of these areas, with much success, as discussed by several of the contributors. Of course, some of these policies have also been among the most controversial of any that the party has introduced.

Effective economic steering – due far more to Brown than to Blair – was one of the party's strong points throughout the first ten years. Rather than only concentrating upon unemployment, New Labour placed the emphasis upon employment. A healthy economy is one in which there is a high proportion of the labour force in jobs, above a decent minimum wage, the latter introduced early on. As of 2006, nearly 75 per cent of the labour force was in work in the UK, a far higher proportion than, for example, other EU countries, such as Germany, France or Italy. Having large numbers of people in work generates the revenue to invest in public goods. A concentration upon employment is also central to Labour's social policy. Being in work is the single most important factor helping individuals and families out of poverty. Such an emphasis has remained a core element in Labour's attempts to deliver upon one of its most radical endeavours, to reduce child poverty by half by 2010 and 'abolish' it altogether by 2020. (See Stephen Driver, below).

Other prime areas among New Labour's concerns receive full attention in the body of this book – constitutional change and devolution (Mark Evans); Tony Blair's 'presidentialism' (Philip Norton); divisions within the party and the shifting relationship between Labour and the unions (Philip Cowley and Mark Stuart; Eric Shaw); Britain and the EU, Blair's doctrine of liberal interventionism and 'Blair's wars' in Bosnia, Kosovo, Sierra Leone, Afghanistan and Iraq (Jim Buller; Raymond Plant; and David Lonsdale).

I argued at the outset that the business of government is always testing and that therefore one should not exaggerate what it is possible for a left of centre government to achieve. It is far, far easier to stand on the outside and criticize than it is actually to achieve real change. This recognition, however, should not stop us seeking a balanced appraisal. Broadly speaking I have been a supporter of New Labour policies and indeed have often defended them against those who have decried them. However in some ways I feel more critical of New Labour than most of the authors in the chapters that follow.

I would have liked Labour from the beginning to have been more explicitly a social democratic party, concerned with a robust re-establishing of the public purpose. Especially during its early days, Labour drew too much upon the New Democrats in the US, and not enough from avant-garde social democracy, such as practised in the Scandinavian countries. I wrote a book in 1998 called *The Third Way*, which was an attempt to synthesize some of what we discussed in the Blair–Clinton dialogues, but the sub-title was *The Renewal of Social Democracy* and that for me is what the third way always meant. Because New Labour did not develop a coherent defence of public institutions and public goods, it was vulnerable to the accusation that it is merely Thatcherism with a human face. PFI, for example, could have been defended much more effectively if its contribution to the public good had been made its main basis. Thus it is a way of embedding long-term investment for social purposes, and if set up properly can instil an ethic of responsibility among the private companies involved (one should remember that private firms still normally do most or all of the work in orthodox state sector procurement).

Much the same applies to Labour's emphasis upon choice and per-sonalization in areas such as health and schooling – which by and large I strongly support. The point should not be just to echo or extend consumer rights as found in the marketplace. Rather, the object should be to empower citizens as part of a transformed citizenship contract. A citizen is not a consumer writ large. It was only realized late on that consumerism itself needs significant political intervention: unhealthy life-styles, the increase in obesity, the courting of the young by corporate advertizing and the widespread nature of clinical depression have a longish history, but responding to them was not a main part of Labour's original programme.

It is often said that New Labour gave up on redistribution and therefore abandoned a good deal of what the party should in fact stand for. In fact, significant redistribution has occurred since 1997. Over two million people have been lifted out of poverty, a significant achievement by any standards. As a result, the long-term tendency of overall economic inequality to increase has been checked. Yet even given the difficulties facing any government concerned to attack inequality, more could have been done. It isn't possible to reduce inequality by concentrating upon the poor alone, as Labour's policies (at least originally) did. The more affluent and the more privileged will inevitably find ways of keeping ahead. Only in the last while are policies being explored that will curb some of these possibilities, such as changes in the charity laws to ensure that private schools recognize and act upon wider social responsibilities. Although it has never found favour with the government, I have long been a supporter of the scheme pioneered by the philanthropist Peter Lampl. By funding needs-blind admission in a private school, the Belvedere School in Liverpool, he has shown that the social composition of such a school can be widened greatly without any sacrifice in academic performance.

I don't know of anyone working in the field who believes that the government will achieve its 2010 target for reducing child poverty. It is a great pity, since lowering child poverty is the single most direct route to a more egalitarian society. Child poverty is a relative measure. Since almost all children live in families of one sort or another, a swingeing reduction in child poverty would ipso facto substantially reduce overall inequality, other things being equal. Labour has largely left the rich alone – or, as Simon Lee argues forcefully in this volume, has pursued policies that have actively fostered a breakaway of income and wealth at the very top. We have reached a point where this situation not only fosters widespread public resentment, but where it threatens to undermine the very legitimacy of business. In *The Third Way* I proposed that 'social exclusion at the top' has to be countered just as does social exclusion at the bottom. I argued more recently for a hypothecated wealth tax on very high earners to support the campaign against child poverty. Why shouldn't the super-rich be obliged to help the super-poor?

In the same book, I addressed ecological modernization as an issue that should be of fundamental importance to the recasting of social democracy. It is another area where New Labour's performance has been less than satisfactory. I hope the editors won't take offence if I point out that environmental questions should brook much larger in this book than they do. Labour has struggled to develop any sort of integrated transport policy; and greenhouse gas emissions have gone up since 1997. The government pushed for the ratification of Kyoto, but it is in sight of reaching its (modest) targets under that Treaty mainly because of the 'rush for gas' that occurred under Mrs Thatcher. The Climate Change Levy was not well thought-through and under pressure the government backed down on the fuel escalator. Tony Blair gave some excellent speeches on climate change and other environmental issues, but only late on in his tenure. It has been left to his successor to steer through the Climate Change Bill, which is certainly in principle a radical document.

There are plenty of other topics for justified criticism. I agree with Mark Evans when he says that devolution to the nations was largely driven by events, and was not part of a wider vision of what sort of country the UK should become. The 'English problem' – what sort of devolution is appropriate in England? – will be with us for some while to come, even should Scotland at some point break away from the rest of Britain. 'Tough on crime, tough on the causes of crime' – the slogan helped propel Tony Blair to the Labour leadership, but it is an area where Labour has struggled to break away from authoritarian populism.

Finally let me make a few brief comments on some very large subjects: our relations with the rest of the EU, and foreign policy. Tony Blair set out explicitly to integrate Britain more closely within the EU and there are some significant achievements to point to. For instance, Britain played an important part in developing the Lisbon Agenda; and the government successfully supported enlargement and the potential accession in the longer term of Turkey. Yet Blair was unable to make any sort of dent at all in the eurosceptic views held by large numbers of the British public (as Jim Butler points out), which are perhaps even stronger now than they were in 1997. Blair's idea that Britain could be a bridge between the US and the EU strikes me as incoherent – we cannot be a bridge to the EU, because we are a member-state of the EU. His metaphor carries an echo of the view so widespread among the British public, that 'Europe' is somewhere else, on the other side of the Channel.

Blair's decision to opt for a referendum on the EU constitution seems to have been driven in large part by domestic expediency. He may have thought such a vote winnable, especially if Britain were the last in line with all the other member-states having ratified. But he probably also wanted to take the issue of the constitution off the agenda with a general election looming not far down the line. The question has come back to haunt Prime Minister Brown as he struggles to push the EU Reform Treaty through parliament.

And then there is Iraq, the episode that is for many critics the defining feature of the Blair era. How it will all turn out in the medium term obviously remains to be seen. It is just possible that, as David Lonsdale observes, Blair's decision to support the invasion may receive some future vindication. At the time of writing, however, and in spite of the recent reduction in violent incidents in the country, such an outcome looks distinctly unlikely; indeed, there may be large-scale ethnic conflict after whatever point the Americans decide to leave.

So far as British politics is concerned, as Alan Milburn has observed, Blair 'is now history'. Gordon Brown is almost certainly not going to get involved in any new military adventures; he is withdrawing British troops from Iraq, although continues to sustain a British military presence in Afghanistan. He has made it clear that he regards his advent to power as a new beginning, in spite of having played such a prominent part in New

Labour's first ten years. I hope he will address some of the shortcomings I have mentioned. At present, however, he seems some way from having created the new synthesis that I hoped for and indeed anticipated that he would develop.

Introductory Preface

Matt Beech

Purpose of the book

What does this volume contribute to our understanding of New Labour? *Ten Years of New Labour* is a collection of essays from leading thinkers who analyse aspects of New Labour's decade in government under Blair, 1997–2007. The volume's objectives can be outlined as follows. First, it will deepen our insight into the New Labour project under the leadership of Tony Blair. Second, it will be a useful teaching resource for undergraduates and postgraduates studying British politics in general and the Labour Party under Tony Blair in particular. As university lecturers, the editors are aware of the value of books which combine accessibility and scholarship. Such books (see Further Reading) become favourites with students, political commentators and academics alike. This is an aspiration for all projects undertaken and produced by the Centre for British Politics.

Ten Years of New Labour provides an in-depth evaluation of the Labour governments since 1997 and examines their successes and failures after a decade in power. When making judgements about Tony Blair's tenure, one can utilize hindsight and attempt a definitive appraisal. But one cannot employ the same method when judging Gordon Brown. The era is therefore not yet over. Although Gordon Brown is currently Prime Minister, and slight differences of public policy have emerged, the post 2007 period marks a change in leadership and tone rather than a break in contemporary Labour politics. Tony Blair and Gordon Brown are New Labour, and although one has gone the other remains. New Labour lives. This volume is thus well placed to offer immediate reflection on the Blair years. Students, scholars and other individuals interested in the direction and future of the Brown premiership would do well to understand New Labour's origins and the ideological, economic, social and foreign policy inheritance bequeathed.

Represented in this volume of essays are the thoughts and judgements of conservatives, liberals and social democrats. So an interesting distinctive feature of this book is that its contributors hold divergent political beliefs. Moreover, contributors whose political preference lies with the Labour

Party include supporters of the Labour left, the Croslandite right, New Labour sympathizers and those in between. Some might say that such a range of political thought would prevent the volume from being a single, coherent critique of New Labour under Tony Blair. In one sense, they would be correct in their assertion. The book has no single thesis like a monograph. It is a collection of topic-specific essays by some of the foremost political scientists who undertake research on New Labour.

One of the most interesting and significant debates about New Labour concerns their philosophical motivations: do they owe more to British social democracy or neo-liberalism? This debate concerning New Labour's ideological fault-line is, perhaps uniquely, manifest in the opposing views of the volume editors. They are both members of the Centre for British Politics, yet Matt Beech and Simon Lee understand New Labour in contrasting ways. The former thinks that although much change has occurred between New Labour and previous Labour governments, significant ideological continuities remain (Beech, 2006). Simon Lee, however, sees New Labour as the product of a generation dominated by neo-liberalism (Lee, 2007). This debate is evident in the editors' respective chapters and can be detected in other contributions in the volume.

Structure of the book

The chapters in *Ten Years of New Labour* are organized thematically with each one appraising the attitudes, intentions and outcomes of specific New Labour policies. In the opening essay Matt Beech argues that New Labour has constructed a new centre-ground in British politics during Blair's decade in power. He states that much of the New Labour project is based on moderate, centre-left principles and that New Labour's politics is best understood as the politics of dominance: electorally and ideologically. Beech states that New Labour's competitors are having to respond to a Labour government that is the author of the contemporary centre-ground in British politics. New Labour's centre-ground has supplanted the dominant neo-liberal agenda. The Conservatives, in particular, have moved leftwards on traditional Labour issues. This chapter is a contribution to the ongoing debate that tries to explain and understand the ideological motivation of New Labour in government.

Simon Lee's chapter stands in contrast to Beech's. Lee examines New Labour's political economy, which he calls the 'British model of political economy', and expands on what is distinctively British about the model. Lee asserts that as Chancellor, Brown co-authored New Labour's economic policy with his economic adviser Ed Balls. Lee analyses Brown's monetary, fiscal and industrial policies and questions whether his reputation as a successful, prudent Chancellor is justified. Moreover, Lee argues that New Labour's political economy has become inextricably linked with the needs and wants of the City of London and the liberalized financial markets. In short, the thesis advanced in Lee's essay is that New Labour's reputation for sound economic management is a myth and the government's alleged desire for economic radicalism is a mirage.

Maurice Mullard and Raymond Swaray's chapter is a comparative analysis of New Labour's record on public expenditure against that of previous Labour administrations since the Second World War. Using extensive data, Mullard and Swaray evaluate New Labour's record on the major spending areas of defence, education, health, law and order, social security, and trade and industry. The authors contend that New Labour has outspent the Attlee, Wilson and Callaghan governments in every area bar subsidies for housing and nationalized industries. Furthermore, they assert that high levels of public expenditure are a central priority for social democrats and that New Labour's record as a government is better than any previous social democratic administration. However, Mullard and Swaray observe that inequalities in income and wealth have grown significantly in Blair's decade in power and that this is a key difference between New Labour and its Labour predecessors.

Stephen Driver's chapter is a study of New Labour's social policy ideas and reforms. He argues that reform of the welfare state and the adoption of market economics are two of the most distinctive aspects of the New Labour project. From here he evaluates notable policy initiatives including the New Deal, tax credits and the national minimum wage. Driver draws attention to the debates within the Labour Party over controversial legislation such as foundation hospitals, university tuition fees and city academies. For example he states that the Private Finance Initiative, which New Labour keenly utilized to fund the building of many schools and hospitals, was the cause of much backbench consternation. Driver concludes his essay by suggesting that New Labour's investment and social policy reforms have succeeded in improving public services and implementing the social democratic principle of social justice through an 'active' state, but that levels of social mobility during ten years of New Labour have remained stubbornly low.

Mark Evans's chapter appraises the constitutional reform agenda of New Labour. He argues that New Labour's approach can best be understood as a 'New Constitutionalism', but one that is based on pragmatism not idealism. Evans considers New Labour's reforms to the Bank of England, devolution, regional development agencies, elections, parliament, and the Human Rights Act. He states that, due to Blair's reforms, new political communities have emerged in Scotland, Wales, and Northern Ireland, in the English regions and in London. Evans asserts that the pragmatic character of Blair's constitutional reforms brings consequences, such as the 'English Question' and the spectre of Scottish separation from the Union. Evans concludes that an absence of a radical plan for constitutional reform where power is wrestled away from centralizing elites, has left the UK in a state of political asymmetry and rising cultural nationalism.

Philip Norton's chapter considers how Blair used the office of Prime Minister and evaluates the consequences for British government. He examines Blair as a person and observes that in terms of institutions including the Labour Party, parliament and government, Blair is rootless. Norton's central thesis is that Blair's disposition is as an individualist as opposed to an institutionalist and that his actions have led to a growing presidentialism which has undermined the relationship between the institutions of British government. Norton evaluates the impact of Blair's behaviour as Prime Minister in relation to the civil service, cabinet, the judiciary, parliament and the crown. In conclusion, Norton states that Blair's unconventional tenure as Prime Minister has caused tensions within the institutional framework of British government that are unsustainable, and that Brown would do well to rectify the current situation.

Philip Cowley and Mark Stuart's chapter examines the level and nature of backbench rebellions under Blair from 1997 to 2007. From their own data, Cowley and Stuart chart a history of rebellions and discuss the reasons for rebellion, the parliamentary and wider political context of rebellions and the government's response. They state that the Blair governments were open to discussion and persuasion, and were willing to strike deals with backbenchers in the hope of minimizing the size and strength of particular rebellions. The authors argue that contrary to popular belief, Labour backbenchers are independent-minded MPs and that under Blair rebellions became increasingly common. This questions the alleged thesis of party discipline and unity expounded by New Labour in government.

Eric Shaw's chapter evaluates New Labour's relationship with the trade unions. He considers New Labour's record on employment, regulation, pay, individual and collective rights, and the use and effect of PFI. Shaw states that the labour movement is changing and to an extent is disappearing in its traditional form. In particular, the normative aspect of the union–party link – in other words its common values – is dwindling but the relationship remains. Shaw argues that a key characteristic of New Labour is that it views trade unions as legitimate but not intrinsically allied to its political objectives. He sees this contemporary situation as a mutually beneficial relationship from which both the trade unions and the Labour Party can work. The Labour Party needs union funding and the unions want their interests met, but New Labour does not see a collaborative role for unions in government.

Jim Buller's chapter examines New Labour's policy towards the European Union under Blair. Buller argues that New Labour's approach to the EU between 1997 and 2001 was informed by its own political concerns such as signing the Social Chapter and securing a 'wait and see' policy on the single currency, whereas the 2001–07 period was affected largely by external factors including 9/11, American unilateralism and the Iraq war. Buller argues that New Labour have been generally successful in their operation of policy towards the European Union because they kept the issue of the euro from dominating British politics; developed bilateral relationships with 'old' and 'new' Europe; and were lucky to work in a favourable political climate brought about by enlargement. In conclusion, Buller states that although Blair is a committed pro-European, pragmatism meant that he opted for the 'special relationship' with the United States rather than a closer union with his European neighbours.

Raymond Plant's chapter assesses Blair's 'Doctrine of the International Community' that was outlined in his Chicago speech in 1999 and through the ideas of his former Chief of Staff, Jonathan Powell. Plant argues that Blair's liberal interventionism is predicated on similar values as his communitarian politics in the domestic sphere: individual rights and concomitant responsibilities. However, according to Plant the international community does not share a universal commitment to human rights, or at least it does not interpret human rights in a shared fashion. Therefore, interventionism is not always undertaken; it is affected by pragmatism. National interests, military preparedness, the domestic appetite for conflict and the likelihood of success are considerations. Plant argues that nations such as Burma or China would not be forced to comply with a Western human rights agenda. Plant further cites communitarian, conservative and realist philosophical objections to Blair's and Powell's liberal interventionism. He concludes that, as it currently stands, Blair's liberal interventionism appears to be a doctrine of national self-interest coupled with a weak conception of the international community.

David Lonsdale's chapter examines New Labour's defence policy including Kosovo, the 'war on terror', Iraq and the replacement of Trident. Lonsdale's assessment considers Blair's actions through the lens of strategic studies analysis. He focuses on Blair as a political leader confronted with a range of strategic choices in the field of defence policy.

Lonsdale argues that Blair's record on strategy is chequered. According to Lonsdale, operation Desert Fox, post-war planning in Iraq and the UK government's current nuclear doctrine do not denote sophisticated strategic thinking. However, he suggests that Blair's personal qualities such as moral courage and his understanding of the importance of the transatlantic alliance with the United States, aided his role as a strategist whilst occupying the office of Prime Minister. Controversially, Lonsdale concludes that although the Iraq war was unnecessary, it was correct for Blair to stand shoulder to shoulder with Bush to secure the future of the 'special relationship'.

The book concludes with the thoughts of Simon Lee on the legacy of Blair's ten years in power. The chapter examines the prospects and difficulties that face his successor, as he seeks to govern in his own way, albeit from the New Labour perspective. Lee argues that New Labour has not won the battle of ideas even though it has won three successive general elections. He asserts that mainstream British politics is still governed by neo-liberal ideas and values. Even though Blair has gone and Brown remains, Thatcher lives.

The Centre for British Politics

The Centre for British Politics is a research centre that promotes the study of British Politics; in particular, it conducts research on British political parties, their ideologies and their public policy. It was designed to unify the research interests of Philip Norton, Simon Lee, Richard Woodward and Matt Beech, thereby creating a research cluster with a British Politics identity and collaborative ethic in the Department of Politics and International Studies at the University of Hull. The establishment of the Centre for British Politics reinforces the tradition of teaching and research in the area of British Government and Politics that the Department has had for over 30 years. The Centre for British Politics strives to produce internationally renowned research in the form of monographs, edited volumes and articles in peer-reviewed journals. It is represented in this volume by Philip Norton, Simon Lee and Matt Beech.

This book was inspired by discussion at the inaugural symposium of the Centre for British Politics at the University of Hull on 28–29 June 2007. The 'Ten Years of New Labour' symposium evaluated Blair's decade as Prime Minister (incidentally it took place the day after Blair left office) and brought together some of the key thinkers in this area. Leading scholars of New Labour discussed and debated specific topics of New Labour's public policy, ideology and institutional reform. The deliberative nature engendered by the symposium is a format that was highly successful and immensely enjoyable for the Centre for British Politics and will form the basis of forthcoming events and inspire future publications.

Acknowledgements

The Centre for British Politics would like to thank and acknowledge Simon Lee for providing the inspiration for this project and Matt Beech for organizing both this publication and the symposium upon which it is based. The project would not have been possible without the funding provided by the University of Hull's Faculty of Arts and Social Sciences Research Support Fund, for which the editors are extremely grateful. In addition, the Centre would like to thank colleagues in the Department of Politics and International Studies for their help in establishing the Centre in June 2007 and for their continued support.

We have been greatly fortunate to have as contributors a team of first rate scholars who made the 'Ten Years of New Labour' symposium, 28–29 June 2007 at the University of Hull a pleasure to participate in. In particular, we were honoured to have Anthony Giddens deliver the keynote speech of the symposium and write the foreword to this book. Moreover, we are very grateful to Raymond Plant and Philip Norton for giving their time and expertise to the project. We would like to thank the publisher and especially Amy Lankester-Owen and her support staff for their continued enthusiasm for the book and for their advice along the way. The editors would also like to thank Ray Addicott and Oliver Howard of Chase Publishing Services for their help and expertise in the delivery of this project.

Finally, Matt as ever would like to thank his wife Claire for her continued support. Simon's contribution would not have been possible without the love and support of Helen McGarry.

1
New Labour and the Politics of Dominance

Matt Beech

So we've prepared the ground by moving to the centre. We've laid the foundations with our big idea, social responsibility. And now with our Policy Groups set to publish their reports, we can move forward to the next stage – showing what we will build for Britain.

(Cameron, 2007a: 3)

Under my leadership I am challenging our party to be bolder, to be more ambitious and to be more thoughtful. Unlike the Tories we don't have to abandon everything we stand for in order to reinvent ourselves. Unlike Labour, we don't have to shore up a crumbling edifice. There is a great opportunity for the Liberal Democrats. Because we are closest to the heartbeat of the British people.

(Campbell, 2006: 6)

Introduction

In attempting to survey New Labour's period in office one aspect appears to stand out. New Labour's politics has been and continues to be the politics of dominance. As a government they have set the tone for political discourse and have been the victors in many policy debates. The purpose of this chapter is to argue that New Labour in government have dominated British politics and by doing so have recast the centre-ground. Implicit in this argument is the assertion that the centre-ground is not fixed and that since 1997, New Labour has moved the centre-ground leftwards.

Previously the political centre was dominated by tenets of neo-liberalism. In policy terms neo-liberals are suspicious of the state, its power and its ability to distribute efficiently goods and services. Therefore, free market economics is promoted as the mechanism for granting liberty to the individual who is seen as the most important of actors. Notions of social justice and egalitarian claims are dismissed as a mirage and a derivation of personal freedom.[1] The Thatcher and Major governments provided the Conservative Party with 18 consecutive years in office and during this long period of Conservative dominance the Thatcher government in particular was given the opportunities to persuade sections of the British electorate of the virtues of their neo-liberal philosophy. In a similar fashion, New Labour has been presented with opportunities to counter some of the 'Thatcher–Major settlement' through the implementation of centre-left principles. These principles include a positive and a negative conception of freedom; a communitarian approach to social theory; equality of opportunity; and mild redistributionism. However, it must be noted that those on the centre-left (New Labourites) endorse market economics and significant aspects of the 'Thatcher–Major settlement', whereas others in the Labour Party further left, desire a more robust egalitarianism with fewer markets in the provision of public goods.[2] The term 'Thatcher–Major settlement' is used here to refer to the economic and political reforms of the Conservative governments from 1979 to 1997 which have been left in place. These include their trade union reforms; direct taxation reforms; some of their welfare reforms (such as curbing universal entitlements); and the proliferation of market disciplines in British public policy. This chapter is divided into four sections. The first outlines the reasons for New Labour's politics of dominance. The second section examines what is understood by the term 'centre-ground'. The third section provides evidence of New Labour's centre-left policies. The final section evaluates contemporary political change in Britain, in the form of the emergence of David Cameron and Menzies Campbell as leaders of the Conservatives and Liberal Democrats respectively.

The politics of dominance

New Labour has been in government since May 1997 and has won three consecutive general elections. In a basic sense they have dominated British politics by maintaining power. In winning the 1997, 2001 and 2005 general elections New Labour have successively defeated their competitors. This is a remarkable achievement for the Labour Party. Until 1997, in its 97 year history, the Labour Party had been in power five times, for a total of 20 years. Of those terms in office, only the Attlee government of 1945–50 and the Wilson government of 1966–70 had substantive majorities, the remaining periods were either minute majority or minority governments. Furthermore, until the 2005 general election was called and parliament was dissolved no Labour government had served two consecutive full terms in office. Such continued electoral success in the post-1945 era was once only associated with the Conservative Party. Their first period of dominance – understood as electoral success and ideological supremacy – was from 1951 to 1964 and their second period was from 1979 to 1997. It is claimed throughout this chapter that New Labour has constructed a politics of dominance in electoral terms by winning three consecutive general elections and in ideological terms by winning many of the key policy debates since 1997. Governments design policy for multiple purposes including problem-solving, electioneering and serving their ideological ends. New Labour's policy design has involved aspects of all three. The starting point for New Labour's policy design for ideological ends is to win the centre-ground in British politics. This was notably achieved. In government, New Labour continued policies aimed at consolidating the centre and ones which demonstrated their governing competence and moderation. Other purposes for policy design follow but the overarching assumption in contemporary British politics is that the centre-ground represents the median voter.[3] Relatively few votes are won at the edges of mainstream politics let alone in the space occupied by the extreme left and right.

Dominating the centre-ground

Political parties are led by elites. Elites are the main actors in the political sphere. These powerful individuals do have to work within the confines of their party organizations and this often involves compromising with other powerful interests or bowing to party traditions. Nonetheless, elite actors are the main decision-makers in the British political system and they sit at the apex of power within the Westminster model of parliamentary democracy. Elite actors seek to both shape and respond to public opinion. They shape it by proposing policies which reflect or underpin their ideas and values or those of their supporters. They respond to public opinion, for amongst other things, to attract potential electoral support. New Labour in government led by Blair and in essence co-led by Brown, has behaved precisely this way. They have sought to shape public attitudes on the need for intervention in Iraq; for high levels of investment in the NHS and in state education; and for the need for anti-terror legislation. They have sought to respond to public opinion by deferring entry to the European single currency; scrapping the fuel price escalator; and by banning hunting with dogs. Elite actors author the centre-ground by deciding upon their policies and ideological direction in their manifestos. For example the 1983 Labour manifesto was by today's standards remarkably left-wing but at the time it was seen as a document of the Labour left though not one beyond the realms of Labour parliamentary and constituency support.[4] Of course no-one seeking to assert the relevance of elite theory[5] can ignore the plurality of events and factors that political elites must consider. Nor is this theory of the agency of elite actors ambivalent about the diffusion of power in British politics. Cabinet government, the media, the rule of law, general elections and the perception of competence all matter. Nevertheless, elite actors more than any other actors in British politics author the centre-ground and seek to shape and respond to public opinion.

It is well known that if a party can occupy the centre-ground it is likely that it will win general elections. Once in government with a workable majority a party can begin to consolidate its power by strategizing for the next general election. Governments are best placed to win general elections in Britain as they have control of when they are called, how long the campaign lasts and what the terms of the debate are going to be. During a significant period in office governments can win arguments; make policy; and ultimately change some people's minds. The politics of dominance begins by occupying the centre-ground, but that in itself is an elusive concept. The imprecision of the term 'centre-ground' is a problem for students of political science. In a recent monograph Andrew Hindmoor suggests a rubric for understanding and conceptualizing the 'centre-ground':

> On the one hand parties are described as being and describe themselves as being at the centre by virtue of their popular appeal. Call this the electoral centre ... On the other hand, parties are described and describe themselves as being at the centre by virtue of their moderation. Call this the political centre. (Hindmoor, 2004: 8)

In this chapter my argument is concerned with the political centre although I acknowledge that the electoral centre is often a precondition for a party to win the political centre-ground. Without power a party cannot attempt to recast the centre-ground politics according to its philosophy. The electoral centre in the case of New Labour came first. In a well-known book entitled *Stranded on the Middle Ground*, Sir Keith Joseph argued that there is a stark difference between the 'middle ground' in politics and 'common ground'. According to Joseph the 'middle ground' is the place on the political spectrum that is between the ideologies of the political parties – in effect it is a process of splitting the philosophical difference – whereas, the 'common ground' reflects the aspirations of most of the electorate. Joseph contended that since the election and tenure of the Attlee administration in 1945 the 'middle ground' had moved further and further to the left and so because of this shift the 'middle ground' by the 1970s was socialist in character: '... the middle ground moved continually to the left by its own internal dynamic ... Because we Conservatives became identified with an unthinkable status quo; we therefore allowed the crisis of British socialism to be presented as the crisis of capitalism by default' (Joseph, 1976: 25). What Joseph's thesis reveals is that the political centre-ground is fluid and dynamic. It does reflect the aspirations of most of the electorate but it is also authored by the political elites within political parties. Additionally, the 'common ground' outlined by Joseph is akin to the 'electoral centre' outlined by Hindmoor. Joseph's 'middle ground' refers to the mid-point between the current policy commitments and ideologies of the main political parties. However, Joseph's definition of the 'common ground' is different from Hindmoor's suggestion of the political centre-ground because Joseph implies that the 'common ground' is a relational concept between the electorate and political parties. Specifically, it is when the programme of a party mirrors the aspirations of the electorate. In this case a lot of political and ideological decision-making is done by the electoral preferences of the public and politicians mainly respond and reflect a given ideological current. This I think is unlikely. Most voters are not deeply interested in ideology and most of us no matter how cynical are affected by the rhetoric, campaigning and persuasion of politicians. Therefore, in contradiction to Joseph's idea, the political centre-ground is authored by elite actors within political parties. Of course, whilst policies are thoroughly tested by pollsters, the political narratives and values that are communicated by politicians in speeches and interviews are acts of political persuasion. Elite actors attempt to persuade the electorate and the political centre-ground is the prize for the party that underpins its ideological agenda in British politics. Joseph believed that Thatcher and the neo-liberals in the Conservative Party needed to reflect the aspirations of the electorate and that in doing so they would have 'common ground' with the British people. In fact what happened was that he and Thatcher were outstanding communicators of neo-liberal values in the face of a philosophically disparate and fractured Labour

Party. Joseph and Thatcher won the political centre-ground by persuading sufficient elements of the British public that their neo-liberal agenda was the correct prescription for Britain's problems. Thus, Joseph is quite wrong in his understanding of the 'common ground'. He is mistaken in his understanding of how ideological battles are won and lost. Nevertheless, he was adept at critiquing social democracy and inspiring Thatcher and a new generation of Conservatives to embrace ideas including rolling-back the welfare state; curbing the dependency culture; reducing the power of the trade unions; ending corporatism; promoting unfettered markets; championing entrepreneurship; and above all connecting British Conservatism with liberal individualism.[6]

New Labour's centrism: stepping away from neo-liberalism

New Labour has constructed an ideological agenda that has become the established political centre in British politics. The centre-ground that New Labour occupies is underpinned by specific values of the centre-left. This is not to suggest that New Labour is either traditionally social democratic or that New Labour has not accepted significant aspects of the Thatcher–Major settlement. On the contrary, New Labour's moderate centre-left politics has assimilated much of the Conservative governments' economic reforms. For example, New Labour is opposed to increases in the upper rate of income tax. Britain's direct taxation model was reformed by the Thatcher government and it is a tenet of New Labour's centrism that the British electorate do not wish to see a 50 per cent band of income tax for the highest earners. New Labour has also wooed the City of London and the wider business community. Furthermore, New Labour has left in place the Thatcherite trade union reforms and by granting independence to the Bank of England New Labour has given control of interest rates to the Monetary Policy Committee. This is an act of deference to the institutions of financial orthodoxy. Perhaps the most overt policy that demonstrates New Labour's acquiescence with the Thatcher–Major settlement is their willingness to perpetuate markets in the provision of public goods. This could be interpreted as a departure from social democracy and an endorsement of a form of neo-liberalism. It could alternatively be viewed as New Labour operating within the dominant economic paradigm of market economics, without fully endorsing neo-liberal ends. One academic who believes that New Labour's centrism is an endorsement of the Thatcher–Major settlement is Richard Heffernan.[7] He suggests that:

While Labour policy in 1970–1987 was cast in a social democratic mould (albeit one cast in a radical form), the politics of 'catch up' since 1987 indicates the nature of contemporary political change. Labour's accommodation to a new neo-liberal centre is a suitable illustration. It is a process which helps explain the emergence of the new neo-liberal paradigm and an instrumental feature of this (as any other) emergent 'post-Thatcher' political consensus. (Heffernan, 2001: 170)

Therefore, Heffernan suggests that New Labour have captured the centre-ground in British politics but that they have accepted the Thatcher–Major settlement. In essence he implies that New Labour has embraced a form of neo-liberalism. So how can one refute Heffernan's claims? What evidence exists for suggesting that New Labour's recasting of the political centre is moderately centre-left? Answering such a question is inherently difficult because there is no consensus on what constitutes centre-left values. I consider New Labour's recasting of the political centre to be moderately centre-left due to four main reasons that I will now outline and explain.[8] Firstly one can argue that New Labour's recasting of the centre-ground is moderately centre-left in character because from their second term onwards, they have given primacy to huge investment in public services. Heffernan's book was published in 2001 and the vast public expenditure began around 2001 and he correctly points out that New Labour ruled out increasing income tax in each of its general election manifestos. With the benefit of hindsight the early New Labour years appear to show acquiescence with the Thatcher–Major settlement. Nevertheless, the investment in health and education was planned and announced in the 1999 Comprehensive Review, after New Labour had fulfilled its commitment of maintaining the Major government's spending plans for two years. They did this to demonstrate their governing competence in managing the economy after being out of office for 18 years. When looking at health spending it can be noted that it has risen from 5.4 per cent of national income in 1996–97 to 7.5 per cent in 2006–07 and is due to rise to 7.8 per cent of national income in 2007–08 (Emmerson et al., 2007: 132). In the words of Emmerson, Frayne and Tetlow of the IFS, '... the NHS has received the largest sustained increase in spending since its inception in 1949' (ibid.). Education spending was 4.8 per cent of national income in 1996–97 and fell to 4.5 per cent in 1999–2000 (ibid.: 137). In the succeeding years spending rose sharply and reached 5.6 per cent of national income in 2006–07 (ibid.). These figures suggest that New Labour want to provide well-funded public services, free at the point of delivery – whereas neo-liberals believe that the state should increasingly leave the provision of such goods to the free market and that it is the responsibility of individual citizens to purchase them independently. New Labour have taxed through an increase in National Insurance Contributions and spent on public services. This approach to public services is commensurate with the centre-left in Britain.

Secondly, and connected to the previous point, New Labour has made government interventionist again. New Labour have continued during their tenure to use 'the active hand of government' to provide services and to expand the size and capacity of the public sector.[9] They have done this by recruiting vast numbers of teachers and non-teaching assistants, nurses, doctors, police officers and community support officers to name merely some of the frontline actors in the public sector. The expansion in the size, cost and remit of the public sector is in contradiction to the neo-liberal idea of rolling-back the size, remit and moral responsibility of the state. The idea that the public sector is permitted to expand and potentially 'crowd out'[10] the private sector in terms of resources is anathema to neo-liberals.

Thirdly, one can point to New Labour's goal of employment opportunity for all as evidence that they are not neo-liberal in philosophy. As is stated in the 2005 Labour manifesto: 'Our goal is employment opportunity for all – the modern definition of full employment. Britain has more people in work than ever before, with the highest employment rate in the G7. Our long-term aim is to raise the employment rate to 80%' (Labour Party, 2005: 17). As well as introducing the National Minimum Wage, the New Deal has been the flagship policy to reduce unemployment across the generations by providing skills training and life-long learning opportunities. It has received significant funding initially through the £5 billion windfall tax that was levied on the privatized utilities in 1998.[11] This was a one-off tax on the profits of former nationalized industries privatized under the Thatcher and Major governments.[12] Such expansion of social programmes to enable employability at considerable expense to the taxpayer is in conflict with the absence of such robust provision under the Thatcher and Major administrations due to neo-liberal ideas that the individual is solely responsible for gaining employment and should expect little support from the neo-liberal state. The goal of employment opportunity for all and the New Deal is a deliberate tax-and-spend approach to public policy, which is indicative of a centre-left politics.

Fourthly, evidence to support the claim that New Labour has recast the political centre-ground along moderate centre-left lines is in the raft of anti-poverty measures and redistributive programmes introduced. The Child Tax Credit is paid in addition to Child Benefit and is given to families with children on the lowest household incomes. The Working Tax Credit is paid to individuals (with and without children) on the lowest incomes as a top-up to earnings. Many better off families with children are entitled to a smaller share of the Child Tax Credit. As HM Revenue and Customs states: 'A family with 2 children over the age of one could receive Child Tax Credit with a family income of up to a maximum of £57,785 per year. If you have a child under the age of one you could receive Child Tax Credit with a family income up to £65,965 per year' (HM Revenue and Customs, 2007). This approach has astutely brought many upper-working-class and middle-class families in to a social coalition that benefits from the Tax Credit programme and therefore tries to associate them as beneficiaries of New Labour's public policy. It is sufficient evidence that New Labour is operating a moderate centre-left approach to government. It is because New Labour has implemented such policies – contrary to the precepts of neo-liberalism – that one can argue that the political centre-ground which they occupy has in some respects altered. One cannot continue to accurately assert that New Labour have continued with a neo-liberal consensus. The four factors outlined above are presented as evidence that New Labour has recast the political centre along moderately centre-left lines. The chapter now moves on to examine contemporary political change in Britain to show that the two main opposition parties – the Conservative Party and the Liberal Democrats – are having to respond to New Labour's dominance of the political centre of British politics.

Response and political change: Cameronites and Liberal Democrats

New Labour's electoral success at the 1997, 2001 and 2005 general elections proves that they occupy the centre-ground in British politics. They have appealed to a sufficient array of voters and have secured a plurality of votes in the majority of constituency contests, which has enabled them to form consecutive governments under the first-past-the-post electoral system. It has been argued that New Labour's politics is the politics of dominance and that they have recast the centre-ground along moderately centre-left lines. A further assertion linked to the idea of New Labour's politics being the politics of dominance is that of a hegemonic enterprise. It is plausible that New Labour as the dominant party has succeeded in communicating its message and agenda to the point where the other elite actors in rival political parties are forced to respond and change their policies, and to a degree, to change their ideas and values. This reduces their political difference or at least reduces the perception of political difference. This in turn enables the rival parties to assert that they too represent the centre-ground. Since the election of David Cameron, the Conservative Party is in the process of responding to New Labour's agenda. This agenda is based around specific policy prescriptions. They include the following: the maintenance of the welfare state (including the NHS, state education and tax credit entitlements); sustained investment in public services; a commitment not to cut direct rates of income tax; an endorsement of the minimum wage; support for the environmental agenda; an acceptance of devolution; a commitment to the communitarian anti-social behaviour agenda; a moral responsibility to help end global poverty, especially in Africa.

It appears as if Cameron is currently accepting many planks of New Labour's moderate centre-left agenda. If we examine some of the speeches made by David Cameron since being elected as Leader of the Conservative Party in December 2005 we can see that he has chosen to address issues on which he believes the Conservatives need to change. For example an early speech was made on public services:

> Tony Blair rightly identified the two things that were needed: investment plus reform. Investment was necessary, for example, to build capacity in the NHS, to improve school buildings and teachers pay, and to fund more police manpower … The very reason we have public services is to look after those without power, wealth and opportunity to provide for themselves. (Cameron, 2005a: 1)

This extract reveals Cameron's pro-public service and pro-investment viewpoints. He overtly credits New Labour with diagnosing what the public services needed and part of that diagnosis was large public investment. In the speech there is no rhetoric of the personal responsibility of citizens to purchase their own healthcare and neither is there an argument posited in defence of the right for parents to be able to send their children to private schools. In essence Cameron's speech is a prime example of reframing; he is accepting New Labour's ideological outlook on public service provision and on its level of funding. This is an extraordinarily significant political side-step which questions the Conservative Party's instinctive neo-liberalism as Cameron is accepting that the public sector needed to be expanded to provide better services – especially for those who really need them. It abandons the crowding out theory, the small state view and accepts an interventionist, tax and spend approach to goods provided by the welfare state. I accept that although this is but one speech it is an early indication of the leftward movement of Cameron's Conservatives in the hope of recasting themselves as centrists. Moreover it is proof that Cameron has to accommodate himself amid the ideological politics that New Labour has authored on the centre-ground.

The following extract is from a speech Cameron made in Norway on climate change. This speech was central in his beginning to communicate a commitment to the green agenda:

> Whether it is at a global, national or local level, all of us, as leaders and decision makers, must play a part in making the green agenda central to everything we do. We can change how we get around; we can change how we build our homes; we can change our lifestyles, change our industrial processes, change our working practices. (Cameron, 2006a: 1)

The green agenda in moderate politics has traditionally been the preserve of social democrats and left-leaning liberals.[13] In Britain, large sections of the Labour Party have campaigned for environmental causes since the 1970s and it is fair to say that the Liberal Democrats are the most pro-environment of the main political parties. Historically, the Conservative Party has been pro-business and pro-economic growth (like significant parts of the Labour Movement) and has been reluctant to argue for – amongst other things – less air travel and for corporations to play their part in combating the greenhouse effect. Cameron authorized the redesign of the Conservative Party's logo and the freedom torch was replaced with an oak tree and the catchphrase 'Think Green, Vote Blue' which was used in the Local Council elections, the Scottish Parliament elections and the Welsh Assembly elections in May 2007. A further extract, from a speech in Oxford to Oxfam supporters, denotes a commitment to combating global poverty. This is an important extract for understanding Cameron's intent to reposition the Conservative Party at the political centre. It is notable for his candour in mildly chiding traditional Conservative attitudes towards a lack of concern for the priority of governmental social responsibility outside of the United Kingdom:

> For too long, politics in this country treated global poverty as a secondary issue. Conservatives used to regard it as a significant, but second-order subject. Labour have helped to raise its significance and we should all acknowledge the personal commitment and leadership of Tony Blair and Gordon Brown in doing so ... And the fundamental challenge for the twenty-first century will, I believe, be a moral one:

how can we bring the rich and the poor world closer together? I describe it as a moral challenge because that, for me, is first and foremost what it is. It is morally unacceptable for billions of people to live in dire and degrading poverty when we know the secret of wealth creation. (Cameron, 2006b: 1)

The fourth and final extract worth exploring is from a speech to the Centre for Social Justice on tackling poverty in Britain. Cameron is trying to suggest that his new, modern Conservatives are compassionate and that they are as sympathetic to the causes of poverty as the Labour Party. This is central to rebranding his party and to recasting their policy perspectives:

Gordon Brown and I share the same objectives. We both want to tackle poverty. But we have different solutions to the entrenched problems of multiple deprivation, and the root causes of poverty in Britain today ... On the one hand, there is a top-down, centralized approach from Labour that means well but fails badly. On the other, I want to develop a forward-looking vision which recognizes that social justice will only be delivered by empowering people to fulfil their potential. (Cameron, 2006c: 1)

This is a fairly ambiguous statement by Cameron, bar noting that Brown is sincere about tackling poverty in the UK. This statement though not full of policy detail is nonetheless important in his trying to move the Conservative Party and the perception of the Conservative Party towards the political centre-ground on the issue of poverty reduction, which historically has been an area dominated by the Labour Party.

From the four extracts it is apparent that on key issues that are Labour policy strongholds – public services, environment, global poverty, and poverty reduction in the UK – Cameron appears to be committed to reframe the Conservative Party's attitudes and arguably their values towards certain public policy standpoints. He does maintain that he is a Conservative and that they have won the battle for ideas as New Labour has accepted much of the Thatcher–Major settlement (Cameron, 2006d: 4). He has espoused the need for the state to 'trust people': in particular, individuals and wider civil society organizations so they can share responsibility in the provision of public services (ibid.). In essence, choice must be given to citizens on issues of healthcare and education. Furthermore, he has stressed his belief in the free market (Cameron, 2006e: 2), in a lower tax economy and a reduction in regulation and in a leaner state (ibid.). Therefore Cameron is not in danger just yet of being called anything but a moderate conservative though he has utilized the term 'compassionate Conservatism' (Cameron, 2006d: 1). Nevertheless, as has been argued, Cameron is moving the Conservative Party leftwards on a range of key issues and by doing so he is attempting to occupy the political centre-ground. The problem he faces is that New Labour dominates the political centre-ground because they are its current authors. The political centre has changed gradually since 1997. If it had stayed the same and continued to be neo-liberal in inspiration Cameron would probably not be Leader of the Conservative Party, nor would he be reframing significant portions of their agenda along moderate, centre-left lines. This is because if the Conservative Party had decided to opt for a more traditional conservative then David Davis would have won the leadership election. The Conservatives would certainly not have moved leftwards to occupy New Labour's territory with such pace and enthusiasm. It is difficult to imagine that Davis would have styled himself as 'the heir to Blair'.

The Liberal Democrats are also in the process of reframing their political identity and are possibly undertaking as thorough a reform process as Cameron's Conservative Party. Since the resignation in March 2006 of the social liberal Charles Kennedy and the election of Sir Menzies Campbell, a group of Liberal Democrat MPs from the party's right-wing have grown in prominence and in policy influence. Campbell himself is the quintessential Liberal in the Jo Grimond mould of mid-twentieth-century Liberalism: an ardent centrist who is not clearly identifiable with the party's left or right wing. However, with Kennedy's resignation the right-wing or as they are sometimes termed, economic liberals, seem to be in the ascendancy. This group includes Vincent Cable, David Laws and Ed Davey. In 2004, these economic liberals and others contributed to a volume of essays entitled *The Orange Book: Reclaiming Liberalism* in which they set out liberal perspectives on a range of public policy issues based around the ideology of economic liberalism. The terms economic liberalism and neo-liberalism are acknowledged synonyms. The Conservative Party in Britain is associated with neo-liberalism and therefore economic liberalism enables the Orange Book liberals to set themselves apart from Conservatism and simultaneously emphasize the economic liberal tradition in their party's history. This includes the desire for a smaller central state, lower taxation, primacy given to the role and rights of the individual, free markets and hostility to the social democratic state. The following extract from an essay by David Laws is a sample of the specific liberal attitude that this group seeks to promote within the

Liberal Democrat Party: 'How did it come about that over the decades up to the 1980s the Liberal belief in economic liberalism was progressively eroded by forms of soggy socialism and corporatism, which have too often been fully perceived as a necessary corollary of social liberalism' (Laws, 2004: 29).

Interestingly, the *Orange Book* has been swiftly succeeded by another Liberal Democrat publication with an introduction and endorsement by Campbell. It is entitled, *Britain After Blair: A Liberal Agenda*. One of its editors, Paul Marshall, states how its goal differs from that of the *Orange Book*:

> *Britain After Blair* is a logical development of the *Orange Book*, although it paints on a broader canvas. It seeks to show, notably through contributions on education, welfare, housing and worklessness, how economic and social liberalism can be fused. It illustrates how economically liberal means – free trade, open markets, competition, choice and accountability – can deliver social liberal objectives: the expansion of life chances and opportunities; the provision of social security; and the reduction of poverty and ill health. (Marshall, 2006: xvi–xvii)

Many economic liberal contributors to the *Orange Book* contribute to *Britain After Blair* but they are counterbalanced by such social liberals as Simon Hughes, Lynne Featherstone and Sarah Teather. The salience of this book is that it represents Campbell's desire to unify the economic and social liberal wings of his party and to counter the straight economic liberal thesis that was the *Orange Book*. The first half of *Britain After Blair* is an audit of New Labour's time in government which was undertaken by the liberal think tank Centre:Forum and the second half is comprised of essays on a variety of issues authored by members of both wings of the Liberal Democrats. Campbell's determination for internal unity and for sensible centrism is encapsulated in a section of his chapter in which he appears to follow Gordon Brown's mantra of fairness and economic efficiency:[14] 'If we want a fairer Britain, we must accept that social justice requires economic prosperity, and economic discipline. This means difficult choices will have to be made, which will require us to move out of the comfort zone of opposition politics' (Campbell, 2006: 7).

This chapter has argued that New Labour's politics has been the politics of dominance. Dominance in electoral and ideological terms to the point where they have recast moderate politics in Britain. This has in turn affected the ideas and policies associated with the centre-ground since 1997. It has been contended that New Labour have constructed a centre-left agenda and because of their dominance their rivals have had to respond – and especially in the case of the Conservative Party – to change their policy positions and, in certain areas, to embrace values that are alien to much of their party. Similarly, the Liberal Democrats are engaged in modernizing and have stepped towards the centre, away from their left of New Labour position under Charles Kennedy. Additionally, the new Liberal Democrat leadership has muted the noisy enthusiasm for economic liberal solutions espoused by Orange Book liberals. Both the Conservatives and the Liberal Democrats are currently concluding their policy reviews and are designing ways to respond to Prime Minister Brown and his style of Labour politics. The most pertinent question is whether New Labour under Brown can maintain the centre that it has fashioned during the decade of dominance. If it can, Brown may well win the next election, subject to the handicap of longevity in office. If it cannot, and Cameron can convey to a sufficient portion of the southern, middle-class, English electorate that he is the 'heir to Blair', then New Labour's politics of dominance will come to an abrupt end.

Notes

1. For more on the doctrine of neo-liberalism, see Hayek (1976).
2. For a more detailed analysis of Labour's political thought, see Beech (2006).
3. For an understanding of the Median Voter Theorem, see Black (1958).
4. See Labour Party (1983).
5. For more on elite theory, see Evans (2004: 39–58).
6. For more on Joseph's political philosophy, see Joseph and Sumption (1978).
7. As well as Richard Heffernan, Colin Hay and Simon Lee are academics who think New Labour owes more to Thatcherism than social democracy. See Hay (1999) and Lee (2007). It should be noted that Lee prefers to class Brown as a liberal in the mode of Adam Smith and suggests that he is influenced by the American liberalism present in Roosevelt's New Deal and Kennedy and Johnson's Great Society programmes. He states that Brown's politics are underpinned by a moral defence of the free market but prefers not to use the term economic-liberal or Thatcherite.
8. For others who think New Labour is centre-left, see Fielding (2002), Meredith (2006) and Hickson (2007). Hickson regards New Labour as centre-left but believes they are not traditional social democrats in the Croslandite model.
9. At the end of the first quarter of 2007 the total number of employees in the public sector was 5.787 million with a total employment figure of 28.924 million. At the end of the first quarter of 2007 approximately 20 per cent of UK employees were employed in the public sector. See www.statistics.gov.uk/statbase/TSDdownload2.asp.
10. For more on the 'crowding out' thesis, see Bacon and Eltis (1978).

16

11. See 'Financial Statement and Budget Report 1997', House of Commons Paper No. HC 85, http://archive.treasury.gov.uk/budget/1997/report/fsbr.htm.
12. For an evaluation of Brown's windfall tax, see Chennells (1997).
13. The Green Party are the ecological party within the United Kingdom, but I do not consider them to represent mainstream, centrist politics.
14. See Brown (1995).

2
The British Model of Political Economy

Simon Lee

Introduction

The political economy of New Labour is central to any evaluation of the legacy of the Blair governments. Consequently, the purpose of this chapter is to outline and evaluate the principal components of New Labour's British model of political economy. This model has received widespread praise, especially from abroad. Highlighting the openness and flexibility of the British model, the Executive Board of the International Monetary Fund praised 'the UK economy's remarkable performance that has lasted for more than a decade' (IMF, 2006). IMF staff also reported that 'During 1996–2005, the growth of real GDP per capita was higher and less volatile than in any other G7 country' (IMF, 2007: 3). By the time of Tony Blair's departure from office, the UK economy had grown for 59 consecutive quarters, including 40 quarters under New Labour. The Treasury noted that this expansion was 'not only without precedent in the post-war history of the UK, but is also the longest on post-war record for any G7 economy and the longest expansion of any OECD country'. Indeed, it would take 'at least nine years before the UK's current expansion could be eclipsed by another G7 country' (HM Treasury, 2006: 14). By redefining on no fewer than three occasions the Treasury's official definition of the UK's economic cycle, so that the previous cycle is held to have begun in 1997–98, and to have ended in early 2007, Gordon Brown ensured that his entire tenure at the Treasury delivered 40 consecutive quarters of growth. This led Brown to boast that Britain was experiencing its longest period of sustained growth not only since the start of the

Industrial Revolution, but also 'since records began in the year seventeen hundred and one' (Brown, 2005a).

This chapter evaluates the British model of political economy by analysing the model's approach to monetary policy, fiscal policy and industrial policy. The chapter then explores the extent to which the Brown Boom delivered prudence and a sustainable prosperity. When Brown redefined the role of the Treasury in May 1999 to become nothing less than the modernization of the British economy, he claimed that it had broken 'decisively with the short-termist, secretive and unstable record of macroeconomic policy-making of the past two decades by setting a credible framework' for monetary and fiscal policy (Brown, 1999). It is undoubtedly true that Brown's economic legacy, in terms of stability, is better than that of any of his modern peacetime predecessors as Chancellor. However, this chapter also demonstrates that the economic legacy of ten years of New Labour is equally one of consistent private and increasing public imprudence. Far from insulating the UK's economy from instability, as the IMF has noted, by encouraging the United Kingdom economy to become even more closely linked to global financial markets, the British model of political economy has increased the vulnerability of the UK to global risks and contagion (IMF, 2007: 22).

The dominance of the Treasury

The role of the Treasury has been central to the political economy of New Labour and the British model of political economy. Under previous Labour governments, the Treasury had superintended sterling's departure from the Gold Standard in 1931 and damaging sterling crises and devaluations in July–August 1947, September 1949 and November 1967. The ultimate economic and political humiliation for Old Labour had occurred in September 1976 when a Labour Chancellor of the Exchequer had applied to the IMF for $3.9 billion, at that juncture the largest credit ever extended by the IMF, to finance the UK's balance of payments crisis and the repayment of short-term credit. Under New Labour, while the Treasury retained its historic role as 'the guardian of the public finances and the guarantor of monetary stability', the British model of political economy redefined the new mission of the Treasury as the modernization of the British economy. Thus, the Treasury was to become 'not just a Ministry of Finance, but also a Ministry working with other departments to deliver long-term economic and social renewal' (Brown, 1999).

The economic policies of the previous Macdonald, Attlee, Wilson and Callaghan Labour governments were undermined by the constraints upon domestic modernization programmes generated by the global commercial interests of the City of London. At the same time, the attempt to create modernizing agencies to rival the Treasury, notably the Department of Economic Affairs and Ministry of Technology in the 1960s and the National Enterprise Board in the 1970s, led to conflict over the Treasury's dominance over economic policy. This pattern reached its zenith in the failed 'social revolution' of the National Plan, when the Wilson government attempted to fashion 'a state of competitive existence' between the Treasury and the newly created Department of Economic Affairs (DEA), led by George Brown, but actually delivered an economic strategy based upon 'two diametrically opposed policies'. Brown had subsequently asserted that 'Some Government, some day, will re-create a department on the lines of the DEA and limit the out-dated authority of the Treasury' (Brown, 1971: 104–5).

Gordon Brown deliberately did not follow George Brown's 1960s model. Rather than limiting the authority of the Treasury, by recreating an alternative focal point for economic modernization, he made modernization the remit of the Treasury. Its power was strengthened and deepened. The British model surmounted that creative tension that once existed within Whitehall between rival economic departments by establishing the Treasury as the pilot agency of the British developmental state. By ceding responsibility for administering monetary policy to the Bank of England's Monetary Policy Committee, the Treasury discovered the policy space and opportunity to intervene, in an unprecedented peacetime way, in economic and social policy, via the institutions of the Treasury-led biennial Spending Reviews, ten-yearly Comprehensive Spending Reviews, and Public Service Agreements. However, because of devolution to elected institutions in other parts of the United Kingdom, the British model's political power was exercised most effectively in England, where no such constitutional checks and balances upon Treasury power operate beyond Greater London.

A model of political economy based upon past lessons

During their ten years of office, the New Labour governments led by Tony Blair and Gordon Brown devised a British model of political economy, rather than just a British model of economic policy. The model reflected a particular understanding of the appropriate relationship between and respective roles for the state and market, based upon a fatal conceit of being able 'not only to support but positively enhance markets'. Indeed, Gordon Brown's closest economic advisers claimed that 'Markets are a powerful means of advancing the public interest' (Balls, Grice and O'Donnell, 2004: 6, 8). New Labour could make markets work better by manipulating the behaviour of private market actors for the general public good, in the manner that Old Labour governments had sought to orchestrate nationalized industries, trades unions and the other component architecture of the public domain. In the mould of Margaret Thatcher, Blair and Brown cast their model in terms of a free economy accompanied by a strong state, prepared to defend the commercial interests of corporations, both at home and abroad. This continuity of party ideology and economic policy led one commentator on British politics to regard the transition from Thatcher to Major, Major to Blair, and from Blair to Brown, as a political and economic revolution in three acts (Jenkins, 2006).

A central feature of the British model was that it claimed to have learnt vital lessons from the mistakes made by previous British governments. Unlike its predecessors, the British model would identify a successful formula for reconciling domestic economic, social and political modernization with the constraints of global financial markets and the need to maintain the UK's international competitiveness. Globalization was mobilized as a political weapon to justify important changes in domestic and social policies, and to discipline popular expectations of what the role of the state should be. The cost of significant areas of public welfare, notably pensions, were increasingly transferred from the state, the corporation and the general taxpayer on to the private individual.

Like Thatcherism before it, the British model regarded the unfettered capitalism of the City of London, the liberalized markets for property and financial services, and the consumer demand that has been driven by those sectors as the key agencies of economic modernization. Where previously the Labour Party had based its electoral strategy on becoming the 'Party of Production' in contrast to the Conservative 'Party of the City', the British model cast New Labour as the champion of the City rather than of manufacturing, and of predominantly consumer rather than producer interests.

For the British model, one vital lesson learnt from past British economic mismanagement was that politicians and policy-makers had paid insufficient attention to economics when making key decisions. This error was manifested in the disastrous return to the pre-1914 'gold standard' of global fixed exchange rates backed by gold reserves, with sterling at its pre-1914 parity of $4.86 which ultimately led in 1931 to the Labour Party acquiring the tag of the 'Party of Devaluation'. It was equally true of the Attlee government's decision in 1946 to re-enter sterling to a fixed exchange rate system with the dollar at sterling's pre-war parity of $4.03. The Wilson government had been equally culpable in its decision in 1964 to reject devaluation, only to be forced into it in November 1967, resulting in deflation, rising unemployment, fiscal retrenchment, and the resignation of James Callaghan as Chancellor. Too little economics also led to the Major government's decision to withdraw an overvalued pound from the Exchange Rate Mechanism on 'Black Wednesday' (16 September 1992), having ushered in the longest recession since 1945 (Balls, 2001).

A model based upon constrained discretion

In his first major announcement as Chancellor of the Exchequer, Gordon Brown identified the central economic objectives of the Blair government as 'high and stable levels of growth and employment', which would be achieved by rebuilding 'British economic strength with a modern industrial base, high levels of investment and a culture of entrepreneurship' (Brown, 1997a). These objectives were located within a reaffirmation of a commitment made in the May 1944 *Employment Policy* White Paper, namely an acceptance 'as one of their primary aims and responsibilities the maintenance of a high and stable level of employment after the war' (Minister of Reconstruction, 1944: 3). Brown contended that in 1997 a 'new paradigm' of monetary and fiscal policy was needed to achieve these goals. A break from 'the short-termism of the past', and the economic instability that had characterized the British economy for most of the twentieth century, would be founded upon 'the solid rock of prudent and consistent economic management, not the shifting sands of boom and bust' (Brown, 1997a). Short-termism would be escaped by making long-term commitments to monetary stability, fiscal stability, higher levels of investment in people and businesses, far-reaching modernization of the welfare state, free trade and 'constructive engagement' with Europe (Keegan, 2003: 130).

From the outset, Brown and Balls based their British model upon the principle of 'constrained discretion', the key principle for policy-making 'in a modern open economy' (Balls, Grice and O'Donnell, 2004: 381). This vital insight was that 'the discretion necessary for effective economic policy – short-term flexibility to meet credible long-term goals – is possible only within an institutional framework that commands market credibility and public trust with the government constrained to deliver clearly defined long-term policy objectives and with maximum openness and transparency' (Balls, 2004). The ERM failure had demonstrated that stability and low inflation required to achieve and sustain high and stable levels of growth and employment would not be achieved by adhering to destabilizing 'fixed and intermediate policy rules' (Balls, 1998: 121).

As the foundation for an alternative British model, constrained discretion would limit the capacity to destabilize macroeconomic policy and performance by pre-committing policy-makers to the delivery of long-term objectives through institutional arrangements. In return for this commitment, policy-makers would benefit from 'the maximum operational flexibility that is consistent with achieving that goal' of stability (Balls, Grice and O'Donnell, 2004: 381). Constrained discretion would deliver credibility, by aligning policy-makers' incentives with long-term objectives; flexibility, through the devolution of operational responsibility for decision-making to front-line agents; and transparency, through both the provision of clear, precise and publicly-stated objectives, and the regular reporting of agents' performance against their objectives.

From the Treasury's perspective, there were two huge political advantages of building the British model upon the principle of constrained discretion. First, it legitimized constraints upon the freedom of policy-makers and other actors, including those in receipt of public expenditure, as dictated by their prior commitment to institutional arrangements and policy objectives prescribed by the Treasury. Second, it simultaneously legitimized a division of labour whereby Gordon Brown, Ed Balls and other elite Treasury officials would be able to design policy and determine resource allocation at the centre, while those in charge of delivering public goods and services would be responsible for administering policy priorities as dictated by the demands of constrained discretion. In this way, policy design would be effectively nationalized, through the institutions of the Treasury's biennial Spending Reviews and attendant Public Service Agreements, and thereby become increasingly divorced from administration in the delivery of public services, with major implications for policy, performance and, above all, democratic accountability in England. Despite Brown's assertion that 'old command and control systems of management are not the way forward' (Brown, 2004a: xiii), constrained discretion had engineered a top-down, technocratic, highly centralized and Treasury-driven approach to domestic economic and social modernization that would become one of the definitive features of policy-making under New Labour.

The British model of monetary policy

The principle of constrained discretion was applied first to monetary policy. This too was an area where the British model had devised policy on the basis of lessons learnt from past experience. During the 1970s, annual inflation had averaged 13 per cent, peaking during Denis Healey's tenure as Chancellor of the Exchequer at nearly 27 per cent in August 1975. During the 1980s, annual inflation had averaged 7 per cent (compared with 3 per cent in Germany and 5 per cent in the United States), and had peaked again in the early 1990s at more than 9 per cent. This meant that the United Kingdom economy had suffered the second highest annual average inflation rate among the Group of Seven (G7) industrialized economies between 1980 and 1997, with only France and Italy having suffered greater variability in inflation (Balls and O'Donnell, 2002: 5–8).

The British model identified four key lessons from this past experience. First, Britain had suffered from poor institutional arrangements. Monetary policy, if set correctly, should be a stabilizing force for the economy. Second, monetary policy had been based on a fundamental misunderstanding of the relationship between inflation and unemployment, namely that unemployment could be cut by stimulating demand, albeit with the trade-off of higher inflation. In practice, any reductions in unemployment had been temporary and inflation had accelerated. Third, because monetary policy decisions had been taken by politicians, the suspicion had been fostered that decisions had been based on short-term political expediency rather than the long-term interests of the economy. Fourth, because monetary policy decisions had been taken in secret, there had been a lack of transparency with little or no explanation for the conduct of policy (Balls and O'Donnell, 2002: 17–18). To rectify these parallel deficits in effectiveness and transparency, in May 1997 one of Gordon Brown's first major policy announcements was the transfer of responsibility for meeting the government's monetary policy objectives to a newly established Monetary Policy Committee (MPC) of the Bank of England.

The MPC would be responsible for honouring the Labour Party's manifesto commitment to match the Major government's inflation target of 2.5 per cent or less (Labour Party, 1997: 25). Constrained discretion would be achieved through three policies. First, sound long-term objectives through a single symmetrical inflation target, whose symmetry would avoid any deflationary bias and which would not target both inflation and the short-term exchange rate. Second, a pre-commitment to credible institutional arrangements, through a division of labour in economic policy. On the one hand, the government would set the broader economic strategy and objectives for monetary policy. On the other, the MPC would take the monthly decisions on how to meet the government's inflation targets. Third, monetary policy would display maximum transparency, through the publication of both monthly minutes and individual votes of the members of the MPC (Balls, 2004). However, the publication of individual voting patterns would inevitably lead to certain MPC members being cast as 'doves' or 'hawks' depending upon their preparedness to adjust interest rates to meet the government's inflation target.

On 10 December 2003, Gordon Brown confirmed that the new inflation target for the MPC would no longer be based upon RPI-X. Instead, the MPC was required to set monetary policy to achieve a target of 2 per cent, as measured by the annual increase in the Consumer Price Index. If inflation deviated by more than 1 per cent from this target, the MPC would be required to send an open letter of explanation to the Chancellor (HM Treasury, 2003a: 3).

The impact of the British model was to deliver a decade of low inflation and macroeconomic stability. Indeed, the Treasury asserted that during the ten years of New Labour, the UK had enjoyed 'more stability in terms of GDP growth and inflation than in any decade since the war'. This was demonstrated by the fact that 'inflation, on the RPI measure, has remained within a range of ¾ to 4¾ per cent over the past 10 years, compared with a range of 1 to 11 per cent in the 1990s, 2½ to 22 per cent in the 1980s and 5 to 27 per cent in the 1970s'. For these reasons, the Treasury also proclaimed 'the longest period of sustained low inflation for the past 30 years', and, Japan apart, lower average inflation in the UK under New Labour than in any other G7 economy (HM Treasury, 2007a: 20–1).

The British model of monetary policy gave 'the MPC the flexibility to respond decisively to unexpected economic events over recent years' (Office for National Statistics, 2007a: 20). However, it meant that during his tenure as Chancellor of the Exchequer, Gordon Brown experienced unprecedented power over the conduct of domestic policy. Granting the Bank of England operational independence over the administration of the government's monetary policy had two key effects. First, unlike his post-war Labour predecessors (Sir Stafford Cripps, James Callaghan, Roy Jenkins and Denis Healey) whose respective tenure at the Treasury had witnessed the sacrificing of modernization programmes upon the altar of sterling crises, devaluation, public spending cuts and trades union unrest, Brown was not preoccupied with the macro-economy, and the immediate responsibility for administering monetary policy. Second, having been freed of the responsibility for setting interest rates, but while retaining the power to devise monetary policy (rendering the Bank of England's 'independence' illusory), Brown experienced the time and policy space to intervene in many areas of domestic policy that were not previously thought to be within the Treasury's compass. This nationalization of policy design and resource allocation was implemented through the new fiscal policy framework, the second element of the British model of political economy.

The British model of fiscal policy

Before New Labour, previous British governments had failed to control public spending. For example, during the tenure of the Wilson governments, public spending had increased from 38.1 per cent of GDP in 1964–65 to a post-war record of 49.5 per cent of GDP in 1975–76. Moreover, despite the Thatcher and Major governments' rhetorical ambition to roll back the frontiers of the state, between 1978–79 and 1996–97, the average annual real growth in public spending had been 1.9 per cent, driven upwards by, for example, a 3.1 per cent average annual increase in health spending (Dilnot and Johnson, 1997: i). There had been a rise in net government debt from 31 per cent of GDP in 1988–89 to 44 per cent of GDP in 1996–97 (Balls and O'Donnell, 2002: 19). The tax burden as a share of GDP had risen slightly, from 34.25 per cent to 36.25 per cent. However, although the UK's tax burden in 1997 was greater than that of either the United States or Japan, Britain remained 'a strikingly low-tax country', especially when compared with its European competitors (Dilnot and Johnson, 1997: 14–16).

The British model identified two key lessons for fiscal policy from this past experience. First, a prudent approach should be taken, adjusting for the economic cycle and building in a margin for uncertainty. Second, policy should be open and transparent, by setting stable fiscal rules and explaining clearly fiscal policy decisions (HM Treasury, 1997: 1). The first principle of constrained discretion, namely sound long-term objectives, would become engrained in fiscal policy by the operation of two fiscal rules. First, the so-called 'golden rule', i.e. that the government would borrow over the economic cycle only 'to finance public investment and not to fund public consumption'. Second, the 'sustainable investment rule', i.e. that the United Kingdom's net debt as proportion of GDP would be kept over the economic cycle 'at a prudent and sensible level' (Brown, 1997b).

In relation to the sustainable investment rule, the Treasury chose to commit the Blair government to maintaining debt below 40 per cent of GDP in each year of the economic cycle. There was no particular reason why this specific figure should have been selected. The British model could equally have chosen 38 per cent or 42 per cent. Indeed, the Maastricht convergence criteria for participation in EMU had set a level of net debt at 60 per cent of GDP, so the United Kingdom already enjoyed one of the lowest figures for net debt among industrialized economies when New Labour took power.

At the same time, the Treasury planned to increase the role of the private finance initiative (PFI) and public–private partnerships (PPPs) in total capital investment. Paradoxically, the government could have borrowed on the City of London's private capital markets to finance public investment at a lower interest rate than the private sector. Sticking to the sustainable investment rule threatened both to put a brake on the capacity to modernize the crumbling national infrastructure and to inflate unnecessarily the cost of modernization by a superfluous reliance on private sector investment which, as the privatization of the railways had already demonstrated, might never materialize.

To implement the third principle of constrained discretion, credibility through maximum transparency, the British model introduced the Code for Fiscal Stability. The Code specified the five principles of the government's fiscal policy – transparency, stability, responsibility, fairness (including between generations), and efficiency – would relate to the formulation and implementation of fiscal policy. The Code demanded that fiscal policy adhere to clearly stated objectives and rules, have its underlying key assumptions independently audited, and its issues regularly and openly reported (Balls, 2004).

The final element of the rules-based British model of fiscal policy was the introduction of a year-long Comprehensive Spending Review (CSR), embracing no fewer than 30 zero-based reviews of not only departmental spending plans but also objectives and policies. The CSR was followed by three biennial Spending Reviews, before a second CSR was announced for 2007. This innovation in fiscal policy in particular signified the manner in which Gordon Brown was to assume an iron grip upon the conduct of domestic economic and social policy, unprecedented during the tenure of previous peacetime Chancellors of the Exchequer. While the conduct of monetary policy had been insulated from manipulation for short-term political gain, fiscal policy had been further politicized.

This overt politicization of fiscal policy was demonstrated in July 2005, when it appeared that Gordon Brown would not meet his first golden rule, namely not to borrow to finance current government spending over the economic cycle. Brown used an appearance before a select committee to announce, without prior warning, that the Treasury had calculated that the economic cycle had actually started in 1997–98, and not in

1999–2000 as had been claimed previously (Brown, 2005b). Had Brown maintained the previous definition of the economic cycle, he would have broken his own golden rule by £5.5 billion, because of the £15.1 billion deficit on the current budget recorded in 2005–06. Brown then announced a second unanticipated redefinition of the economic cycle in December 2005, extending the economic cycle by three years, to end in 2008–09 (HM Treasury, 2005: 208). Once more, the redefinition was little more than a political convenience to ensure that Brown met his golden rule. Brown's hat-trick of unannounced redefinitions of the economic cycle came a year later, when again he used the platform of his Pre-Budget Report statement to announce that the end of the economic cycle, which the 2006 Budget had confirmed at 2008–09, would be 'early 2007' (HM Treasury, 2006: 218). This would conveniently define the economic cycle as having coincided precisely with the beginning and end of Brown's tenure as Chancellor, and thereby enable him to claim that his economic legacy for Britain would be one of unbroken economic growth.

Brown's politically-driven redefinitions of the economic cycle meant that the golden rule of fiscal policy was met with a margin of around £11.6 billion or 0.1 per cent of GDP (Institute for Fiscal Studies, 2007a: 2). As the Treasury itself noted, 'the introduction of strict fiscal rules and clear objectives for fiscal policy have put the public finances on a more sound and sustainable footing than in previous economic cycles'. Indeed, a surplus for the current cycle of 0.1 per cent of GDP was 'in contrast to the last cycle's average deficit of 2.0 per cent of GDP, and the 1977–78 to 1986–87 cycle's average deficit of 1.8 per cent of GDP' (HM Treasury, 2007a: 15). However, this performance appears less creditable when it is remembered that, in his 2001 Budget statement, Brown had confidently forecast that the current budget would be in surplus to the tune of £118 billion over the economic cycle. By the time of his pre-Election 2005 Budget, that forecast surplus had evaporated to only £5 billion. The Institute for Fiscal Studies has estimated that around one quarter of this fiscal deterioration was the consequence of policy decisions to increasing spending, but the remainder reflected unexpected weakness in tax revenues, a further indictment of Brown's flawed economic management (Chote and Emmerson, 2005: 4).

The central weakness of the British model of fiscal policy was that it delivered only short-lived fiscal prudence. Brown's initial austerity was sufficient to reduce public spending to 37.7 per cent of GDP in 1999–2000, its lowest level since 1960–61. Brown was able to reduce public sector net debt, as a share of national income, from 43.6 per cent of GDP in May 1997 to 31.3 per cent by the time of the 2001 general election. By contrast, during the Blair government's second term, Brown's increasing fiscal imprudence led to public sector net debt rising by 3.7 per cent to 35.0 per cent of GDP by the time of the 2005 general election. Subsequently, a further deterioration saw net debt increase to 37.5 per cent of GDP by June 2005 (Office for National Statistics, 2007b: 1).

The legacy of the British model of fiscal policy was fourfold. First, it increased public spending from 40.8 per cent of GDP in 1997–98 to 42.0 per cent in 2007–08, or about £25.0 billion in cash terms. Second, during the same period, it increased tax and revenue receipts by about 2.8 per cent of GDP, or about £39.6 billion. Third, it reduced net borrowing by around 1.1 per cent of GDP, or £14.6 billion. Fourth, it reduced net public debt by 5.4 per cent of GDP, or around £74.4 billion (Frayne, 2007). Following Gordon Brown's third redefinition of the economic cycle, which abbreviated the economic cycle by two years, Brown engineered a small surplus on the cycle, but at the expense of starting the next economic cycle with two years of likely current budget deficits (House of Commons Treasury Committee, 2007: 20).

The British model of industrial policy

One of the most distinctive features of the British model of political economy was its abandonment of civilian manufacturing industries, and the Labour Party's longstanding commitment to state-led industrial modernization. The British model of industrial policy chose instead to champion increasingly the interests of the City of London. Gordon Brown claimed that a 'new industrial policy' had replaced 'the old centralization of national champions, picking winners or offering special subsidies to loss makers with a level playing field for all' (Brown, 2004a: xii). In practice, the British model of industrial policy continued the tradition of picking winners. Indeed, precisely the same winners were picked by New Labour as had been by the Thatcher and Major governments, namely the City of London and the financial services sector; the property market; defence manufacturing; civil aerospace; nuclear energy; and pharmaceuticals. Each of these sectors was supported by major policy initiatives, institutional innovation or large-scale subsidies.

The City of London was identified as the key winner to be backed by the British model of industrial policy. It provided the most tangible evidence of the benefits for innovation and entrepreneurship of meeting the challenges of globalization with a policy approach based upon competition, liberalization and deregulation of markets. London was championed as the home for 20 per cent of all cross-border lending, 30 per cent of world foreign exchange turnover, 40 per cent of the over-the-counter derivatives market, and 70 per cent of the global secondary bond market (Balls, 2006a). Consequently, long before the £25 billion of taxpayer loans to Northern Rock, the major beneficiaries of the British model were the major UK banks, whose net earnings totalled more than £40 billion in 2006 (Business Guardian, 2007).

Where previous Labour Chancellors had regarded the capitalists of the City of London as the Labour Party's class enemy, likely to undermine the prospects of domestic modernization by serving as the catalyst for balance-of-payments and devaluation crises, New Labour's Treasury ministers, led by Gordon Brown and Ed Balls, paid fulsome homage to the global centre of casino capitalism. Indeed, Brown boldly asserted that 'we can demonstrate that just as in the nineteenth century industriali-zation was made for Britain, in the twenty-first century globalization is made for Britain' (Brown, 2006b).

The British model of industrial policy did not neglect manufacturing altogether. The Blair governments maintained the longstanding tradition of the British state's provision of large-scale financial assistance to the aerospace industry. The Treasury under New Labour sanctioned a total of £980 million of repayable launch investment to British Aerospace (BAe) and Rolls-Royce for the Airbus A380 'super-jumbo' aircraft, even though these companies are highly profitable transnational corporations. Despite these subsidies, the Treasury refused to intervene in BAe's subsequent sale of its 20 per cent stake in the Airbus consortium, a commercial decision that threatened the long-term future of civil aircraft manufacturing in Britain. BAe had chosen to concentrate upon the defence sector which under New Labour had remained the manufacturing sector that has received the largest public investment. For example, in December 2005, the Blair government published its Defence Industrial Strategy, setting out its vision for the United Kingdom's future defence requirements and the industrial capacity that would be needed to procure the requisite equipment. Outside of the realms of the City of London and the warfare state, it would have been unthinkable for the British model to sanction such large-scale state intervention.

The extent of the failure of the British model to redress any of the longstanding supply-side weaknesses of the United Kingdom economy was demonstrated when Ed Balls contended that 'raising skills levels is the central economic challenge of the next decade' (Balls, 2006b). This comment invited the question of what the British model had been doing to redress these shortcomings during the past decade. Business investment in the UK reflected the lack of progress in supply-side performance under New Labour. On the one hand, corporate profitability and company balance sheets had appeared 'unusually healthy'. On the other hand, investment expenditure had appeared 'anaemic', despite the cost of capital being low, and with pre-tax real rates of return on corporate capital (both net and gross of depreciation, and relative to net or gross capital employed) being 'close to 40-year highs' (Institute for Fiscal Studies, 2006: 61).

During 2006, business investment fell by 4.7 per cent, having grown by a meagre 3.25 per cent during 2005 (Office for National Statistics, 2007c: 1). Leading analysts described this performance as 'disappointing' (House of Commons Treasury Committee, 2007: 7–8). However, the reality was that investors continued to prefer to exploit the freedom offered to them by the City of London's liberalized markets to invest overseas, or to trade speculatively, rather than to invest in the opportunities afforded by the British model.

The British model also failed to bridge the productivity gap between the UK and its leading competitors. In 2005, UK productivity per worker remained 9 per cent below the Group of Seven (G7) average, and 25 per cent behind the United States. This marked a considerable improvement on 1997, when the United Kingdom had been 15 per cent behind the G7 average, and 28 per cent behind the United States (Office for National Statistics, 2007d: 10). The productivity gap had been narrowed, but not bridged.

The most damning evidence that the British model had failed to remedy supply-side weaknesses lay in its failure to reverse the trend of UK current account deficits. Indeed, those deficits had strengthened and deepened during the ten years of New Labour. The UK had experienced current account deficits in every year since 1984 and a trade deficit in every year since 1982 (and in all but six years since 1900). In 2006, the UK recorded a deficit of £50.2 billion (or –3.9 per cent of GDP), an increase from the deficit in 2005 of £29.2 billion (or –2.4 per cent of GDP). The deficit on trade in goods was no less than £77.4 billion. This deficit was in no sense balanced by a £31.1 billion surplus on the UK's trade in services. Thus, the overall deficit on trade in goods and services was £46.3 billion, compared to £44.5 billion in 2005 (or –3.6 per cent of GDP) (Office for National Statistics, 2007e: 1–3; 2007f: 1; 2007g: 1).

The legacy of the British model: private imprudence, debt and volatility

One of the most frequent boasts by Gordon Brown was that the British model had 'locked in' stability. In practice, the British model could not possibly lock in stability because the openness of the City of London's financial markets meant that the door remained wide open to potential volatility and contagion. The UK had to borrow from abroad to finance its continuing current account deficit, with the consequence that inward investment (UK liabilities) came to exceed outward investment (UK assets). Since 1995, the level of the UK's external assets and liabilities had more than trebled. At the end of 2006, net assets stood at £5,279 billion, but net liabilities had risen to £5,544 billion. This meant that during the year, the UK's net liabilities had risen by £124.8 billion, from £140.4 billion at the end of 2005. This signified a deterioration from liabilities equivalent to –11.4 per cent of GDP at the end of 2005 to –20.6 per cent of GDP at the end of 2006 (Office for National Statistics, 2007e: 10). Indeed, this meant that 'net UK overseas liabilities as a percentage of GDP were at their highest in 30 years' (Institute for Fiscal Studies, 2006: 58).

Under previous Labour and Conservative governments, between 1966 and 1994, assets had tended to exceed liabilities, reaching a record £86.4 billion in 1986. However, from 1995 and throughout Brown's tenure as Chancellor, 'the UK has recorded a net liability position in every year' (Office for National Statistics, 2006: 96). Furthermore, in 2005 direct investment in the UK was greater than direct investment abroad for the first time since 1990 (Office for National Statistics, 2006: 78). That trend continued during 2006, with direct investment abroad of £43.2 billion far exceeded by direct investment in the UK of £75.8 billion (Office for National Statistics, 2007e: 8). Such imbalances risked a potential loss of confidence and willingness among foreign investors to continue to fund the United Kingdom's deficits, with potentially destabilizing consequences for the future value of sterling, especially since sterling operates outside the collective stability of the Eurozone.

Under New Labour's British model of political economy, economic growth was overwhelmingly consumer-led and borrowing-driven. It was neither investment-led nor savings-driven. Consumers had taken advantage of the opportunities offered by liberalized and deregulated financial and property markets to borrow record amounts of money, set against the rising value of assets – notably house prices and share values. This capacity to borrow had been facilitated by the innovative way in which liberalized financial markets had discovered new ways to finance debt. Where once home-buyers would have been limited to borrowing up to three times their current salary, it was now possible for them to borrow up to six times their salary.

Gordon Brown's sense of moral purpose did not extend to prudence and thrift in the use of credit cards. During 2006 total spending in the

UK on credit cards did actually fall by 2 per cent, from £122 billion to £120 billion. However, that decline, which was the first fall for more than forty years, was more than offset by a 15 per cent increase in spending on debit cards, which rose to £195 billion. Indeed, spending on plastic cards in December 2006 reached a record high of £31 billion, including £19.6 billion from 472 million transactions conducted on debit cards, a 15.3 per cent rise on a year earlier (APACS, 2007).

Total UK personal debt stood at £1,291 billion by the end of December 2006, an annual increase of 10.6 per cent or around £114 billion. Of this total, £1,078 billion was lending secured against property, an annual increase of 11.5 per cent. The remaining £213 billion was consumer credit lending to individuals, an annual increase of 6.2 per cent, of which £54.9 billion was owed on credit cards. That meant that, by the end of December 2006, the average UK household debt was £53,326 (including mortgages) or £8,791 (excluding mortgages). These debts cost an average of £3,400 a year to service. Indeed, the average UK adult owed £27,445 (including mortgages), including £4,524 of debt held on credit cards, motor and retail finance deals, overdrafts or unsecured personal loans (Credit Action, 2007).

An increasing number of people are incapable of managing their debts. During the financial year 2005–06, the Citizens Advice Bureau (CAB) received 1.4 million requests for advice with debt problems, an annual increase of 11 per cent. However, during January 2007 alone, the number of cases of debt problems rose to 83,000, an annual increase of 15 per cent. Indeed, the CAB estimated that it would take its clients an average of 77 years to pay back their average debt of £13,000, because that amount is nearly 17.5 times their average monthly income (Citizens Advice, 2007). Therefore, the British model had done little to curb the UK's addiction to credit and borrowing. On the contrary, it had fed that habit by making it the principal motive force behind a decade of economic growth. At the end of New Labour's decade in office, personal debt was increasing by £1 million every 3.85 minutes (Credit Action, 2007).

These very high levels of personal private debt may have important and damaging consequences for the UK's economic performance during the next economic cycle. New Labour did not contemplate a tax on consumer credit, in an attempt to dampen the growth of debt. However, during the 1980s, with Nigel Lawson as Chancellor, the Treasury had contemplated the introduction of a 1 per cent tax on outstanding consumer credit (including mortgages). Lawson concluded that the consumer- and property-led boom of the late 1980s was 'to a considerable extent a once-and-for-all occurrence: the change from a financially regulated to a financially deregulated economy' (Lawson, 1992: 366–7, 631). He was wrong. Rather than being a one-off, the UK had become locked under Lawson's successors, notably Gordon Brown, into a permanent condition of financial risk, volatility and debt-financed consumption.

Conclusion

During ten years of New Labour government, the British model of political economy delivered 40 consecutive quarters of economic growth. This constituted a superior economic performance than that achieved by any previous Labour government. However, despite that success, and the general election victories in 2001 and 2005 that it helped to inspire, the British model failed in its attempt to rally the private sector to a shared sense of national economic purpose. At the start of New Labour's tenure, Gordon Brown had promised not to pursue 'a policy of "Whitehall knows best"', but instead to be 'a supporter and friend of all that is best in British entrepreneurial culture' (Brown, 1997c). In the event, New Labour discovered that, when left to themselves to enjoy the freedom of liberalized markets, British entrepreneurs might choose to engage in the very culture of short-termism and domestic under-investment that had prompted Whitehall intervention by previous Labour governments.

The impact of the British model of political economy was to reinforce both competitive advantage and societal inequalities in income and wealth by rewarding the rich and successful. The winners from the British model of political economy were the City of London, investors in the housing market, and the Treasury itself, which enjoyed unprecedented power over the design of policy and the allocation of resources in England. The losers under the British model were manufacturing industry, and first time buyers on the property market. Moreover, the implementation of the British model of political economy was a quintessentially top-down, technocratic exercise. Despite its claims to have accorded primacy to economics over politics, it remained a highly politicized agenda, driven by a committee of two, namely Gordon Brown and his Chief Economic Adviser and closest political confidant, Ed Balls. Vital decisions concerning macro and microeconomic policy were delegated to a series of unelected committees and experts appointed or approved by Brown, much of whose work has been beyond the democratic scrutiny of the British people.

At the end of a decade of New Labour government, the long tail of under-performing companies and individuals first highlighted by the Commission on Public Policy and British Business immediately prior to the election of the Blair government was still evident (CPPBB, 1997). Furthermore, that Gordon Brown's tenth and final Pre-Budget Report identified the challenge for the next decade as the creation of 'a new British framework for investment and innovation, a British strategy to make the next stage of globalisation work for the British people' (Brown, 2006a), was testament to the failure of the British model during ten years of New Labour to redress significantly the long-term supply-side weaknesses of the United Kingdom economy.

3
New Labour and Public Expenditure

Maurice Mullard and Raymond Swaray

Introduction

This chapter compares the record of the Blair governments on public expenditure with that of the previous Labour governments of Clement Attlee, Harold Wilson and James Callaghan. A study of the data confirms that public expenditure during the years of the Blair government had increased significantly above the levels reached by the previous Labour governments. This applies not only for the total levels of public expenditure but also for individual programmes, including health, education, social security, defence, law and order, and trade and industry. However, the Wilson and Callaghan governments did spend more than the Blair governments on subsidies to the nationalized industries and on housing capital and housing subsidies.

May 2007 marked a decade of uninterrupted Labour government, an unprecedented experience for the Labour Party and modern British political history. During the period 1884 to 1996, the Conservatives had been in government for 80 out of a possible 102 years. In a previous study (Mullard and Swaray, 2006), it had been shown that politics does make a difference to public expenditure trends. Both Labour and Conservative governments' public spending outturns did reflect competing political ideologies, with Labour governments spending more on health, housing, education and social security while Conservative governments tended to spend more on defence and law and order. This chapter explores whether, after ten years of New Labour, the Blair governments delivered a qualitative shift in their public spending outputs when compared to previous Labour governments.

Public expenditure has always been at the heart of the Labour Party's thinking because it has provided the means for achieving Labour's plurality of major policy commitments. These have included nationalization, subsidies to industry and to regional policy, income redistribution, incomes policy and subsidies on rents, gas and electricity prices. Furthermore, a central assumption of Labour's thinking that connects the Fabian socialist and social democratic traditions has been the assumption that higher levels of spending on health, education and social security would improve the quality of public services, while access to universal benefits would in turn reduce income inequalities. For example, the Diamond Commission, set up by the Wilson government in August 1974, measured incomes at three levels that included original income, income after expenditure in kind (health and education) and income after transfers (social security). It found that the share of wealth possessed by the richest 1 per cent of the UK population had declined dramatically from 69 per cent in 1911–13, to 42 per cent in 1960, and to only 28 per cent in 1972 (Diamond, 1975).

There is now a growing body of academic literature that seeks to argue that the Blair governments represented a departure from Labour's historic commitments to collectivism, equality and social democratic values (Panitch and Leys, 2001; Heffernan, 1999; Hay, 1999). According to these authors, the Labour Party under Blair has accepted the logic of free markets, and that the role of government is limited in the context of the globalized economy. The celebration of individualism and market-based choice has included the implicit acceptance of growing income inequalities. In terms of social policy, the concern has been the reduction of poverty rather than seeking to deal with issues of structure and income inequalities. From this perspective, the Blair governments have represented continuity within the New Right settlement that had been defined and shaped during the years of the Thatcher governments.

An alternative interpretation points to the social policy achievements of the Blair government including the minimum wage, Working Families Tax Credit, increases in child benefits, the lower rates of unemployment and continued economic growth, policy successes that allowed the government to combine economic prosperity with growth in social provision. This interpretation points to the high levels of spending on health and education as being trends that have reversed the neglect of public services the Blair government had inherited after 17 years of Conservative governments. New Labour under Blair has remained loyal to the Croslandite tradition and belief in high quality public services (Leonard and Crosland, 1999; Finlayson, 2003; Fielding, 2002).

The principal conclusions of this chapter are that, during the tenure of the Blair governments, total expenditure on law and order, health, education and social security rose faster than under the Attlee, Wilson and Callaghan governments. However, during the tenure of the Wilson and Callaghan governments, total expenditure on housing subsidies and subsidies to nationalized industries increased at a faster rate than under New Labour. These findings, at one level, suggest that the Blair governments have remained committed to the Croslandite tradition of increasing public expenditure to improve the quality of public provision. However, previous Labour governments tended to increase subsidies for gas, water and electricity, housing rents, price controls and incomes policies, which in turn contributed to reducing income inequalities. Under the Blair governments income inequalities have continued to increase.

The study of post-war British political history confirms that each Labour government had different priorities that reflected changing contexts. During the Wilson and Callaghan governments of the 1960s and 1970s, housing subsidies, price controls and income policies were crucial to those governments' anti-inflation strategies (Callaghan, 1987; O'Hara and Parr, 2006; Coopey et al., 1993; Morgan, 1997). Those Labour governments were involved in securing trade union agreements on wages while the government pledged to hold down prices on housing and other public utilities. At the same time, both the Wilson and Callaghan governments showed commitments to reducing income inequalities. The Wilson government of 1964 made commitments on building more social housing, the expansion of higher education, comprehensive schools, increases in pensions and social transfers. For its part, the Callaghan government introduced child benefits.

By contrast, during the years of the Blair governments there was no explicit incomes policy and no attempt to reintroduce price controls. However, there was an implicit incomes policy. Delegating responsibility to the Bank of England to deal with inflation meant that any hints of pressures in wage settlements would result in higher interest rates and therefore higher mortgage costs. Utilities had been privatized and the government did not seek to secure incomes policy or trade union agreements to deal with inflation. Anti-inflation policy became the responsibility of the Bank of England. While recognizing the achievements of the Attlee governments, Tony Blair tended to live in denial of both the Wilson and Callaghan governments (Skidelsky, 2004; Riddell, 2004). According to Blair's interpretation of history, both those governments had made promises to increase public expenditure but had to reverse their commitments because of lower rates of economic growth that could not sustain their spending plans. Blair pledged to break with the cycle of boom and bust and to put the economy on a sustainable growth path that would sustain his government's plans for additional spending.

Income inequality declined during the period 1964 to 1979. The average Gini coefficient during this period was 0.25 (Institute for Fiscal Studies, 2007b). By contrast, since 1980 the Gini coefficient has expanded to 0.35, which makes the UK the most unequal society within the Organization for Economic Cooperation and Development (OECD) area after the United States and the Republic of Ireland (Institute for Fiscal Studies, 2007b). The expansion of income inequality attributed mainly to the tax reductions of the Thatcher years had not been reversed after ten years of New Labour. During the Wilson and Callaghan years, full employment and incomes policy helped to reduce wage differentials, while subsidies on housing, electricity, gas and coal increased the social wage. Since the 1980s, incomes for the top 1 per cent of earners have increased from 20 times the median wage to 400 times the median wage in 2005.

The Attlee government and the post-war settlement

From its inception, the Labour Party interpreted Clause IV of its 1918 constitution as the written confirmation of Labour's core values. The commitment to nationalization aimed to challenge the axioms of the logic of free markets and instead provide a means for managing the economy. Within Clause IV was embedded the argument for income redistribution. In 1937, for example, Hugh Gaitskell, who was to become the Leader of the Labour Party in 1959 wrote:

So long as production is left to the uncontrolled decisions of private individuals, conducted, guided and inspired by the motive of profit, so long will Poverty, Insecurity and Injustice continue. (Gaitskell cited in Williams, 1982: 72)

This quote is significant because in 1937 Gaitskell seemed to be making the important statement that Labour needed to reject the values both of competitive markets driven by profits and of an uncontrolled capitalism that seemed to reproduce injustice and inequality. Labour Party policy in the inter-war years therefore made the connections between the structure of capitalism, class and inequalities. The priorities of the Labour government elected in 1945 were outlined in two major policy statements; first in 1937 in *Labour's Immediate Programme* (Labour Party, 1937), and, second, in Labour's general election manifesto of 1945, *Let Us Face the*

Future (Labour Party, 1945). The Attlee government nationalized coal, steel, the railways, gas and electricity and also established the National Health Service, and reformed pensions and social security in line with the recommendations of the Beveridge Report of 1942. When Aneurin Bevan became Housing Minister in 1945, he had envisioned a sector of public housing that would offer people the choice to live in owner occupation or in the public sector:

> We should try to introduce in our modern villages and towns what was always the lovely feature of English and Welsh villages, where the doctor, the grocer, the butcher and the farm labourer all lived in the same street. I believe that is essential for the full life of a citizen ... to see the living tapestry of a mixed community. (Bevan cited in Foot, 1973: 76)

Ernest Bevin, leader of the Transport and General Workers' Union, was brought in as Minister of Labour in the Attlee government. The Trade Disputes Act of 1927, passed by a Conservative government in the aftermath of the 1926 General Strike, was repealed and trade union immunities were restored. The Attlee government had by 1951 delivered an economy in better shape than it had inherited in 1945. The years 1946 to 1951 were a period of continuous full employment with living standards increasing by about 10 per cent and the economy growing at 3 per cent per annum. Britain by 1951 had the best economic performance in Europe, while output per person was increasing faster than in the United States (Williams, 1982; Cairncross, 1985).

Labour's programme of rationing, food subsidies and rent controls was described as providing justice and avoiding profiteering in a context of shortages. The problem of austerity was that although by 1951 everyone was healthier, people were feeling increasingly restricted and deprived of choice:

> Although the nation as a whole was healthier by 1951 than it had ever been, due to the even distribution of basic foods, the average adult's resistance to infection was often like his spirits: low ... The adult world continued to be one of queues and shortages ... It seemed sometimes as if no one could go anywhere or do anything without producing some kind of permit or coupon (or as Sir Stafford Cripps would have it 'couponing'). (Sissons and French, 1964: 36)

The Conservative Party that won the elections in 1951, 1955 and 1959 did not seek to undo the Attlee government's post-war settlement.

The Industrial Charter of 1947 had committed a future Conservative government to the policy of full employment, the welfare state and trade union rights. The Conservative Party proclaimed:

> We are not a Party of unbridled brutal capitalism and never have been. Although we believe in personal responsibility and personal initiative in business we are not the political children of the laissez-faire school. We opposed them decade after decade. Where did the Tories stand when the greed and squalor of the industrial revolution were darkening our land? I am content with Keir Hardie's testimony: 'As a matter of hard dry fact, from which there can be no getting away, there is more labour legislation standing to the credit of the Conservative Party on the Statute Book than there is to that of their opponents.' (Anthony Eden cited in Conservative Party, 1947: 42–3)

The Attlee government accepted the argument that the shaping and the defining of economic decisions could not be left to private individuals or markets. A modern economy needed national decisions to improve investment in the infrastructure including electricity, railways and telecommunications. Housing provision was obviously a priority as well as economic re-structuring.

By contrast, the economic contours inherited by Blair in 1997 were qualitatively different to the economic landscape that confronted the Attlee government in the aftermath of six years of total warfare. The nationalized industries of Attlee had been de-nationalized during the years of the Thatcher governments. Railways had been returned to railway companies, while gas and electricity were broken into generating companies and local suppliers. The vision of public housing being one of choice of high-quality housing in the public sector and people choosing their landlords had become residual social housing that caters for poor families. Coal, gas, electricity and steel had been nationalized during the Attlee governments because of the lack of financial investment. During the years of the Thatcher governments, the arguments had been reversed. The financial investment needed in these sectors would now come from the private sector.

The revisionists and the Wilson government, 1964–70

During the 1950s, and after three successive electoral defeats under the direction of Hugh Gaitskell and Anthony Crosland, the Labour Party was urged to move away from the ideas of nationalization and to adopt a social democratic approach. It was argued that improving the quality of public expenditure would result in the making of the classless society since people irrespective of income will want to use high quality public services (Crosland, 1956). Gaitskell, after the third consecutive general election defeat in 1959, was more determined that it was crucial for the Labour Party to abandon Clause IV from its 1918 constitution since he believed that the party no longer believed in 100 per cent public ownership of the economy, but that public ownership will always be only one of the means to the classless society. He argued:

> We should make two things clear ... that we have no intention of abandoning public ownership ... that we regard public ownership not as an end in itself but as a means to certain ends ... While we certainly wish to extend social ownership our goal is not 100 per cent State ownership. Our goal is a society in which Socialist goals are realised ... The pace at which we can go depends on how quickly we can persuade our fellow citizens to back us. (Gaitskell cited in Labour Party, 1959)

Hugh Gaitskell died in 1963, so it was under Wilson's leadership that the Labour Party won the 1964 and 1966 general elections. Wilson had argued that the years of Conservative governments had been 13 wasted years and that a Labour government would embrace the 'white heat' of technology, essential to the modernization of the British economy:

> In all our plans for the future, we are re-defining and we are re-stating our Socialism in terms of the scientific revolution. But that revolution cannot become a reality unless we are prepared to make far-reaching changes in economic and social attitudes which permeate our whole system of society. The Britain that is going to be forged in the white heat of this revolution will be no place for restrictive practices or for outdated methods on either side of industry ... we must use all the resources of democratic planning, all the latent and underdeveloped energies and skills of our people, to ensure Britain's standing in the world. (Labour Party, 1963: 139–40)

The Wilson government of 1964 to 1970 accepted the logic of Crosland's argument for increased public spending and soon made education and housing the priorities for the Labour government. The late John Macintosh had no hesitation in arguing that the Labour governments of 1964–70 and 1974–79 were dominated by Crosland's views on equality:

Crosland's ideas continued to be almost unchallenged and dominated the Labour Governments of 1964–1970 .... the Labour Government which came into office in 1974 edged back towards a Croslandite position ... if any ideas or policies could be said to have characterised Mr Callaghan's very matter-of-fact and cautious government, they were the continuation of an approach which Crosland had set out in 1956. (Macintosh, 1978: 260)

During the years 1964–70, Prime Minister Wilson made the expansion of education central to Labour's public expenditure commitments. The government accepted the recommendations of the 1963 Robbins Report advocating a major expansion in higher education. Robbins fitted in with Wilson's commitment to the 'scientific age'. Pimlott (1992) described this era as the 'golden age' for higher education. The Wilson governments established 29 polytechnics and the Open University, and expanded student participation rates from 5 per cent to 10 per cent. The Housing Minister, Richard Crossman, managed to get a commitment from the Prime Minister to build 500,000 houses. There was also an expansion in the road building programme. Capital expenditure increased to 8 per cent of GDP – the highest level achieved by any post-war government.

Despite this public investment, industrial militancy was on the increase after 1966. Agitation had started with the informal system of industrial relations of joint shop stewards committees, which in turn resulted in an upsurge of wildcat strikes. Trade union leaders who wanted to work with the Labour government through tripartite structures were undermined by their shop stewards. The proposal outlined by Barbara Castle *In Place of Strife* (HM Government, 1969) aimed to introduce cooling-off periods, regulate secondary pickets and introduce ballots before a strike. Because of opposition to the reforms within the cabinet, Harold Wilson decided not to introduce the legislation, but many of the recommendations in that White Paper became the central themes of trade union legislation introduced by the Heath and Thatcher governments.

The Wilson and Callaghan governments, 1974–79

Both the Wilson government in 1969 and the Heath government in 1970 had come to the conclusion that the reform of industrial relations was connected to Britain's economic performance. Too many days were being lost at work because of strike action while trade unions were still seen as crucial to dealing with the problem of rising inflation. Both governments were committed to the post-war settlement of full employment and were therefore reluctant to use unemployment as a means of disciplining labour markets.

The Heath government did attempt to secure trade union agreements on wage moderation but trade union demands on price controls and school meals were seen as being too high a price to pay to secure a wage settlement. The Heath government Trade Disputes Acts of 1972 had been made unworkable. As a consequence, the February and October 1974 Conservative Party general election manifestos focused upon 'The Danger from Within' posed by the trade unions to economic performance, political stability and the rule of law, and the need for the British people to recognize that the unions were 'not the government of the country' (Conservative Party, 1974b: 3). Labour won the election arguing the case that it had a special understanding with the trade unions and that it would seek to govern through harmony rather than confrontation. The Social Contract agreed between the trade unions and the Labour Party was central to the government's anti-inflation strategy. Implicit in the social contract was the concept of the social wage. Trade unions would recognize increases in spending on health, education, pensions and subsidies as part of their take-home pay.

Between 1974 and 1976, the government expanded spending on housing rents, price control, health and education. Public sector borrowing had increased to 9 per cent of GDP. The government had to resort to borrowing from the International Monetary Fund (IMF). The Letter of Intent signed by the Chancellor Denis Healey committed the government to reduce public expenditure. A study of debates within the cabinet and the key committees of the Labour Party during the period 1975–77 reveals the tensions between some members of the cabinet. Lord Barnett and Denis Healey argued that the government had made too many concessions to the trade unions, while other cabinet ministers including Anthony Crosland and Tony Benn resisted the IMF Letter of Intent of 1975 and argued for an alternative economic strategy (Mullard, 1993).

The Callaghan government did succeed in securing three consecutive years of incomes policy from 1976 through to 1979 and the anti-inflation policy was in many ways a success when compared with the experiences of the Thatcher governments. The Thatcher government did manage to squeeze out inflation but throughout the years of that government unemployment never fell below 2 million and there were periods in 1983, 1987 and 1990 when unemployment peaked at over 3 million. By contrast, after 1976 the inflation rate did fall without any major increases in unemployment. Furthermore, the unemployment rate had started to fall in late 1978. However, the Winter of Discontent and the unsettled industrial relations climate of 1978 and early 1979 did contribute to Labour's defeat in 1979.

The making of New Labour

During the period 1979 to 1997, all three leaders of the Labour Party including Kinnock, Smith and Blair had argued the case for the need to modernize the structure and constitution of the Labour Party. Reforms including one member, one vote (OMOV), reforms to the Electoral College and the creation of policy forums all aimed to reduce the influence of Labour activists and the trade unions. The aim was to give the party back to the moderates. The lesson drawn by Tony Blair was the need to accept the political settlement defined by Mrs Thatcher. The post-war settlement ushered in by the Attlee government had been eclipsed by Thatcherism, and like the Conservatives of the 1950s Labour in 1997 had to accept the new political contours.

There would be no social contract or incomes policy under a Blair government. After four election defeats, Blair had argued that the Labour Party needed to make itself relevant to changing expectations if the party still aspired to win office. Embracing the Thatcher political settlement including the housing right-to-buy policy, the process of privatization, trade union reform and the commitment of not increasing income tax rates for higher earners (Powell, 1999), Blair could present the Labour Party as New Labour (Rawnsley, 2000). The jettisoning of Clause IV, a symbol of Labour's commitment to nationalization, economic planning and redistribution of income, confirmed that Labour would embrace the open market economy. Any policies on redistribution and public expenditure would therefore in future depend on the success of the market economy to provide the necessary economic growth and tax revenues to finance increases in public expenditure. Where Gaitskell had failed in 1959, Blair prevailed in 1995 (Fairclough, 2000).

Desperate to win office, the Labour Party was willing to follow a new leader who promised electoral success. In re-branding the party as New Labour, Blair was accused of breaking with the layers of thinking that defined Labour's history. In re-making the party as New Labour, there implicitly had to be a break with what was to be defined as Old Labour and implicitly to picture previous Labour governments as failed governments. New Labour also had to break with the social democratic politics of Gaitskell and Crosland by making commitments not to increase income tax rates on higher incomes to finance increases in public spending:

a party agenda that seemed to revolve around more state control and higher taxes was out of tune with the times, that it was not enough to be a caring party if the caring could not be paid for ... That a party that seemed to be the prisoner of outside interests could not pursue the public interest. That a party that represented producer interests could not properly represent consumers. (Wright, 1997: 23)

Trends in public expenditure under Old Labour and New Labour

In a previous study (Mullard and Swaray, 2006), we argued that in the study of public expenditure politics does matter. In our study for the period 1948 to 2003, we focused on individual expenditure programmes to show that Labour governments had always spent more on health, education and social security while Conservative governments tended to spend more on law and order and defence. However, the key question after ten years of New Labour concerns whether the Blair governments have behaved differently on public expenditure when compared to previous Labour governments. Consequently, the same statistical methodology for analysing expenditure statistics has now been applied to the New Labour governments (for an explanation of this methodology, see Mullard and Swaray, 2006).

In terms of total expenditure, between 1997 and 2005, spending expanded from 41 per cent of GDP to 44 per cent of GDP. During the years of the Attlee government expenditure increased from 29 per cent to 32 per cent of GDP. Between 1964 and 1970, the Wilson government increased expenditure from 38 to 42 per cent of GDP, while during the period 1974–79, the Wilson and Callaghan governments increased spending from 41 per cent in 1974 to 48 per cent in 1976 but then decreased it to 43 per cent of GDP by 1979. However, statistical testing has confirmed that the Blair governments' record on total spending was significantly higher than that for previous Labour governments.

In relation to health expenditure, during the period 1948–51, the Attlee government increased spending rapidly from £6 billion to £11 billion, an increase of over 50 per cent, and from 2.1 per cent of GDP to 3.6 per cent of GDP. Over the period 1964–70, during the tenure of the Wilson government, expenditure increased from 3.6 per cent to 4.1 per cent of GDP, while over the period 1974–79, the Wilson and Callaghan governments reduced expenditure from 5.4 per cent of GDP to 4.7 per cent, and from £31 billion to £29 billion. During the Blair governments, health expenditure again increased from 6.3 per cent of GDP to 7.2 per cent and from £58 billion to £84 billion by 2005. Again, the record of the Blair governments was that of the state spending significantly more on health than previous Labour governments.

With regard to education spending, during the years of the Attlee government, expenditure increased from £6.5 billion to £10 billion, an increase of over 50 per cent. Expenditure also expanded from 2.3 per cent of GDP to 3.4 per cent of GDP. During the period 1964–70, expenditure expanded from 4.3 per cent of GDP to 4.8 per cent and from £19 billion to £24 billion. During the period from 1970 to 1979, spending on education increased from 5.5 per cent of GDP to 6.2 per cent, but declined to 5.5 per cent after the IMF cuts of 1976. Under New Labour, expenditure increased from 4.5 per cent of GDP to 5.6 per cent and from £42 billion to £65 billion by 2005, an increase of 54 per cent. The Blair governments' expenditure record on education is significantly better than those of previous Labour governments.

Under New Labour, public spending on social housing increased from £8.4 billion to £10 billion, while as a ratio of GDP expenditure totalled some 0.8 per cent of GDP. This needs to be compared with the years of the Attlee government when expenditure was around 2.5 per cent of GDP, and the years of the Callaghan government when expenditure peaked at 5 per cent of GDP, increasing from £18 billion to £28 billion. Statistical testing has confirmed that both the Wilson and Wilson/Callaghan governments spent more on housing than the Blair government. The Labour government of 1964 spent more on capital expenditure on housing, while the Callaghan government focused on increasing subsidies on rents as part of its anti-inflation strategy and the government's commitment to the Social Contract.

In relation to social security, our research has confirmed that New Labour under Blair has been spending significantly more than previous Old Labour governments, because of increases in child benefits, pensions and the Working Families Tax Credit. During the years of the Blair governments, incomes for the bottom 10 per cent of earners increased because of transfers through the social security system. Furthermore, expenditure on social security increased despite the falls in unemployment. The rate of unemployment during the past decade averaged around 1 million, compared with 2 million during the Thatcher years.

In 1948, the Attlee government had spent in real terms (2005 prices) around £13 billion, which amounted to about 5 per cent of GDP. In 1964, the Wilson government expenditure inherited spending of around £28 billion, but by 1970 Labour was spending £39 billion on social security, or around 7.6 per cent of GDP. During the years of the Callaghan government, social security expenditure had reached £67 billion or 10 per cent of GDP. Under the Blair governments, social security expenditure increased from £151 billion to £183 billion by 2005. Expenditure on social security in 2005 totalled some 16 per cent of GDP.

The trade and industry programme during the period 1950–76 included initiatives such as regional assistance and regional aid programmes which tended to provide incentives for industries to relocate. Prominent examples included relocation of parts of the car industry to Liverpool and Scotland during the 1960s. During the years of the Wilson government, the programme reached a peak of £17 billion, equivalent to 4.3 per cent of GDP. During the Callaghan years, the roads and environment programme peaked at £12 billion, but then was reduced drastically by 50 per cent. During the years of the Blair governments, despite their rhetorical commitment not to intervene in industry, expenditure increased to £31 billion by 2005.

For public expenditure on the environment and roads, both programmes historically have incorporated a high capital component. Under the Callaghan government, both programmes experienced the bulk of reductions after the IMF's intervention in 1976. Previously, the Wilson government had increased spending on the environment from £7 billion to £9 billion. Under the Callaghan government, expenditure reached a peak of £13.7 billion. However, by the time Labour had left office in 1979, expenditure had fallen to £3.4 billion. As a ratio of GDP, expenditure reached a peak of 2.4 per cent in 1975. By 1979, this had fallen to 0.4 per cent of GDP. From 1997 to 2005, expenditure under New Labour increased to £10 billion, but was still at 0.9 per cent of GDP, well below the levels of 1.7 per cent in 1966 and 2.4 per cent in 1975.

Finally, in relation to public spending on law and order, the statistics have shown that the Blair governments spent significantly more on tackling crime and disorder than any previous Labour government. In 1948, expenditure on law and order was only £1.2 billion, or equivalent to 0.4 per cent of GDP. In 2005 expenditure had increased to £29 billion, or the equivalent of 2.5 per cent of GDP. By contrast, the Attlee government in 1948 had spent as much as £17 billion on defence, equivalent to 6 per cent of GDP. In 2005, despite the UK's involvement in major military operations in Iraq and Afghanistan, defence spending of £30 billion was equivalent to only 3 per cent of GDP, a very significant decline in total spending and bucking the trend in other public spending programmes.

Conclusion

Public expenditure on health, education and social security increased more rapidly under New Labour than under previous Conservative and Labour governments. At the same time, the Old Labour governments of the 1960s and 1970s did spend more on house building and housing subsidies, and on subsidies to electricity and gas. Consequently, not just the total amount spent, but also the amount spent on individual programmes, had changed significantly after ten years of New Labour. However, the increases in spending on social protection during the past decade have not reversed the trend in income inequalities that started with the election of Margaret Thatcher in May 1979. The increases in spending have not addressed the issue of the structure of income inequalities.

Previous Labour governments had made connections between the structure and nature of capitalism, issues of social class and inequalities in income and wealth. The Labour Party's historic relationship with the trade unions had been the mechanism for attempting to create a policy framework that would seek to address issues of structures and inequality. Trade union recognition, trade union immunities and the growth of trade union membership had been integral to the thinking of the Labour Party of Attlee, Wilson and Callaghan. For example, the Callaghan government had introduced legislation on the closed shop, which in turn resulted in increases in trade union membership. By 1976, trade union density had reached a peak of 50 per cent of the UK workforce. By contrast, in 2007, trade union membership had fallen to well below 30 per cent of the workforce.

To justify their changes in the pattern of New Labour's public spending priorities, the Blair governments embraced the arguments that economic prosperity depended upon competing in the global economy. This meant not only living with but actively embracing competitive markets, and a highly educated and trained labour force prepared to be flexible to meet the global challenges of competition. Power no longer belonged to organizations but to individuals able to sell their ideas. In the new knowledge economy, trade unions and collective forms of resistance had become irrelevant. The Blair governments have therefore embraced the concept of the individual, that life is made up of individualized biographies and the role of government is therefore limited to providing contexts for market-based opportunities. Failure and success depend on individual endeavour. New Labour did not define the economy as a capitalist economy of structure, class and inequality but in terms of markets, competition and individual enterprise. The role of government was simply to provide the context for individuals to succeed, and to reduce child and pensioner poverty. Income inequality, which for previous Labour governments had been a focal point for public spending priorities and programmes, had therefore become a non-issue.

4
New Labour and Social Policy

Stephen Driver

Preparing for power

Social policy was always likely to make headlines for the Labour Party once it got into power in 1997. It had the potential to touch many raw political nerves. And with social policy defining so much of what was new about New Labour, the government's policies on welfare to work, education and the National Health Service, in particular, would be critical political battlegrounds for the party modernizers led by Tony Blair and Gordon Brown. As it turned out, social policy would also prove a key battleground *between* Blair and Brown over the next ten years.

Since the Labour Party's election defeat in 1992, the reform of the welfare state had become a dominant theme alongside market economics in the emerging New Labour story. The Commission on Social Justice, established by Labour leader John Smith, set the new course: the welfare state should promote work; and that by investing in education and training, the government could boost the human capital of the nation, leading to economic growth and social justice. There was a future for social democracy in Britain, but Labour had to rethink what centre-left governments did, how collective action was organized and the balance between welfare rights and responsibilities.

In important respects, the Commission's work did not do much more than nudge nascent New Labour back into the mainstream of European social democratic politics, in particular, in terms of more active labour market policies. But some on the Left in Britain were damning: the Commission had given up on welfare rights and on any real commitment to egalitarian political economy. Blair, as would become familiar, was unrepentant. In a 1995 lecture to the Fabian Society, the future prime minister told his audience that Labour had to move on, whatever its past achievements. 'We need a new settlement on welfare for a new age', Blair said, 'where opportunity and responsibility go together.' The party's new social policies, he continued, 'should and will cross the old boundaries between Left and Right, progressive and conservative' (Blair, 1995). This was not exactly an olive branch to New Labour's critics on the Left.

After ten years, then, do Labour's reforms amount to a coherent attempt at re-fashioning the British welfare state within the social democratic tradition? This chapter will cover two broad, and what for the Labour government have been key areas of social policy. The first is employment and social security, with the main policies being the New Deal, tax credits and the minimum wage. The second area covers those collective public services that were integral to the post-war welfare state's cradle to grave service: education and the National Health Service. Both are devolved policy areas and in Scotland and Wales governments have attempted to stake out distinct policies on the NHS and the funding of higher education, as well as personal care for the elderly. This chapter will focus on policy in England.

Taking over from the Tories

In opposition, New Labour promised to 'think the unthinkable' on welfare reform. But in truth, it had been the Conservative Party, not Labour, which had been doing just that for more than two decades. And as Mrs Thatcher's governments set about reforming education, health, housing, social security and social care (and not always getting very far), Labour retreated into a political bunker.

By the time Labour took over from the Tories in 1997, however, it was clear that the party had shaken off its bunker mentality. Labour modernizers conceded that Thatcherism might have a point. Public policy had to move on, not go backwards. The welfare state did need reforming – and money in itself was not the answer to the provision of welfare services (a view that echoed James Callaghan's 'Great Debate' speech on education standards in 1976). Post-Thatcherite politics took hold. But where would it lead?

The coherence of Labour's social policy programme ten years ago was not helped by a string of commitments to 'abolishing the internal market' in the NHS, to 'standards not structures' in schooling and to being 'wise spenders not big spenders' that the party in opposition had picked up on the way to power. These commitments said as much about New

Labour's tough electoral balancing act in the 1990s, between appeals to its traditional supporters as well as to those who were thinking of voting Labour against the grain, as it did about coherent programmes of public sector reform. Only where Gordon Brown reigned supreme – over the party's emerging welfare-to-work programme, the New Deal – was there any consistent guide to future policy making. But even on social security, it was not clear where the promise to 'examine the interaction of the tax and benefits system' might lead – the answer it proved was tax credits.

Significantly, Labour's first period in office was overshadowed by Brown's announcement made before the 1997 election that the party would for two years stick to the Conservative spending plans as set out in Chancellor Kenneth Clarke's last budget. In simple terms, Labour's social policies would not involve any new money, except for the much talked about 'windfall tax' on the privatized utilities, which would pay for the New Deal. This may have helped bury Labour's image as a party of tax and spend, but it did little to build a coherent strategy for reform of the welfare state.

Labour's first two years in power, then, saw Gordon Brown live up to his reputation as an iron chancellor. Extra money (£2.2 billion) did go to health and education from the contingency fund in 1999. Otherwise, the combination of a strong economy and the prudence of Mr Brown saw public spending as a share of national income fall to a 30 year low. The 2000 comprehensive spending review changed all this. Public spending was back on the political agenda – and there it would stay.

The big spend

The 2000 comprehensive spending review set out the government's plans for the rest of the parliament and beyond. After three years of a shrinking state, the size of government was set to grow again. Public spending went back above 40 per cent of national income. The big social policy winners after 2000 were health and education, as well as targeted support to lower-income families, in particular via tax credits (see Institute for Fiscal Studies, 2007c). After declining slightly in the first three years of Labour's term in office, health spending as a proportion of national income rose from 5.3 per cent to 7.5 per cent in 2006–07. Never since its creation in 1949 had the NHS been given such a sustained injection of cash. The health budget increased on average by 7 per cent a year, a marked increase in government spending compared with the rate under the Conservatives. Public spending on education also rose substantially after the 2000 comprehensive spending review with an annual average increase of over

6 per cent. However, the growth in spending on education over the first two terms of the Labour government fell behind transport; was only just ahead of policing and public order; and was less than one percentage point above the long-term growth rate in education spending.

While the 2004 spending review marked a tightening of Labour's spending plans – and in terms of social policy, the big losers were social services – since 2000, the clear policy of the government was to increase public spending on certain areas of the welfare state, principally health, education and targeted support to lower-income families. But how effective has all this spending been in tackling those issues central to Labour and social democratic politics?

Welfare to work

Central to the Labour government's anti-poverty strategy over the past ten years has been to get the unemployed and the economically inactive back into work. This meant rethinking social security entitlements, including the tightening of employment tests, and a shift in the balance between the duties of the state to provide welfare and the duties of the welfare recipient in return for the right to public support. Once in power, Labour's New Deal programmes quickly expanded to cover 18–24 year olds, the long-term unemployed, the over 50s, lone parents, disabled people and partners of the unemployed. By 2001, most of those not in work or full-time education were in one of the New Deal programmes. The point of the New Deal was to offer support finding employment not just cash benefits for people not in work – the idea of an 'active' rather than 'passive' welfare state. The New Deal also introduced time limits, education and work options and sanctions for non-compliance. However, the new deals for lone parents and the disabled – new deals that cover key groups who are economically inactive – were in effect voluntary, though in both cases the government has introduced in subsequent parliaments measures to engage those on long-term disabilities benefits and to tighten the rules covering these groups.

The other side to Labour's New Deal was its policy to 'make work pay'. This meant two things. First, the introduction of a policy commitment dating back to the early twentieth century: a minimum wage. The starting rate of £3.60 and young people exempt from its provisions did little to win support from sceptical trade unions, or from equally sceptical employers who feared that governments telling them how much to pay their workers would increase costs and lead to higher unemployment.

These fears have largely been proved false, even as the minimum wage was raised to £4.10 at the start of the second term and to £5.35 in 2006.

The second aspect of the Labour government's policies to 'make work pay' has been the introduction of tax credits paid to working families on lower wages – and a national childcare strategy to increase the number of childcare places for working parents. Launched in the autumn of 1999, the Working Families Tax Credit (WFTC) replaced the Conservative government's in-work benefit, Family Credit. Controversially, the new credits were to be paid by HM Revenue and Customs through wage packets not the Benefit Agency. In 2003, the WFTC was split into two: a Working Tax Credit payable to all those in work; and a Child Tax Credit payable to all families with children, whether in work or not (and paid directly to the claimant).

Labour's tax credits policy has drawn considerable fire from, among others, the House of Commons Public Accounts Committee. While the policy has worked to support the incomes of low-paid workers, thereby increasing incentives to take employment and pulling families out of poverty, its administrative problems are legion. Critics suggest that the culture and practice of Revenue and Customs is ill-suited to the role of a benefits agency; and the method of predicting income has led to endemic problems of overpayment and claw-back for families on low and often unstable incomes. Moreover, tax credits, along with Labour's pension reforms, including a Pensions Credit as part of a minimum income guarantee for the retired, has further extended means-testing which, critics such as Labour MP Frank Field argue, discourages saving, promotes dependency and social security fraud and penalizes families that do the right thing (such as sticking together).

Labour's welfare-to-work policies have drawn criticism from those that view welfare rights as unconditional – although how far social security was unconditional in practice is the subject of some debate. Moreover, these policies have, in effect, acknowledged that welfare dependency is a problem for social policy; and that the behaviour of those dependent on state support matters, thereby challenging the underlying assumptions of post-war social democratic social policy (see Deacon, 2002). And the unrelenting focus on work has led the Left to accuse the government of moving away from a model of active labour market intervention based on human capital to one that gives priority to 'labour force attachment'. This, critics suggest, has turned the British welfare state into an Americanized 'workfare state', no longer offering a haven of support for people in need away from the market economy. 'Social inclusion' in New Labour's hands has meant little more than getting a job, however poorly paid (see Levitas, 2005).

Employment, poverty and inequality

How successful have Labour's policies been in raising employment levels *and* tackling poverty and inequality – issues at the heart of any Labour politics? Since 1997, helped by a buoyant and well-managed economy, Britain has enjoyed high levels of employment. Ten years after taking office, the overall rate of economic activity stands at 74.3 per cent – having fallen half a percentage point since the start of 2005. There is a debate about how effective the government's welfare-to-work programme has been in boosting employment. Since 1997, the numbers working have increased by over 2 million to just under 29 million. Estimates of the New Deal's contribution to this figure are below 1 million. Evaluations suggest that the New Deal increases the chances of finding work by 5–7 per cent. Sanctions and job search are seen to be the most cost-effective parts of the New Deal – although there are some concerns that sanctions have led to individuals leaving the labour market (and becoming economically inactive) and criminality. The education and training side of the New Deal is seen as the least effective and most expensive part, although in the longer term, it may be the most important in Labour's 'social investment state' (Centre for Economic Performance, 2005).

While employment has grown under Labour, however, rates of economic inactivity have remained stubbornly high – stuck at around 21 per cent of the working age population (all figures from the Office for National Statistics). Increasing student numbers account for a proportion of the economically active, though the number of people looking after the family and home has fallen. Indeed, the employment rate for lone parents has increased by over 5 per cent since 2001. Nonetheless, falling unemployment rates over the past ten years have not been matched by similar falls in the number of people outside the labour market. Over 2 million people of working age are on long-term sickness benefits, a greater proportion of them men – and a significant number aged under 25.

What about income distribution? During the 1980s, the income gap between rich and poor widened as a result of fiscal policy, deregulation, globalization, new technology, changing patterns of work and a booming economy that stretched income differentials. During the early 1990s, the income gap stabilized as the British economy sank into recession, but it grew again as the economy took off in the second half of the 1990s. Labour's fiscal policies since 1997 have been egalitarian in outcome, certainly by comparison with Conservative fiscal policy. Comparing the tax and benefit regimes in 1997 and 2004, whether adjusted for prices or earnings, the poorest are considerably better off and the richest worse off (Hills, 2004). The pattern of winners and losers is complicated by consumption and direct taxes. But the clear winners of Labour's policies have been the working poor, especially those with dependent children, as a result of the tax credits, the minimum wage and substantial increases to Child Benefit, all of which led to faster growth in earnings at the bottom end of the income distribution scale. The biggest losers are those households not in work without dependent children; households which in the main have seen benefits rise only with inflation.

Despite these fiscal redistributions under Labour, the gap between rich and poor in Britain remains wide. Comparing income inequality in 2004 with 1979, when Margaret Thatcher first took office, inequality is 40 per cent higher. Indeed, income inequality grew in 2004/05, partly as a result of growing wage differentials between skilled and unskilled workers. But after ten years of Labour government, while the very rich have got richer, many of the poorest are catching up with the middle. This, as John Hills argues, has been one of the major drivers for the fall in poverty rates, especially for children (Hills, 2004). Since the mid-1990s, there has been a steady decline in households living below the official poverty line. According to figures from the Office for National Statistics, in 2004/05, 16 per cent of the population was in low-income households, down from a high of 21 per cent in the early 1990s. But levels of poverty among working-age adults without dependent children have grown since the mid-1990s; stark differences in income levels persist between ethnic communities; and poverty rates among pensioners have not fallen as quickly as might be expected, partly as a result of the low take-up of means-tested benefits, in particular, the Pensions Credit. Labour's target to reduce child poverty has not proved as easy to reach once early gains were made from people finding work. The number of children in low-income households remained at 21 per cent between 2000 and 2004, before falling to 19 per cent in 2005.

'Modernizing' public services

Back in 1995, Tony Blair argued in a *Spectator* lecture that a Labour government should find new ways of bringing about social change. The old social democratic state was in need of reform – and New Labour would take a more pragmatic approach to the delivery of collective public services. 'What works' was the new motto. During much of Labour's first term in government, it was not clear what did work. But as the first part of this chapter has shown, with the 2000 comprehensive spending review in place, it became apparent that dealing with the Conservative legacy was in part about changing government priorities to target resources on the poor – and spending on the collective public services that benefit poorer families more than richer ones was central to this agenda.

However, these funding increases for public services came with strings attached. The public sector would have to 'modernize' in return for extra resources. Working practices would have to change. Terms and conditions of employment could be different, especially as services switched to the private sector. It is perhaps of little surprise then that the reform of the public sector has proved one of Labour's major domestic challenges over its ten years in power.

At the heart of Labour's modernization agenda was the idea that public services should become more 'customer-focused' and 'user-led' – and that within a national framework of minimum standards, the delivery of services should be devolved and delegated to meet the needs of local people. Furthermore, decentralization would underpin strategies that sought to break the culture of turf wars between government departments and develop 'joined-up' policies and multi-agency partnership working, such as the Sure Start programme for families in poor communities.

What the government left unsaid was that much of the new public management introduced under the Conservatives was here to stay. Business planning and performance management, inevitably driven by targets set by Whitehall (the 2000 NHS plan being a prime example), was necessary to deliver better public services. This set the government on collision course with professional bodies and public sector trade unions (who quickly joined other opponents of the government as part of the 'forces of conservatism').

In certain respects, Labour's first term reforms to the public services, limited as they were, were taking public policy beyond Thatcherism. In health, for example, certain aspects of the devolved governance of the Conservatives' health reforms were being retained – local purchasing, trust hospitals – but the quasi market features of these devolved forms were being replaced by a more collaborative network or partnership approach through the introduction of primary care trusts (PCTs). The powers of central government, however, remained much in evidence. Far from decentralizing public administration, the NHS plan and its associated policy of target setting were extending the powers of the central state.

This tension between centralism and localism was evident in Labour's education policies. Having abolished the assisted places scheme and returned grant maintained schools back to the local education authority as 'foundation schools', Labour retained the basic architecture of Conservative reforms to schooling. Parents could choose the school for their child, if that choice was available, when it frequently was not due to the competition for limited places. Schools continued to compete for pupils and be funded on a largely per capita basis. Local management of schools was kept (and reinforced, for example, through the policy of 'earned autonomy' in the 2002 Education Act), as was the National Curriculum, national testing and the revamped schools inspectorate, Ofsted.

But Labour also intervened directly in local schools and education authorities. These interventions largely concerned teaching, assessment, the curriculum and class sizes in primary schools, and included the introduction of national literacy and numeracy hours and their associated targets. The early 'fresh start' policy also gave ministers the powers to close down 'failing schools' and re-open them with a new head and senior management.

Going private

The role of the private sector in Labour's social policies has proved one of the most controversial areas since the party's coming to power in 1997. And embracing the Conservatives' private finance initiative (PFI) was bound to cause friction with Labour backbenchers. The initiative sees the private sector invest in public sector capital projects, such as new schools and hospitals; and then in effect the government rents the new facility from the private sector for a given period of time. Today's private sector investment is tomorrow's public spending. According to figures from the Economic and Social Research Council, between 1997 and 2004, just over 600 PFI deals were signed. By July 2003, 451 PFI projects had been completed, including the building of 34 hospitals, 119 other health schemes and 239 new and refurbished schools. From 1997 onwards, nearly all hospital schemes – either complete hospitals or major extensions – have been financed and built under PFI.

The government argued that PFI brought much needed investment, skills and expertise to public sector provision. Critics, however, responded by saying that more private sector involvement was creating worse working conditions for public sector employees; locking public bodies into private sector suppliers; distorting clinical priorities; and diverting resources away from front-line services. Critics also argued that the contracts offer poor value for money and that the evidence for the transfer of risk from the public to the private sector has not been established (Pollock, 2004).

For the government, the logical extension of the private finance initiative was to bring in more private sector businesses to deliver public services. In fact, the private sector had been informally working with the NHS for many years. But this relationship was formalized in October 2000 when a concordat between the government and the Independent Healthcare Association was signed by then health minister Alan Milburn – a measure that blurred the distinction between public and private in the health economy. By 2004, private sector providers were performing 4 per cent of elective treatments – and the government set a target of 15 per cent by 2008.

But as with PFI, value for money concerns have been raised about the costs of these treatments, as well as the long-term implications of increasing the dependency on the private sector to solve Britain's healthcare problems. Private sector costs have often proved higher than comparable costs in the public sector, usually because 'spot purchasing' of treatments by the NHS has increased private sector prices. In 2002, the government introduced an independent treatment centre programme to cut waiting lists and drive down prices by bulk-buying health procedures from the private sector. There continues to be a robust debate about the value to taxpayers of using the private sector in this way. While important, however, this debate does not go to the heart of the *political* controversy over private sector involvement in Labour's social policies. Privately financed and delivered public services not only bring in private sector management and private sector ways of doing things, they also breach the great political divide for social democrats between public collective services and private markets in providing for social need. And it was a divide that many thought was breached again by Labour's reforms to hospitals, schooling and university funding.

The return of the market: foundation hospitals and health commissioning

Foundation hospitals were at the heart of the government's second term reforms to the NHS. In important respects, creating foundation hospitals is a logical extension of trust hospital status, key to the Conservative policy of giving greater freedom and responsibilities to local health managers in the internal market. In basic terms, NHS hospitals would be given more independence and allowed to be more like private sector bodies (while remaining not-for-profit).

The extent of these freedoms was at the heart of the disagreements between the Department of Health (and Downing Street) and the Treasury. The freedoms the new foundation trusts have to make decisions include powers to raise money on the open market (subject to a limit set by a regulator) and to retain surpluses and proceeds from the sale of assets and land. Foundation trusts are expected to use these financial freedoms to improve patient care by recruiting staff, building new facilities and funding treatments in the private sector.

But just as going private caused alarm among government backbenchers, so allowing public service providers to behave like private sector businesses caused headaches for the Labour government. The creation of foundation hospitals revealed tensions between the government and its backbench supporters, as well as cracks in the New Labour coalition – between Gordon Brown and Tony Blair. The 2003 Health and Social Care Act, paving the way for foundation hospitals, was passed with the government's massive majority cut to 17 amid fears that the new style trusts would lead to a two-tier health service and that foundation hospitals were a cloak for the further privatization of the NHS. The government's commitment to 'modernization' was leading to growing rebelliousness on Labour's backbenches in its second term. Despite some of the powers of the new hospitals being cut, the first wave of ten foundation hospitals was launched in England in April 2004, followed by another wave of ten hospitals in June 2004 and more in January 2005. Tony Blair, who staked much of his domestic reputation on public sector reform, promised that all hospitals in England could be of Foundation status by 2008.

As the full extent of the funding crisis facing so many hospitals became apparent in 2006, it was clear that the policy of creating foundation hospitals was part of a broader shift back to market forms of governance under Labour. Alongside a new health commissioning system of 'payment-by-results' (whereby hospital budgets are tied to clinical activity, priced against a national tariff based on average hospital costs), health policy under Labour has seen the return of the internal market between purchasers and providers. Today, most of the purchasing is done by PCTs rather than GPs, though this may shift back to surgery level with 'practice-based commissioning'. The government has extended these policies by guaranteeing that all NHS patients should be offered a choice of secondary healthcare one of which will be from the private sector. Despite the return of the market, however, the governance of healthcare provision in England remains caught between command and control management and a more 'pluralistic, quasi-market model' (Klein, 2005). And this is where it looks likely to stay.

More diversity and choice: city academies and trust schools

The government's policies to create city academies and trust schools have caused similar controversy as foundation hospitals. Labour came to power not just promising 'education, education, education', but that standards in schooling could be raised without major structural reforms. By 2001, however, the intention of the government was to introduce more significant reforms to secondary schooling. The problem it seemed lay with that bastion of Labour education policy, the comprehensive school (or the 'bog standard comprehensive', to be more precise). The Labour government, like the Conservatives before them, moved to promote school specialization in subject areas. And those former grant-maintained schools retained important freedoms to own and manage their own land, assets and admissions under their new Foundation status.

Where Labour has tested the patience of its supporters has been on its plans for independent state schools – city academies and later trust schools – where existing school provision is seen to be failing. The policy, driven forward by Andrew Adonis first in the Downing Street policy unit, then in the Department for Education and Skills, has drawn fire from a broad political coalition (including some Labour modernizers) which accuses the government of undermining the universalism of state education and fostering social inequalities. The government responded by arguing that as in health, giving all parents, not just middle-class ones, greater choice over their children's schooling put pressure on the education system to raise its game.

City academies have many of the features of the Conservative policy to develop city technology colleges. Both involve the private sector in establishing new schools. Under the policy, academies remain state funded and are free to students. But they have much more independence than most secondary schools. The sponsors of city academies – typically a business, faith or voluntary group – put £2 million towards the new school. Taxpayers provide the remaining £20 million or more in start-up costs. The new schools have greater powers over the curriculum and staffing. By 2006, 46 academies were open or in development, with another 100 planned.

Labour had already signalled its future intentions in a new education white paper published in October 2005. This promised to push secondary school reform further by proposing that all schools should become self-governing trusts and making it easier to open new schools. The proposals, which even loyalists like former leader Neil Kinnock opposed, reinforced the thrust in education policy since the early 1980s away from local education authorities. Education secretary Ruth Kelly made some concessions to head off a potential backbench revolt, which happened anyway, and the legislation was passed with generous support from the Conservatives.

Paying for higher education

Paying for higher education has proved a further test of New Labour's commitment to the old social democratic state. Soon after the 1997 election, the Mr Fix-it of education policy, Lord Dearing, published a report on the funding of university education. In it, Dearing recommended the ending of fifty years of free tuition by the introduction of fees amounting to 25 per cent of course costs. Then education secretary David Blunkett agreed, arguing that those who benefited from a university education in terms of higher lifetime earnings could reasonably be expected to make an additional contribution to its costs. Critics argued that having a well-educated population would benefit the whole of society – and should, therefore, be paid for out of general taxation. Access to higher education was also an issue. Would tuition fees, at around £1,150 in 2005, deter those from poorer backgrounds, especially those from families with no history of higher education, from applying to study at university? Would mature students, who were being encouraged back into education under the policy of 'lifelong learning', be put off by the extra costs of university fees?

Blunkett argued in July 1997 that the government was 'determined to ensure that there is access to higher education for all those who can benefit from it'. The 1998 Teacher and Higher Education Act brought in tuition fees and included measures to support students from low-income families. By 2003/04, 43 per cent of students paid the full tuition fee, 43 per cent were exempt and the remainder paid part fees. For those students deemed independent, mostly over 25s, over 80 per cent paid no tuition fee.

Labour's 2001 manifesto promised, or at least appeared to promise, that the government would not allow universities to cover the full costs of courses through 'top-up fees' – in other words, to top up the existing flat rate tuition fee. University vice-chancellors argued that higher education needed more money if the sector was not to fall behind in the global education market. Labour agreed. In January 2004, the government's Higher Education bill, which allowed universities to increase tuition fees, scraped through its first big test in the House of Commons with a majority of just five (the government majority at the time was 161). But concerns about access to higher education – what is known as 'widening participation' – became a central feature of the often difficult passage of the legislation through both houses of parliament.

A 2004 report from the Higher Education Steering Group into access to higher education further confirmed what most people knew: that a class divide marks going to university. The final legislation on top-up fees saw a series of measures designed to temper the market in higher education, including that the new fees would not be paid in advance but out of graduate earnings (i.e. a form of graduate tax); and that students from poorer backgrounds would get a fee remission and a maintenance grant worth around £2,700. Figures in 2007 on university admissions suggest that fees are not putting students off going on to higher education. However, there remain concerns that university life will continue to be dominated by the middle classes (Bekhradria, 2007).

Delivering better public services?

The success of Labour's reforms to health and education has relied on the equation of money and 'modernization' equalling better public services. But what evidence is there of the taxpayer getting value for money from the government's policies? According to official figures, public sector employment rose 10 per cent between 1998 and 2004 – up from 4.95 million to 5.45 million. The numbers of nurses, doctors and teachers have all increased – but so has the number of NHS managers. Pay has also risen, with inflation in the public sector running ahead of the increase in prices elsewhere.

In the health service, inputs have run ahead of outputs. According to the Office for National Statistics, in 2003 for every extra 10 per cent in public health spending, output increased by only 4 per cent. Some but not all health targets have been met; while hospital waiting times have generally fallen, there remain significant variations in waiting times for medical procedures in different health areas. In education, primary school class sizes have fallen as promised and post-16 participation rates have risen. Academic achievement in primary schools increased significantly during Labour's first term, but then stopped rising. GCSE and A level pass rates have gone up year-by-year, but doubts persist on what standard is being measured. Nearly half of children entering secondary school at age 11 continue to fall below the expected standard in literacy and numeracy. Education performance among the country's poorest social groups remains low. And the schools inspectorate, Ofsted, still reports problems with the numbers of 'failing schools'.

Labour's end of ten years report on public sector reform is certainly mixed: but how to deliver better public services? Tensions between the firm hand of central government and a more pluralist model of public administration in Labour's reform plans have been a continuing feature of the government's social policies. While Gordon Brown at the Treasury was open to private finance in the public sector, giving greater autonomy to public agencies, whether foundation hospitals or city academies, was viewed by the then chancellor with suspicion. This was partly Treasury worry about the ability of these agencies to bear risk – and who would pick up the tab if things went wrong. But it also reflected the unresolved tensions within the government about how best to reform the public services.

Brown's view was that greater autonomy (and greater choice and diversity) in public service provision – he called it 'marketization' – undermines the public service ethos and egalitarian political economy of the welfare state (the 'two-tier' welfare state argument) (see Brown, 2003). For this reason, for example, choice in the public sector should be limited, to areas such as the booking of hospital appointments managed by collective agencies such as PCTs. Otherwise, in Brown's world, the provision of key public goods like health and education should remain in the hands of nationalized monopoly providers, albeit with greater provision for ensuring that these providers are more accountable – that local patients, parents and communities have more 'voice'.

Leading Blairites such as Alan Milburn, Stephen Byers and John Reid took a different view (e.g. Reid, 2005). Their perspective gives far greater weight to increasing the diversity of public sector provision and to a more radical notion of 'personalized' public services. Choice and diversity challenge public service providers to improve standards for all (and therefore, bring a measure of social justice to that provision); whether or not choice leads to exit, the potential for such an exit might be just as significant as whether public sector consumers actually switch suppliers (Le Grand, 2003).

With Labour's transfer of power at Number 10 complete, these differences of perspective on public sector reform become blurred. Gordon Brown backed foundation hospitals and the city academy programme and argued the case for 'contestability' and 'personalized' public services. Leading Blairite David Miliband, echoed Brown's stress on localism as a driver for reform (strangely it sounded more convincing coming from Miliband than it did from Brown); and just to confuse everyone, the Cameron Conservatives announced that they – and not Brown – were the true heirs to New Labour's public service reforms. Then just to confuse everyone even more, promptly changed their minds.

For Labour modernizers looking to build on ten years in power, and to strengthen their claim that New Labour is a new social democracy not neo-liberalism by another name, the question remains: how to combine commitments to greater choice and diversity in public service provision – and the inevitable role of markets in making that choice and diversity possible – with traditional social democratic commitments to collective public provision available to all on the basis of need? Moreover, it remains uncertain how New Labour's combination of market and democratic models of governance – the choice/voice dilemma – are to work, in particular, in conditions where exit is limited. Giving people power to make choices as consumers is one thing; giving them a voice as citizens to influence public policy delivery is something else.

New Labour and the social democratic state

For over ten years now, social policy has provided the Labour government with some of its biggest domestic headaches. Its policies on foundation hospitals, city academy schools, university funding, tax credits and welfare rights have caused controversy and raised the hackles of the party's backbenchers and others who doubt the radical credentials of New Labour. But has New Labour's ten years in power set a social agenda beyond Thatcherism: one that combines a commitment to poverty reduction and social inclusion as well as to equality and social justice?

Dealing with the Conservative legacy since 1997 has in part been about changing government priorities to target resources on the poor through investments in social security and public services. Social justice and state activism returned to the political agenda. Over a decade in government, public spending increased and private spending fell as a proportion of national income. Indeed, New Labour proved just as 'tax and spend' as old Labour – it was just rather better at managing the economy and keeping the nation's books just about in the black. This sweetened the bitter pill of tighter welfare entitlements and the government's public sector reforms. Paradoxically, it also enabled those devolved governments who disagreed with some of New Labour's social policies to do something different, as happened in Scotland over university funding and social care for the elderly.

The prime concern of this New Labour government has been with the provision of initial endowments that are seen to shape individual life chances – what is called the 'new egalitarianism' (Giddens and Diamond, 2005). The role of the state is to intervene to promote individual opportunities through the provision of public goods, social welfare and targeted programmes aimed at disadvantaged communities. Investments in, as well as reforms to, education and health; programmes such as Sure Start and the provision of childcare places; as well as policies such as 'baby bonds', are aimed at ensuring that there is some minimum, though not necessarily equal, starting point in society that gives everyone, regardless of their family background, a fair chance of making the most of their lives given their abilities and effort. This 'asset-based' approach to social justice sees such policies as offering not simply more opportunities for poorer groups but also stakes as citizens in a market society.

Such an approach demands early intervention – and problems of reaching those families who might benefit most from such intervention has undermined the effectiveness of programmes such as Sure Start. But even if policies such as the proposed 'family nurses' attached to disadvantaged mothers prove more effective, asset-based approaches are unlikely on their own to narrow the gap in the overall distribution of wealth and income between different social groups. The focus on what individuals have to sell in the market place (their marketable assets, such as skills and education qualifications) leaves the distribution of resources to the market.

This creates a problem for social democratic political economy that recognizes that the distributions of wealth and income remain major determinants of the opportunities an individual has in life. For social democrats, the demands of social justice reach beyond establishing some minimum standard in society. Dealing with poverty requires a commitment to egalitarianism. The freedom to make choices is nothing without the capacity and capability to enact those choices (Lister, 2004).

In practice, as we have seen, the government's fiscal policies have redistributed resources from the better off to the poor (although the non-working poor have not benefited to anywhere near the same extent as the working poor). This has done much to address levels of relative poverty. But it has not made Britain a more equal society in terms of the gap between rich and poor; and Britain remains, by comparison to other similar European countries, an unequal society.

Moreover, while any strategy to improve opportunities for the less well off will always be long term – it is easier to change tax and benefit levels than the chances facing a new generation – the evidence on how meritocratic British society is is not promising. Indeed, a 2005 study by researchers at the London School of Economics suggests that social mobility in Britain lags behind other countries and is on the decline because of widening income inequalities and the greater educational opportunities being taken up disproportionately by the better off (Blanden et al., 2005). The investments in, and reforms to, Britain's public services that Labour has started – and at best they can be described as work in progress – are central to this social policy goal of enhancing social opportunities, as Labour promised ten years ago, 'for the many not the few'. But after a decade of social policy-making, there remains a 'significant few'. As Tony Blair admitted shortly before he left office, the rising tide of economic prosperity – and ten years of record spending and public service reforms – that the many in Britain have enjoyed, has not lifted the ships of the 'tail of underachievers' that remain. This is still the challenge for social policy whichever party wins the next election.

5
New Labour and the Rise of the New Constitutionalism

Mark Evans

> The old constitution is dissolving beneath our eyes. The only question is what will replace it. To that question the authors of the revolution have no answer.
>
> (Marquand, 2000: 269)

Arguments

Unlike Margaret Thatcher Tony Blair was no conviction politician but he was a committed pragmatist driven by the desire to reverse the Labour Party's electoral fortunes and replace the Conservative Party as the natural party of British government. Nowhere is this better illustrated than constitutional reform. He possessed a keen analysis of Britain's constitutional dilemmas in a post-Thatcherite world but with the exception of those areas where there was a ready-made solution he was less certain about what needed to be done (Giddens, 2007). The main dilemma he confronted was that the essence of the constitutional crisis his government inherited was the product of the sovereignty of parliament which afforded untrammelled powers to the executive as long as it was able to discipline its majority. It was impossible, however, given the constraints of the British political tradition, to mitigate the sovereignty of parliament except through the constitution of a new sovereign. To do so would be federalism and federalism would inevitably constitute a radical assault on both English interests and his own powers as Prime Minister. This strategic paradox remains the fault line for understanding constitutional reformism in the Blair era, the contestation between centralism and reform and Blair's governing style.

Nevertheless, the constitutional reform programme which emerged from this crisis of conviction has galvanized institutional and political forces across the 'nations' and 'regions' in a way that is fundamentally altering the nature of British constitutionalism. For the political scientist they are of consuming interest, for we can now observe the processes whereby political and social actors have moved beyond Whitehall as a basic framework for individual and collective action, establishing new political communities in their wake and exercising newly found rights of citizenship. It is these processes that in combination, I refer to as the New Constitutionalism and which form the subject of this chapter (Evans, 2003).

The analysis, which follows, proceeds from two definitions – of constitutional reform and of the New Constitutionalism. Constitutional reform is defined here as any change to the institutional design of government in a country and the collection of rules, written and unwritten, which regulate the government and inform the relationship between the government and the people. The New Constitutionalism within the New Labour project is understood as a strategy of integration – a countervailing method for coping with the defects of the Westminster model of parliamentary democracy through a process of statecraft (Bulpitt, 1986) in which new and old political institutions and communities are either redefined, created or discarded in both institutional and attitudinal terms. This emphasis on the strategic rationale for constitutional reform has a long historical lineage. For example, since 1707 the Union has endured due to the development of intra-institutional learning, adaptation and the evolution of shared tasks, as well as the emergence of mechanisms for resolving conflict and reaching compromise. Through various forms of devolution, Westminster's economic, political and ideological hegemony has been sustained over the periphery and 'Britishness' became a pseudonym for 'English questions' (Anderson, 1992). For unlike a federal system in which each level of government is, in theory, autonomous, devolution preserves the sovereignty and therefore, the supremacy of parliament. Its prime purpose is to integrate dispersed elite political power in an over-centralized state and the success of the project rests on the degree of institutionalization and interdependence that result from the process of building new political communities across the 'nations' and 'regions' of Britain.

By implication, the study of constitutional reform is a normative enterprise in which the institutions and political activities studied provide a living laboratory for observing the processes which lead to the creation and consolidation of new types of political community and forms of political action. The discussion is organized into five sections. The first traces the emergence and development of a leadership view, which has challenged the Labour Party's traditional satisfaction with Britain's constitutional arrangements. The second section then provides a contextual understanding of the state of play in the constitutional reform project and a normative investigation of the gaps which have emerged in its implementation. In the third, fourth and fifth sections the chapter moves on to investigate Britain's changing constitutional landscape. It contends that the impact of constitutional reform can usefully be examined through the lens of a neo-functionalist approach (Haas, 1970). This can help us to measure the extent to which the creation of a programme of constitutional reform and the activities, which take place in its framework, give rise to factors of integration (spill-over) and disintegration (spill-back). It observes that although the New Constitutionalism has been plagued by factors of disintegration (spill-back), these have been counterbalanced by factors of integration (spill-over) which will ultimately lead to greater constitutional radicalism. This is a classic story, as old as politics itself, about the struggle between two types of political project: on the one hand, the relentless struggle by elites for power and control; on the other hand, liberal constitutionalism and the concept of popular control through effective constitutional checks and balances (Beetham, 1994).

Constitutional revisionism

By the late 1980s, the utility of Britain's unwritten constitution was experiencing a profound and historic challenge. The restructuring of the British economy, the unresolved Irish and Scottish questions, the mounting pressures of European integration and public dissatisfaction with the way the UK was being governed all placed an almighty stretch on the elasticity of Britain's unwritten constitution. The excesses of Thatcherite statecraft had undermined constitutional fundamentals and a profound constitutional crisis loomed as Britain's unwritten constitution no longer provided a 'political sociology of the British'. The transformation of the Labour leadership's standpoint on constitutional matters can be viewed as an elite response to both external party dynamics and internal party concerns. With regard to the former, the Labour Party adopted a policy agenda, which in its most crucial aspects reflected the aspiration of transforming the British Industrial-Welfare State into a Competition State (Cerny and Evans, 2004; Evans, 2003). As Blair put it:

We on the centre-left must try to put ourselves at the forefront of those who are trying to manage social change in the global economy. The old left resisted that change. The new right did not want to manage it. We have to manage that change to produce social solidarity and prosperity. (Blair, 1998c)

New Labour's Competition State project focuses on the transformation of the state from within with regard to the reform of political institutions, functions and processes in an attempt to adapt state action to cope more effectively with what they defined as global 'realities'. State intervention was aimed at not only adjusting to, but also sustaining, promoting, and expanding an open global economy in order to capture its perceived benefits. In Gordon Brown's words, this calls for 'balanced budgets', 'tight control of interest rates', and the need to deal with unemployment through the marketplace and not through government intervention. The New Constitutionalism formed a key element of this broader political project. It is well documented that constitutions structure domestic economic systems and pattern social relationships and politics (Hutton, 1995). In this sense the constitutional reform project may partly be understood as an attempt to reform the constitutional order in line with the economic order, and most significantly, to alter pre-existing patterns of social relationships and politics to allow the state to deal better with the imperatives of globalization.

At the same time, there is no ignoring the pragmatic dimension of the constitutional reform project. The transformation of the leadership view on constitutional matters was also a response to electoral despair and the perceived need by party elites for political pragmatism in order to secure electoral success. The Labour Party's traditional approach to the constitution rested on a centralist tradition in which strong executive government was viewed to be the key instrument of statecraft for achieving and promoting greater social equality. Indeed Labour and Conservative governments had conspired in a High Tory approach to the constitution in praise of existing constitutional arrangements for much of the twentieth century and with few exceptions stoutly opposed proposals for change unless political expediency demanded it. The view of the Labour leadership on constitutional reform had been in flux since Roy Hattersley and Neil Kinnock drew up a scoping document, *Statement of Democratic Socialist Aims and Values* in 1988, which aimed at providing an ethical framework for the Labour Party Policy Review. In the opening paragraph of the document the two authors stated that: 'The true purpose of democratic socialism, and, therefore, the true aim of the Labour Party, is the creation of a genuinely free society, in which the fundamental objective of government is the protection and extension of individual liberty, irrespective of class, sex, age, race, colour or creed.'

The document revised the party's position on constitutional matters and laid the foundations for the publication of *Meet the Challenge, Make the Change* in 1989, which placed piecemeal constitutional reform at the heart of the Labour Party's reform programme. In January 1991, Hattersley launched his alternative to a Bill of Rights, the *Charter of Rights*, which included proposals for a range of statutory rights that would be protected by a parliamentary select committee. A commitment to constitutional reform was then included as a central plank of Labour's 1992 election manifesto; although the project remained temperate in its radicalism in so far as these reforms would not have addressed the problem of executive dominance. Indeed, it was not until the aftermath of the Conservative government's fourth successive election victory that the Labour Party's constitutional project would start to become truly radical and question the key assumptions underpinning Labour's constitutional doctrine.

John Smith took Kinnock's revisionism one step further. He began with the establishment of the principle of 'one member, one vote' which limited the political power of the trade unions within the party and then moved on to the constitutional sphere. Partly as a response to Labour's longstanding commitment to Scottish devolution and partly due to a further electoral defeat in 1992, Smith had become convinced of the need for constitutional reform. In a lecture to the constitutional reform group Charter 88 in 1993, he stated: 'I want to see a fundamental shift in balance of power between the citizen and the state – a shift away from an overpowering state to a citizens' democracy where people have rights and powers and where they are served by accountable and responsive government' (Smith, 1993: 1). Smith set up a policy commission on the constitution under Tony Blair's convenorship which led to the first comprehensive statement on Labour's partial conversion to constitutional radicalism.

However, it was not until the untimely death of John Smith in May 1994 and the election of Tony Blair to the Labour leadership in July of that year that Labour's constitutional revisionism took on a temporary evangelical zeal. The rewriting of Clause IV of the Party Constitution provided a political moment for re-evaluating the key policy instruments for delivering democratic socialism. It was also evident that the Labour Party leadership had been influenced to varying degrees on different areas of reform by reform groups such as Charter 88, the Campaign for Freedom of Information and the Scottish Constitutional Convention, together with the Liberal Democrats, who all argued that a project focusing on democratic renewal could provide a cohesive, energizing focus of common identity for a new coalition of working and middle-class public sector oriented citizens (Evans, 1995).

Labour's pre-1997 election policy statements focused on what could be achieved within one term of government (Blair, 1996a, 1996b; Labour Party, 1996a, 1996b, 1996c). Blair chose not to opt for a written constitution and thus held New Labour back from fully embracing a radical approach to the constitution. At the 1997 general election New Labour presented a flawed pluralist interpretation of the problems in British government. This analysis of British government is best summarized in the following extract from David Marquand's book, *The Unprincipled Society*: '... the conception of power and authority which has underpinned Britain's political order since the 18th century has become an obstacle to successful adjustment. The notion of politics as mutual education is not only alien to that conception; it is also subversive of it' (Marquand, 1988: 246). The flawed pluralist interpretation is associated with radical approaches that seek constitutional reform to defend the individual in society and allow for the generation of consensus building constitutional rules. This was the ideological 'space' in which the New Constitutionalism emerged.

The reform programme

Blair claimed that constitutional reform would not be '... the politics of 100 days that dazzles for a time, and then fizzles out. It is not the politics of a revolution, but of a fresh start, the patient rebuilding and renewing of this country – renewal that can take root and build over time' (Labour Party, 1997: 2). Labour has introduced major constitutional reforms in five main areas since 1997 – the economy, territory, elections, parliament, and citizenship.

The economy

The former chancellor, Gordon Brown launched three main initiatives within the financial area which have all sought to challenge a financial system which has, for much of the post-war period, valued short-term profit over long-term growth or income generated in trading through what Will Hutton has termed the cult of the 'gentlemanly capitalist' (Hutton, 1995: 21). These initiatives are: the introduction of an independent central bank and a code for fiscal stability to create a more open, transparent and accountable approach to economic policy-making; the stripping of the Bank of England's watchdog role and the creation of a new finance regulator; and, measures to make the Bank of England's operations in currency markets more transparent. The first of these reforms represented a significant constitutional innovation as a key instrument of economic policy-making was devolved to a non-elected body. Although it was based on sound reason – the need to prevent governments engaging in short-term shock therapy with interest rates – it does mean that the British people no longer have 'direct' control through their elected representatives of economic policy-making. While most other central banks also set interest rates, in the Bank of England's case this is done within the framework of government policy and included the low inflation target of 2.5 per cent. Central Bank independence provides institutional recognition of Brown's view that as a consequence of the globalization of financial markets if inflation rises, or the ratio of public debt to GDP rises, the cost of borrowing will rise further. As Brown himself puts it, '… the war on inflation is a Labour war … Brown's law is that the government will only borrow to invest, public debt will remain stable and the cost effectiveness of public spending must be proved … nobody should doubt my iron resolve for stability and fiscal prudence.'[1]

Central Bank reform has left something to be desired in terms of both its independence and accountability. The three-year tenure of the 'independent' members of the Monetary Policy Committee leaves them vulnerable to political manipulation. Moreover, it is difficult to see how the existing forms of scrutiny by the House of Commons Treasury and Civil Service Select Committee will be able to hold the Governor of the Bank of England fully to account. This is a potential source for future constitutional conflict in times of economic recession.

Territory

The introduction of asymmetrical devolution in Scotland, Wales and Northern Ireland under New Labour has been a strategy of integration, a counterweight to separatist forces and a method for coordinating multi-level governance downwards across the nations and regions of the UK and upwards to the European Union. As Blair put it: 'Subsidiarity is as sound a principle in Britain as it is in Europe. Our proposal is for devolution not federation. A sovereign Westminster parliament will devolve power to Scotland and Wales. The Union will be strengthened and the threat of separatism removed' (Labour Party, 1997: 33).

Labour also adopted a bi-partisan, all-Ireland approach to the peace process in Northern Ireland. In the short term this approach led to the Good Friday Agreement in April 1998 which lay the foundations for a gradualist approach to peace-building culminating in the restoration of devolution and the creation of a Northern Ireland Assembly and Executive in May 2007. The appointment of loyalist Dr Ian Paisley as First Minister and republican Martin McGuinness as deputy First Minister of the new NI Executive has to be viewed as one of Labour's greatest achievements in office, demonstrating that major advances have been made in both reconciling the differences between the two traditions and establishing a new political settlement which can command the support of the majority in both communities.

The most significant constitutional reform with regard to local government lies in the establishment of Regional Development Agencies (RDAs) to coordinate regional economic development and transport. This reform built on the Conservative government's creation of a tier of regional government in England through the use of quangos and the creation of government regional offices. At the same time some rather half-hearted attempts have been made to make local decision-making less constrained by central government, and, more accountable to local people. An emphasis has been placed on providing the necessary powers to help facilitate public–private partnerships with local businesses and voluntary organizations. A range of democratic innovations have also been introduced to ensure greater accountability: a proportion of councillors in each locality are elected annually; and, elected mayors and/or cabinet government with executive powers have been introduced in City government. Moreover, in London, following a referendum to confirm popular demand, a directly elected London Strategic Authority was created with an elected Mayor.

The Blair government's attempts to deepen democratization has also been reflected in the introduction of a public participation agenda in local government and the National Health Service (NHS) which has included broader consultation with the local citizenry through such devices as the creation of NHS Patient Public Involvement Forums, citizens' juries, and deliberative opinion polls. The decisive test of a democracy is its capacity to encourage its population to play an active role in its government. It remains to be seen whether these reforms can achieve this aspiration. However, technological advances and mature consumerism should make participatory decision-making ever more feasible in the future.

In short, major constitutional reforms have been introduced at the level of the 'nations' and, to a lesser extent, the 'regions' of the UK. However, three main gaps currently exist in the devolution programme. The first is the English Question or meeting the demand for downward devolution to an independent English parliament or regional assemblies to redress inequalities in representation and public expenditure. Scotland currently receives 23 per cent more funding per head than England, and Wales 16 per cent more (Jones, 2004: 320). Labour's attempts to decentralize powers and 'strengthen regional policy through the creation of directly elected assemblies in (English) regions where people want them', ultimately failed to win the support of regional communities in referenda.[2] The English Question remains unanswered and as the gains from the devolution settlement for the other nations have grown, the democratic deficit in England has become profoundly salient. It is therefore unsurprising that in his first speech as Labour leader, Gordon Brown should announce his commitment to 'devolution within a Union of nations: England, Scotland, Wales and Northern Ireland'.[3] Nor should we be surprised to see Brown's regional agenda refocusing around the empowerment of the big English cities (Stoker, 2000).

The second gap in the devolution project lies in the absence of sufficient upward devolution to the European Union in both an economic and a political sense and downward devolution from the EU to European publics. Blair has consistently emphasized Britain's commitment to Europe in an attempt to shed Britain's reputation for being an 'awkward partner' (George, 1990). However, partly as a consequence of Blair's personal embarrassment at failing to join EMU and partly due to the negative impact of his decision to wage war in Iraq, the government has made little attempt to address the EU's democratic deficit (Gamble, 2002). Such a policy agenda would focus on: the unaccountable nature of the European Commission; the limited decision-making competencies of the European Parliament; the poor scrutiny of European legislation in national parliaments; the ineffective implementation of European policy; and, the failure of the EU to engage with the European citizenry with respect to history making decisions as evidenced by the debacle of the European Constitution.

The third gap in the devolution project lies with the undemocratic character of Networked Governance. The concept of Networked Governance proceeds from two simple assumptions about the nature of policy-making in Britain. First, policy-making is the outcome of the interaction between policy networks, hierarchies (i.e. governmental structures), markets and/or third sector organizations; and secondly, this constitutes a mode of governance. The task of government in Networked Governance is to select participants, coordinate, steer, integrate and regulate network activities. Recent research on Networked Governance has characterized networks as imprisoned zones of elite decision-making characterized by conflict and power asymmetries (Marsh et al., 2003; Davies, 2005). Moreover, a wealth of empirical studies has argued that networks are not sufficiently deliberative or democratic (Diamond, 2004; Stoker, 2004; Skelcher, 2005; Sorensen and Torfing, 2005) and nor are they efficient because they are not responsive to societal demands (Davies, 2005). A deepening of the New Constitutionalism therefore needs to occur through the reformation of network norms, values and operational rules aimed at achieving 'public value' (Stoker, 2004; Moore, 1995).

Elections

New electoral systems based on different forms of proportional representation (PR) have been introduced for Scotland's Parliament (AMS), the Wales (AMS) and Northern Ireland (STV) assemblies, the European Parliament (AMS) and even for contests for the deputy leadership of the Labour Party (STV). Yet despite this *de facto* recognition that proportional electoral systems are both more democratic and efficient in maximizing the value of a vote, the government's 1997 manifesto commitment to a referendum on the voting system for the House of Commons remains in abeyance. The Labour Party's position on electoral reform continues to be in keeping with the British political tradition reflecting the leadership's preoccupation with the party's immediate electoral prospects. The determining factor for most frontbench Labour politicians has not been the democratic merits or demerits of various electoral systems, but rather the benefits that a particular system might offer the party at election time. Hence, once in government, issues of fairness have tended to slip from view and 'end-state' justifications for an electoral system have taken precedence over 'procedural' or democratic ones (Plant, 1991).

Parliament

Tony Blair wrote in 1996: '[S]ome British institutions ... are actually pre-First Age. Think of the way Parliament works, sometimes seeming more private club than modern democratic forum; or the composition of the House of Lords; or constitutional conventions established in the 18th and 19th centuries' (Blair, 1996a: 33). The Blair government was quick to establish a select committee to review general parliamentary procedures and working conditions, together with the process of scrutinizing European legislation. This ultimately led to the reform of Prime Minister's Questions, the implementation of the Nolan Committee recommendations on standards in public life, which were fully implemented and extended to all public bodies, and the improvement of working conditions in parliament.

Yet despite Blair's apparent indignation with the *ancien régime*, the government has done little to improve the power imbalance between the executive and the legislature or the democratic credentials of the House of Lords (Russell, 2000). Indeed attempts to modernize parliament have fallen foul to the government's intent to retain the policy instruments of executive dominance. For example, the House of Commons Modernization Committee reported in February 2002 making 22 recommendations aimed at guaranteeing 'the independence of the select committees ... [and] ... strengthening the ability of Parliament to keep the Executive under effective scrutiny' but was rejected by cabinet.[4] Moreover, since 1997, there have been a royal commission, two Joint Committee reports and four government White Papers on Lords reform but thus far only stage one of the reforms (the abolition of 92 hereditary peers) has been completed.

The reform of the House of Lords is presently gridlocked. The source of contestation centres on a disagreement over the future composition of the second chamber, between those who oppose an elected membership on the basis that in time it would accrue powers that would challenge the supremacy of the first chamber and those who argue that unless the new second chamber is at least in part elected it will lack legitimacy. The new Prime Minister is promising prompt action which is likely to lead to a second chamber with a much larger elected element than previously envisaged (60–80 per cent). Moreover, he has already signalled his intention to give parliament voting rights on 'all the major issues of our time including peace and war'.[5] Nonetheless, the process of reforming the House of Lords provides a telling illustration of the capacity of centralists to resist change.

Citizenship

Labour's rights approach derives partly from traditional liberal theory and partly from Blair's communitarian belief that rights should be bonded with obligations (Giddens, 2002). With regard to the former, the Thatcher years demonstrated the increased isolation of the individual in contrast with the strong centralized state. As we have seen, this was largely attributed to the failure of the unwritten constitution to safeguard individual rights and its tendency to provide an enabling context for big government. New Labour became strongly committed to the idea that citizens should have statutory rights to enforce their human rights in the UK courts. However, since 1997 the economic obligations of the citizenry have expanded, while little has been done to increase the political obligations of citizenship. Regardless of one's views on the merits and demerits of the reforms that have taken place, the efficacy of citizens' rights in Britain has been strengthened considerably under

New Labour: a Human Rights Act (HRA) has been introduced which allows judges to declare that legislation is incompatible with the European Convention on Human Rights (ECHR); a Freedom of Information Act has been implemented; and the 2005 Constitutional Reform Act legislated for the establishment of an independently appointed Supreme Court – leading to the establishment of a formal separation of powers at the heart of Britain's constitution from 2008.

It is noteworthy, however, that the incorporation of the ECHR into British law fell short of the British Bill of Rights that Blair had previously advocated in 1994. A British Bill of Rights to complement a *written* British Constitution remains a logical corollary of the HRA, particularly if the pace of European integration quickens and a need arises to reassert national sovereignty to safeguard UK based rights.

Assessing the impact of the New Constitutionalism

One problem with this analysis thus far is that it has created the impression that governments have the capacity to control the implementation of reform programmes free from constraints. This is where I introduce a further twist in this cautionary tale. Although Labour's project does not match the radicalism of the agendas of some groups such as Charter 88 and the Power Inquiry, existing reforms 'spill-back' and 'spill-over' increasing the radicalism of reform and the scope and intensity of change. The New Constitutionalism has created the space for further constitutional reform because institutionalization has a momentum of its own. I will refer to this process of institutionalization as the dynamic of spill-over (Evans, 1999, 2003).

The concept of spill-over is used in this study in the following way – the introduction of a wide-ranging programme of constitutional reform creates situations that can be dealt with only by further expanding the nature of reform and the delegation of power. Spill-over manifests in three main ways. *Political spill-over* consists of a convergence of the expectations and interests of national elites as a response to constitutional change. This may result in a transfer of loyalties (for example, authority-legitimacy transfers from Westminster to Brussels, Cardiff, Edinburgh or Stormont) or, at minimum, in a transformation in the political activities of political elites (for example, the increase in lobbying at Brussels, Cardiff, Edinburgh, Strasbourg or Stormont). *Technical spill-over* refers to a situation in which the attempt to achieve a goal agreed upon at the outset (for example, freedom of information) becomes possible only if other (unanticipated) cooperative activities are also carried out (for example, its harmonization with human rights legislation). In this way cooperation in one sector can spill-over into cooperation in another, previously unrelated sector. Moreover, once introduced, constitutional reform creates the possibility for further reform because it shows that constitutional change is possible. This inspires political parties and groups to pressure for further change. *Geographical spill-over* can also be identified with reference to the territorial dimension of constitutional reform, as the creation of Scotland's Parliament paved the way for assemblies in Wales and Northern Ireland.

In all of these categories, the possibility of political, technical and geographical spill-back effects exists. These may be understood as factors of disintegration which stem from resistance to the New Constitutionalism, the popularity of competing constitutional discourses or unintended consequences of action that undermine central goals. Moreover, factors of integration may be introduced to militate against harmful factors of disintegration. The following two sections explore some prominent examples of political, technical and geographical spill-back and spill-over. The study of these forms of spill-over will allow us to investigate both the integrating (spill-over) and disintegrating (spill-back) effects of the constitutional reform process. For organizational purposes we will begin by exploring various case studies in spill-back as these have often given rise to spill-over effects.

Case studies in spill-back

This section provides a selective survey of the political, technical and geographical spill-back effects which have emerged with the implementation of constitutional reform.

Political spill-back – constitutional containment and the 'clammy hands of centralism'

A story will now unfold about a political party that comes to power with radical aspirations after a long period in opposition which then diminish when confronted by the forces of constitutional conservatism. While the rise of the New Constitutionalism has gone some way towards challenging conventional constitutional wisdoms, from 1999 to 2005, the Labour government initiated a policy of constitutional containment in defence of the constitutional status quo. Any reform that threatened the ability of government at the centre to steer a New Labour course was diluted in its radicalism so it could no longer pose a threat. Five prominent examples may be highlighted here.

Firstly, David Clarke's sacking as the minister in charge of developing freedom of information legislation in May 1998 and the handing-over of responsibility for freedom of information legislation to the constitutional traditionalist Jack Straw, symbolized the reassertion of constitutional conservatism and the adoption of a policy of constitutional containment.[6] Clarke had produced an outstanding White Paper that was popularly viewed as a radical package of reforms that would establish a Freedom of Information Act of international standing.[7] But it was clearly too radical for the conservative sensibilities of some, particularly civil service mandarins. The implementation of the 2000 Freedom of Information Act was subsequently delayed until 2005. Secondly, the HRA was introduced in 1998 incorporating the ECHR into British law but the absence of a Supreme Court with the power to enforce convention rights and hold the executive to account has meant that it cannot provide an effective constitutional check. This will hopefully be rectified with the creation of a genuinely independent Supreme Court in 2008. Thirdly, the second stage of the reform of the House of Lords faltered due to worries in certain quarters of government that an elected second chamber would provide too great a check on the first chamber. Fourthly, the recommendation from the Jenkins Commission on Electoral Reform to replace the first-past-the-post electoral systems for House of Commons elections with the 'alternative vote top-up' system was rejected and the manifesto pledge of a referendum on the issue was ignored. Fifthly, manifesto pledges to address the democratic deficit in the European Union through extending the powers of the European Parliament have been disregarded.

The clammy hands of centralism had resurfaced; but how do we make sense of this struggle between constitutional idealism and pragmatism? Specific changes to constitutional policy have had much more to do with making the Labour Party electable than an ideological commitment to constitutional reform. Once in power constitutional radicalism has appeared less attractive. As one minister of state put it: 'Do you really think that when it comes down to it we're going to give away real power? That's what you come into politics for – to change things – and anything that threatens that aim is bound to fail.'[8]

The constant reference by prime movers of debate to a restrictive notion of democracy and the preference for an 'executive-friendly' constitution over a liberal 'restricting' one is a key feature of elite political discourse on constitutional matters both historically and contemporaneously (Evans, 2003). A cabinet minister confirmed this prejudice to me: 'I soon began to realize that constitutional reform is about placing constraints on the ability to make things happen. I got involved in politics to make things happen – it's as simple as that really.'[9] It is noteworthy, however, that probably the most radical Labour politician on the constitution in opposition, Robin Cook, remained committed to the implementation of Labour's 1997 election manifesto until his untimely death. He stated, 'I came into politics to change things and I'm still committed to changing things. We'll get there in the end.'[10] In the view of the governing elite, the main reason why constitutional traditionalists are presently in the ascendancy on Labour's front bench is that certain aspects of the 1997 election manifesto were impractical. Moreover, 'New Labour friendly' mandarins at the apex of the civil service have been successful in diluting the radicalism of the open government agenda. This has certainly been the case with regard to freedom of information legislation. A senior civil servant observes:

> What people have to understand, and some clearly do which is why they don't bother to vote, is that most politicians know very little about government. They spend their time in opposition thinking and talking about ideas for change that are totally impractical and at odds with the way we do things. It is our job to convince them otherwise.[11]

A former cabinet minister drew my attention to the difficulties of engineering policy change:

> Once you become part of a government it becomes clear very early on that it takes a great deal of time and energy to change anything. Our electoral system makes this slightly easier because we don't have to engage in a difficult bargaining process and to be honest we need all the help we can get.[12]

These narratives tend to confirm the argument that was presented in the first section of this chapter; that the contestation between reformism and centralism at the heart of the core executive remains the fault line for understanding constitutional reform in the Blair era.

Technical spill-back – the problem of disjointed constitutionalism

Some of the more problematic examples of technical spill-back have arisen as a consequence of disjointed constitutionalism. A fundamental flaw has characterized New Labour's constitutional reform project. The government would have been better placed if at the outset they had plotted a course towards its achievement through the creation of a written and/or a federal constitutional blueprint. The failure of New Labour to develop a holistic approach to constitutional reform has meant that Blair's reforms have been beset with implementation gaps. These problems have occurred due to: insufficient policy instruments for coordinating multi-level governance; the provision of inadequate resources for meeting policy objectives (e.g. FOI); resistance from bureaucratic (e.g. FOI) and political elites (e.g. Lords reform); and, the paucity of civic education. For example, the Seventh Report of the Select Committee on Constitutional Affairs (SCCA) provides us with insights into the technical spill-back effects in the implementation of FOI. It proclaims that the Act is a 'significant success', bringing about 'new releases of information' for 'a range of different individuals and organisations' (SCCA, 2006: 8.1). However, major implementation gaps were identified including: failure to meet the statutory response time for internal reviews (ibid.: 8.2); poor record management practices by the National Archives (ibid.: 8.5); failure of public authorities to comply with effective records management practices (ibid.: 8.5); long delays in the conduct of investigations by the Information Commissioner's Office (ICO) followed by 'inadequate' investigations and decision notices (ibid.: 8.8); inadequate costings of the work of the ICO (ibid.: 8.8); an inefficient complaints procedure (ibid.: 8.9); and, an ineffective working relationship between the DCA and the ICO (ibid.: 8.21, 8.22). Indeed the Select Committee questioned the independence of the ICO and recommended that it should become 'directly responsible to, and funded by, Parliament'. Although it has to be accepted that the FOI Act is in its infancy these serious problems in operational delivery severely impede the ability of British citizens to exercise their rights to public information.

A similar dynamic of institutionalization can be seen in the case of HRA. The HRA has provided only limited remedies for violations of Convention rights. For example, after *A. v. Secretary of State for the Home Department* (2005, 2 WLR 87) the suspected international terrorists had to remain in Belmarsh prison to await new legislation despite the decision that their detention violated Articles 5 and 14 of the ECHR. In effect Convention rights can only be enforced against public authorities. This is largely because of the careful preservation of the principle of parliamentary sovereignty which makes it impossible to strike down primary legislation which is held to be incompatible with a Convention right under Section 4 of the 1998 Human Rights Act. Nonetheless, the political process has proved to be responsive to the introduction of human rights standards and thus far the government has responded to every declaration of incompatibility by introducing amending legislation. Hence the HRA has provided a moral rather than legal check on the core executive.

The main weakness of the HRA, however, lies not in its policy design but in the policy instruments (or lack of them), which have informed its implementation. This is reflected both in the consistent failure to provide decision-makers with adequate training, guidance and legal advice, and in the relative absence of public education on the HRA. The most important measure of the institutionalization of the HRA lies in the extent to which it has become socially embedded. This is particularly important given that the Blair government intended the Act to do more than provide legal remedies for violations of Convention rights. Although there is evidence that a growing number of 'special' groups benefit from the Act (such as asylum-seekers, foreign suspected international terrorists, and victims of violent crimes and their families) it is amongst the general public that the HRA is having its least impact.

Geographical spill-back – the English and Scottish questions

Perhaps the most important question in this regard relates to whether the creation of a Scottish Parliament with the power to pursue its own social and tax policies will stimulate a dynamic of separatism (Hobsbawm, 1977). Despite the recent upsurge in support for the SNP leading to a narrow one-seat victory in the 2007 elections to the Scottish Parliament, devolution has not necessarily strengthened support for Scottish independence. The 1999 referendum result itself always raised the prospect of a new consensual style of politics north of the border – 56 of the 129 members of the Scottish Parliament were elected in 1999 by PR – and no party was ever likely to enjoy an overall majority for very long. Hence, as Labour's popularity at Westminster has waned, the likelihood of a coalition arrangement in Edinburgh has always been probable. However, as John Curtice and Ben Seyd observe, there are clear pluralities in both Scotland and England in support of devolution in its current guise: '... the Scottish Parliament is the "settled will of the people" not only in Scotland but England, too' (Curtice and Seyd, 2001: 227). While there is no evidence to suggest that devolution has led to an increase in public approval for the way that Britain is governed, there is evidence of new sources of conflict between the Scots and the English with regard both to the English Question and the West Lothian Question.

The government's proposal for English regional assemblies was partly a response to mounting pressure within both the Labour Party and the English regions to tackle the English Question and partly a response to the results of several polls, which highlighted significant majorities in favour of change (*The Economist*, 11 May 2002).[13] However, in October 2004, referenda in the northwest, northeast and Yorkshire and the Humber failed to win the support of regional communities and the bandwagon for English regionalism stalled. Although very little empirical research has been conducted on the reasons behind the debacle, anecdotal evidence suggests that the inability of the 'Yes' campaigns to convince regional electors that regional assemblies would not lead to higher local council taxes and become the preserve of a new regional political elite were the deciding factors. This geographical spill-back effect has meant that the English Question has remained unanswered, at least for the time being.

Case studies in spill-over

This section provides a selective survey of the political, technical and geographical spill-over effects which have emerged both as a consequence of the implementation of constitutional reform and in response to damaging spill-back effects.

Political spill-over – changing domains of political action

There is already evidence to support the argument that there has been an upsurge in conventional forms of political participation as a consequence of the establishment of Scotland's Parliament and assemblies in Wales and Northern Ireland. The number of registered pressure groups focusing their lobbying activities on the new political institutions has doubled in Scotland, quadrupled in Wales and increased in Northern Ireland.[14] These include some new pressure groups such as the Scottish Youth Parliament, and, the Parliament for Wales Campaign, together with a broad range of community based organizations. This growth in the scope and intensity of pressure group activity has been reflected in the emergence of professional lobbying organizations in the Wales Assembly and Scottish Parliament as people and groups have sought to influence new decision-making processes. For example, the Royal Society for the Protection of Birds has refocused its lobbying activities on the Wales Assembly in an attempt to get the Assembly to unfreeze funding for the Countryside Council of Wales. Elites in sub-national administrations have also started to pursue their aims more vigorously in the EU policy arena. They now focus both on lobbying central government and on making direct contact in Brussels. Hence, the UK government is increasingly viewed as a 'partner' rather than a 'gatekeeper', and it remains the view of elites in both Scotland and Wales that both Scotland and Wales have more clout in the EU by virtue of their Union with the UK.

Technical spill-over – methods of constitutional coordination

The search for the most efficient institutional machinery to deliver joined-up constitutionalism provides the most telling demonstration of technical spill-over since 1997. Four institutions have been created to coordinate constitutional reform. From the outset it was perceived as necessary to have a central coordinating institution and this emerged in the shape of the Cabinet Office Constitution Secretariat (CS) which was set up in July 1997 to handle the raft of constitutional legislation. Secondly, as the new reforms passed through the legislative process, the CS's role diminished, and in 2001 devolution management was passed over to the Office of the Deputy Prime Minister (ODPM) where it resided until 2003 and HRA and FOI management was delegated to the Lord Chancellor's Department.[15] This was initially seen as a logical move as it fitted well with the issues that the ODPM was addressing, such as English regional government and the Lord Chancellor, Derry Irvine's interest in FOI (Croft, 2002). Thirdly, Joint Ministerial Committees covering Health, Poverty, and the Knowledge Economy were also created to ensure a coordinated approach to public policy-making and implementation across new organizational and territorial boundaries and to consider disputes between new and old administrations.[16] Fourthly, a new form of institutional machinery was introduced to deliver joined-up constitutionalism in 2003 as part of a new constitutional reform bill (later to become the 2005 Constitutional Reform Act). Blair had earlier abolished the post of Lord Chancellor in a cabinet reshuffle; a measure which was viewed to be a response to the growing desire to increase the separation of powers between the judiciary and the executive thus ensuring compliance with Article 6 of the ECHR on judicial independence. As noted above, this proved to be just one part of a wider agenda for reform which encompassed: the abolition of the Lord Chancellor's Department and its replacement with the Department for Constitutional Affairs (DCA); the establishment of a Supreme Court with independently appointed judges to replace the Law Lords; and, changes to the appointment of judges. The DCA was subsequently established in June 2003 combining responsibility for the judiciary and the constitution. It is evident from this brief survey that constitutional reform has precipitated a dynamic of institutionalization through technical spill-over that has been exacerbated by the need to negotiate the demands of multi-level governance.

Geographical spill-over

The dynamic of geographical spill-over has already been amply demonstrated by the establishment of the Wales and Northern Ireland assemblies and the upgrading of the power of RDAs in the wake of the creation of the Scottish Parliament. The potential for further significant geographical spill-over can also be identified. The asymmetric character of the present devolution settlement provides two potential sources of geographical spill-over. The first is the possibility for further devolution in Wales and Northern Ireland, where there is a great deal of frustration at Scotland's possession of primary legislative and tax raising powers. The second is the potential for the creation of an English Parliament. It can also be argued that the introduction of devolution has had a positive geographical spill-over effect with regard to the Northern Ireland peace process. The creation of the Wales Assembly and Scotland's Parliament bolstered Sinn Fein's confidence in the Blair government as it provided systemic evidence that this was a government that was committed to constitutional change.

Blair and the constitution – the sorcerer's apprentice

The main argument that has been advanced in this chapter has been a relatively simple one; the launch of a radical constitutional project by the Labour government in 1997 posed a historic challenge to Britain's elitist political tradition that led to certain participatory gains for the 'nations' of Britain and for British citizens. But this radicalism was short lived because the development of the constitutional reform project was born from electoral despair, the imperatives of globalization and political pragmatism rather than idealism; and it failed to confront the strategic paradox at the heart of the British constitution – that radical constitutional change could only be achieved by limiting the powers of the executive. Indeed, the emergence of a period of constitutional containment post-1999 to 2003 is testimony to the continued strength of this elite tradition in shaping our central institutions and processes of government and insulating them from participatory reform. Yet this is where we can identify the key twist in the tale of constitutional reform. In 1997 Blair set in motion a whole range of processes over which he and his government had little control. He became the sorcerer's apprentice in Walt Disney's *Fantasia*, desperately trying to stem the flood of unintended consequences that flow from constitutional reform. Hence, attempts to contain certain aspects of constitutional change ultimately failed as existing reforms began to spill over, increasing the radicalism of reform and the scope and intensity of change culminating in the 2005 Constitutional Reform Act and a decisive move towards the separation of powers.

Whether the Labour government will complete the transition to a New Constitutionalism under the premiership of Gordon Brown remains to be seen, but the early signs should provide grounds for optimism for constitutional radicals. In his inaugural speech as leader of the Labour Party, Brown declared:

> I want a new constitutional settlement for Britain. And the principles of my reforms are these: Government giving more power to Parliament; both government and Parliament giving more power to the people; Parliament voting on all the major issues of our time including peace and war; civil liberties safeguarded and enhanced; devolution within a Union of nations: England, Scotland, Wales and Northern Ireland – a Union that I believe in and will defend; local government strengthened with new powers – local communities empowered to hold those who make the decisions to account; and with community ownership of assets – greater power for more people to control their lives. (Brown, 2006c)

The logic of joined-up constitutionalism in the context of multi-level governance points inexorably towards Federalism and the constitution of a new sovereign, but given the strength of Britain's elitist political tradition there is nothing inevitable about it and would require a considerable leap of faith and political will.

Notes

1. 'Notebook: Brown's meeting with American sage sealed his plans for new regime', *Guardian*, 7 May 1997.
2. See www.cabinet-office.gov.uk/2002/news/020509_yourregion.htm.
3. G. Brown, 'I joined this party as a teenager ... Its values are my moral compass', *Guardian*, 25 June 2007.
4. Modernization Committee of the House of Commons, First Report, Select Committees, HC 224, 2001–2002.
5. Brown, 'I joined this party as a teenager'.
6. David Clarke MP was Chancellor of the Duchy of Lancaster from 1997 to 1998.
7. HMSO, *Rights Brought Home. The Human Rights Bill, CM 3782* (London: HMSO, 1997).
8. Interview, junior minister, September 2000.
9. Interview, cabinet minister, September 2000.
10. Interview, cabinet minister, June 2001.
11. Interview, senior civil servant, September 2001.
12. Interview, cabinet minister, September 2002.
13. See www.cabinet-office.gov.uk/2002/news/020509_yourregion.htm.
14. See www.politicsdirect.com/info/Pgrps/pregrlist.htm and www.walesindex.co.uk/pages/1356_624.html.
15. Ibid.
16. See House of Commons, Cmnd. 4444.

6
Tony Blair and the Office of Prime Minister

Philip Norton

When Tony Blair stepped down as Prime Minister in June 2007 he was the ninth longest-serving holder of the office since the time of Sir Robert Walpole. One survey of political scientists and historians in 2004 rated him as the sixth most successful of twentieth-century Prime Ministers (Theakston and Gill, 2006: 198). However, the pattern was not uniform. Historians rated him less highly than political scientists. Much depends on the criteria employed. Peter Riddell, in his book *The Unfulfilled Prime Minister*, identified ten tests for being a successful Prime Minister (Riddell, 2005: 9–13). Tony Blair, he argued, met over half the tests, but failed some critical ones.

According to Riddell, Blair was reluctant to take risks in domestic policy and appeared to many to lack a sense of direction (Riddell, 2005: 14–15). I share Riddell's views about ends. One of the areas in which the Blair government achieved substantial change was that of the constitution of the United Kingdom, yet it is an area in which there was no clear and coherent direction, no clear stipulated goal. That is a point I have developed elsewhere and has a relevance to what I shall argue (Norton, 2007a: 269–81; Norton, 2007b). My concern in this chapter is not with ends but rather with means; my focus is not policy but rather the institutional means of achieving policy goals. In the case of Tony Blair, how did he use the office of Prime Minister and – as institutions are not neutral in their effect – what have been the consequences for the British political system?

Given that the title of my chapter is 'Tony Blair and the Office of Prime Minister', I propose to address each part individually before explaining the relationship and the consequences for British government.

Tony Blair

In institutional terms, Tony Blair was arguably the first truly rootless Prime Minister. By that, I mean he had no roots, no clear grounding, in politics, the Labour Party, parliament or government. His view of all these appears to be instrumental. He was the quintessential outsider; therein may lie some benefits but it has also created major problems for the health of the political process.

Tony Blair's interests at university were in law and religion. He later lost his enthusiasm for law but developed his interest in religion. He developed some interest in ideas but he had no interest in student politics. He did not join the Labour Party until 1975, when he was 22, seeing it as a way of achieving his Christian goals. Both he and his flatmate, Charlie Falconer, became members of the Fairfield Branch of the Battersea Labour Party. As Blair's biographer, Anthony Seldon, noted:

> ... neither Blair nor Falconer proved much good at the hard graft of local politics – delivering notices and canvassing was not for them, despite it being a time of intense activity with the Tories .... This became the source of some resentment among fellow party members, not least because of Blair's lack of roots in the Labour movement. (Seldon, 2004: 50–1)

Blair failed to get selected to fight a council seat. Despite his lack of experience, he applied in 1980 – just one month after joining the local party in Hackney – to contest a parliamentary seat, and had to ask how to go about getting nominated by a trade union. Within two years of applying, he was selected to contest a by-election – Beaconsfield in 1982. He was seeking election to an institution that he had never visited. He was pushed into third place and lost his deposit. The following year, despite this less than auspicious performance, he was adopted, at the eleventh hour, as the Labour candidate for the new constituency of Sedgefield, the result, as John Rentoul noted, of hard work and luck (Rentoul, 2001: 108). It was safe Labour territory and selection was tantamount to election. I quote again from Anthony Seldon:

Tony Blair arrived in the House of Commons in June 1983, aged thirty and one month, the youngest Labour Member of Parliament. He had made no significant impact on the Labour Party up to that point, either at university or local government, or as a special adviser, speechwriter or on party bodies. Beaconsfield had given him a fleeting exposure, and he was regarded as the very lucky beneficiary of Sedgefield. But he had no standing or base in the Labour Party. He was a blank slate. (Seldon, 2004: 93)

After being elected to parliament, he spent little time on the back benches. The individual is important but so too is the political context. The Labour Party was defeated heavily in the 1983 general election. There were more than 100 new Conservative MPs elected but fewer than 40 Labour Members (Criddle, 1984: 233). In a House in which Labour's ranks were much reduced, the more able among them were soon recruited to the front bench. Blair was the first was to be chosen. The year following his election, he was appointed to the shadow treasury team. He was variously promoted and in 1988 – five years after entering the House of Commons – he was elected to the shadow cabinet. Four years later, he was Shadow Home Secretary and two years after that, when the leadership of the party came unexpectedly vacant, Leader of the Labour Party. His Leadership Election Statement, entitled *Change and National Renewal* (Blair, 1994), was good at identifying goals but not for stating specific policies. Three years later, he entered 10 Downing Street. Again, context is important. His rise to the top was made possible by the sudden death of John Smith in 1994 and the persistent unpopularity of the Conservative government following Britain's withdrawal from the European exchange rate mechanism in 1992. He entered office with no experience of government.

None of Blair's predecessors in the period of modern British politics (that is, since 1832) lacked institutional roots to the extent that he did. Some were somewhat detached from their own parties; one thinks especially of Harold Macmillan, who at one stage had the party whip withdrawn, and also of Benjamin Disraeli and Winston Churchill. Some spent little time on the back benches before being invited to join the government; one thinks especially of Harold Wilson, but also of Edward Heath and Margaret Thatcher. One of his predecessors, Ramsay MacDonald, also entered the premiership with no experience of government.[1] However, each had some grounding in their party, parliament or government. MacDonald had been a leading national figure in the Independent Labour Party for ten years before his election to parliament and held leading party posts, including secretary of the National Executive, before becoming party leader. John Major served for a shorter period of time than Blair in parliament before becoming Prime Minister, but he had held seven ministerial posts (the same number as Macmillan) before kissing hands as Prime Minister. Wilson served a shorter period on the back benches, but held three ministerial posts before entering No.10. Churchill has the record of modern Prime Ministers for the number of ministerial posts held before reaching the top of the 'greasy pole' – a total of ten – and he served in parliament for more than 37 years before the call came. Disraeli only held one ministerial post before being appointed Prime Minister, but he had spent more than 30 years in the Commons.

Blair thus lacked roots to an extent unparalleled in modern British politics. I revert to the combination of individual and political context. The timing of Blair's coming to the premiership is significant. It can be argued that the Conservative Party in 1997 had been in government for too long. Similarly, it can be argued that Labour had been in opposition for too long. Both conditions had consequences, I would contend negative consequences, for the health of the political process. The Conservatives in government developed an arrogance born of familiarity. Labour entered office with an arrogance born of ignorance. The party, and especially its leader, did not understand government and operated as if still in opposition. After ten years in Downing Street, Tony Blair left office still not understanding government. The nature of the office of Prime Minister enabled him to exist in such a state.

The office of Prime Minister

The office of Prime Minister is, as Asquith noted, what the holder of the office makes of it. The office is hardly mentioned in statute and little constrained by statute. The Prime Minister is the Queen's principal adviser. As such, he has at his disposal a vast array of prerogative powers. The scope for utilizing those powers to achieve prime ministerial goals is considerable.

There are few formal limitations. The Queen has significant legal powers but does not exercise an independent judgement in their exercise; she works on the basis of precedent and advice. Parliament has the formal power to say 'no' to government but does not usually exercise that power; the House of Commons is dominated by the party headed by the Prime Minister. The cabinet determines the policy to be laid before parliament, but the Prime Minister chairs the cabinet, determines who is in it, when it will meet, what it will discuss, and what it has decided. Mrs Thatcher changed the practice of summing up discussion in cabinet; she summed up at the beginning.

The scope for moulding the office, and pushing the boundaries, is considerable. There have been some weak Prime Ministers, constrained by other political actors and, as Harold Macmillan would have it, 'events, dear boy, events'. But equally there have been some strong Prime Ministers, dominating party, parliament and cabinet. Edward Heath is a good example, especially in dominating cabinet. Margaret Thatcher is another, especially in dominating parliament.

The individual in the office has determined how much he, or she, has wanted to use and shape the office. Much depends on their purpose in office (see Norton, 1987a: 325–45). Some have not wished to achieve much, seeing themselves as consolidators. Others – innovators, reformers and egoists – have had clear future goals (Norton, 1987a). The extent to which they have been able to achieve their goals has been affected by their capacity to mobilize the political, institutional and personal resources at their disposal (Heffernan, 2005; Norton, 1987a). Some have had the personal skills necessary to achieve the results they want; some have relied on oratory, some have utilized their skills as party managers, others their acute political antennae, and some have utilized all of these and more.

However, even those who have been determined to achieve their programme – an Attlee, Heath or Thatcher – have been constrained by their socialization in the political process. Their grounding has given them an appreciation of that process and that has worked both ways. They understand how to use the process but equally they understand the nuances and intricacies of that process. They recognize the inter-relationships at the heart of the system and the extent to which that constrains them. In effect, they have learned to respect it.

The political system comprises different bodies, each with a distinct role to play but where the system depends on each understanding not only that role but also the role fulfilled by others in the system. There is an interdependence – ministers rely on civil servants to carry out policy, civil servants depend on ministers to take a view – and usually mutual respect for what each does. There was a perception during the Thatcher years that ministers were adopting an arm's length relationship with civil servants. My own research, as part of the ESRC Whitehall programme, challenged that perception. As I wrote:

> Though there have been major changes in the structure and organisation of government, what is remarkable about recent years is how little has changed in terms of how ministers view officials and what officials

expect of ministers. Ministers have generally found the civil service supportive and able. Headey found that civil servants preferred ministers who could take decisions and fight (and win) departmental battles … That still appears to be the case. (Norton, 2000: 113)

The political process has worked on the basis of mutual respect, not necessarily at the individual level – Margaret Thatcher had a notably prickly relationship with some senior civil servants – but at the institutional level. There may be occasional tensions, sometimes personal clashes, but those in each part of the system knew their role and, equally and fundamentally important, the role of the other players.

Blair was fundamentally different. He benefited from being swept to office at a time of massive unpopularity of a Conservative government. Labour would have won in 1997 regardless of who led the party; Blair may have made some difference, but if he did it was only in the terms of the size of Labour's majority. He entered office with a massive parliamentary majority. He also brought to bear a number of political skills, especially the oratorical. But what set him apart was his lack of grounding.

He combined self-confidence with ignorance of government. He was not the first to be supremely self-confident but this has to be combined with his lack of understanding of government in order to make sense of how he has used the office. As Philip Stephens noted:

The story of Tony Blair's rise in politics is one of a politician blessed with unshakeable self-belief; principle and personal ambition unite in the conviction that he has both the capacity, and in a curious way, the duty to change things. His religious faith is a guiding presence. (Stephens, 2004: 26)

Someone who saw Blair at close quarters – Michael Barber, who headed the Prime Minister's Delivery Unit – has similarly made the point:

He has always had a tendency … to believe that in the end, through an act of his own personal will and the exercise of his own formidable powers of persuasion, he could achieve almost anything: pass a law, change a system, stop a revolt by backbenchers or bring a conflict to an end. (Barber, 2007: 305)

He believed in what he was doing. Government existed to enable him to deliver what he believed was right.

He wanted to use government to achieve his ends and he believed government was there to serve him in achieving those ends. He could not understand why he should be limited by other parts of the system, be it the civil service, the courts, parliament or the crown. He lacked an appreciation of the distinct role of the civil service. He complained about what he termed 'departmentalitis'. He treated the civil service as an adjunct of the party in government, not as a body to serve Her Majesty's government. He created his own units within No.10 for overseeing the actions of departments. His director of communications, Alastair Campbell, and his chief of staff, Jonathan Powell, were empowered to give directions to civil servants. 'There was', reported Peter Riddell, 'continual friction, particularly in the first two years, between senior civil servants and political appointees over the boundaries between government and party – reflecting both the inexperience of Whitehall of the New Labour team and their "permanent campaign" style of operating' (Riddell, 2001: 30). Within the government's first term, the civil service felt 'badly demoralised and out of the loop' (Hazell, quoted in Morrison 2001: 284). In an interview in 2002, the general secretary of the First Division Association of civil servants 'painted a picture of a battered Civil Service being undermined by ministers who had unrealistic demands and who underestimated the complications of government' (Sherman, 2002). The relationship faltered to the extent that there were demands for a Civil Service Act to ensure that the role of the civil service was enshrined, and protected, in statute, something promptly conceded by Blair's successor.

Blair did not fully appreciate the role of the cabinet as a linking mechanism to the rest of government. It was seen as a meeting for recording discussions, not discussing issues and ensuring departmental heads were committed to policies as a result of cabinet engagement. Meetings were short and sometimes perfunctory. As James Naughtie recorded, 'No Prime Minister since the nineteenth century has spent more time avoiding formal meetings with cabinet colleagues than Tony Blair' (Naughtie, 2001: 104). Whereas cabinets previously had sometimes lasted more than an hour, and on some occasions the cabinet met twice a week, under Blair the emphasis was on going through the motions as expeditiously as possible. 'The agenda was the same for almost every meeting and simply listed home affairs and foreign affairs and then Tony would bring up whatever he had in mind' (Short, 2004: 70). When one member, Clare Short, expressed publicly reservations about government policy and was criticized for not adhering to collective responsibility, her response was to point out that there was no cabinet discussion that was the basis of collective responsibility (Short, 2004: 71). There was little attempt to draw cabinet ministers together. Ministerial away days at Chequers appeared to be rather desultory affairs (Campbell, 2007: 321–2, 446–7). 'Sitting there listening, you had no real sense of a discussion leading to a conclusion, more a group of people who felt they had to speak and who made essentially random points' (Campbell, 2007: 322). When Frank Dobson suggested to Blair that he could hold team-building dinners for the whole cabinet at Chequers, 'Blair did not even think this was worthy of a reply' (Beckett and Hencke, 2004: 254). Blair was content to rely on his own coterie of advisers, with significant results for public policy. One example cited by Beckett and Hencke was the decision to press ahead with the Millennium Dome:

> If the cabinet had taken the decision, the project would have been scrapped. If the minister responsible for it at that time, Chris Smith, had taken the decision, it would have been a totally different project. It went ahead in what proved to be a disastrous fashion because the decision was taken by the prime minister and his new, all-powerful court without taking the heed of the views of either the cabinet or the minister responsible. (Beckett and Hencke, 2004: 195)

Nor did Blair understand the courts. Despite the government having passed the Human Rights Act, the Prime Minister's stance on combating terrorism led him, and some of his ministers, to question judicial decisions and for him to order a review of the Act. When the courts held certain provisions of anti-terrorism legislation to be incompatible with the European Convention on Human Rights, Blair and his ministers criticized the judges. In August 2005, in his monthly press briefing, Blair announced new measures to deal with terrorism and declared, 'Let no-one be in any doubt, the rules of the game are changing' (PM Press Conference, 2005). He conceded that it was likely that the provisions would be tested in the courts, and declared 'there will be lots of battles in the months ahead on this, let's be quite clear because of the way that the law has been interpreted over a long period of time, and I am prepared for those battles in the months ahead. I am absolutely and completely determined to make sure that this happens' (PM Press Conference, 2005). His attacks, and those of his ministers, led both the Lord Chancellor, Lord Falconer, and the Lord Chief Justice, Lord Phillips of Worth Matravers, to defend publicly the judges and to explain that what they were doing was their job of interpreting the law as passed by parliament. In evidence to the House of Lords Constitution Committee, Lord Phillips said 'The judge is just doing his job of applying the law and enforcing the rule of law. It is the law that has changed' (Constitution Committee, 2006: Q59). In 2006, Blair conceded, following a review of the Human Rights Act by the Department for Constitutional Affairs (2006), that it may not be possible to make major amendments.

Blair appeared to have no regard for the judiciary in deciding in 2003 to abolish the office of Lord Chancellor and create a Supreme Court – the announcement 'took place without any apparent understanding of the legal status of the Lord Chancellor and without consultation with the judiciary (or anyone else outside government)' (Constitution Committee, 2007: para. 12) – and in 2007 in creating a new Ministry of Justice. The judiciary were concerned both by the way in which the Ministry of Justice was created – the first the Lord Chief Justice knew of the proposal was when a story appeared in the press – and in its implications for resources and sentencing. When Blair left office, the relationship between the executive and the courts was arguably at an all-time low.

Nor did he understand parliament. He exhibited no intellectual curiosity about the British constitution or about parliament. As one senior politician put it to me, whenever he mentioned the constitution to Blair, 'his eyes just glazed over'. As Peter Riddell has reported, 'He has made virtually no speeches about the constitution since 1997, and during conversations with him I have never had a sustained discussion about the subject' (Riddell, 2005: 158). Blair's attitude towards the subject, and in particular parliament, was demonstrated in July 2000 when he was replying to a debate on the Norton Commission report on parliament. I have quoted the passage elsewhere and it is one also picked up by Riddell. The Prime Minister poured scorn on the Leader of the Opposition, William Hague, for choosing to discuss parliamentary reform:

He could have discussed jobs, the economy, schools, hospitals or even crime. I do not know whether people in his pubs and clubs are discussing pre-legislative scrutiny, but they are not in mine. (HC Deb., vol. 353, col. 1097, 13 July 2000; see Norton, 2003a: 550; Riddell, 2005: 158–9)

It was a crude populist approach. The fact that the health of parliament was crucial to a healthy polity seemed to pass him by.

His lack of interest in parliament was reflected in his absence from it. There has been a decline in involvement in parliamentary activities by Prime Ministers since the 1860s (Dunleavy and Jones, 1993), but Blair's lack of interest was especially pronounced. He had the worst voting record of modern Prime Ministers (Tyrie, 2000). On the face of it, this may seem of no great consequence, given the government's overall majority, but going through the lobbies when a vote is called provides a rare opportunity for MPs to see and have a word with ministers, including the Prime Minister. When a fixed Prime Minister's Question Time came into being in 1961, it was the result of the Prime Minister, Harold Macmillan, accepting the recommendation of the House of Commons Procedure Committee that there should be separate fixed slots on Tuesdays and Thursdays. In 1997, Blair unilaterally decided that there should be a single slot on a Wednesday. His only nod in the direction of parliament was to agree, after some pressure, to appear twice a year before the Liaison Committee, comprising the chairmen of Select Committees, but the environment of a committee room in Portcullis House was not that of the chamber of the House.

Blair also seemed oblivious at times of the constitutional relationship with the crown. He acted as the sovereign's principal adviser and in practice exercised prerogative powers in the name of the crown. Though the power rested with the Prime Minister, there were constitutional proprieties to be observed, such as consulting or advising the monarch in advance of announcements that affected her prerogative. The Queen was one of those not consulted or informed when Blair decided to abolish the ancient office of Lord Chancellor and to create a new Supreme Court. It was symptomatic of Blair's attitude to the royal family. 'Both of Blair's predecessors had been punctilious in following centuries of custom and practice in acknowledging the status of the royals' (Beckett and Hencke, 2004: 246). Blair was less punctilious and there was also a well-reported clash between Downing Street and Black Rod – the serjeant at arms in the House of Lords and the official responsible for royal ceremonials in Westminster Hall – over attempts to give Blair a prominent role in the funeral arrangements for the Queen Mother (Beckett and Hencke, 2004: 249–52).

This lack of grounding resulted in prime ministerial attempts to control the political system creating a new paradigm. Blair was accused of a presidential style of government (see Foley, 2004). In that, he was not alone. However, his premiership was more than a case of a creeping extension of presidentialism in British politics (Foley, 1993, 2000). Rather, it took prime ministerial power to a new plane (Norton, 2003a, 2003b). There has clearly been the development of presidentialism – of the Prime Minister becoming more and more detached from party, cabinet and parliament, acting as if directly elected by the people and not through parliament. Political imperatives have tended to make premiers more detached; what Bennister has termed 'institution stretch' has not been peculiar to the United Kingdom (Bennister, 2007: 2–19). However, none of Blair's predecessors were detached to the extent that he was. They were too grounded in the system. Heath had a prickly relationship with parliament, but relied heavily on the civil service; the then head of the civil service, Sir William Armstrong, was once dubbed the deputy prime minister (Campbell, 1993: 491). 'Senior Civil Servants felt that he [Heath] was one of them, a Permanent Secretary *manqué'* (Campbell, 1993: 490). (Heath's predecessor and successor, Wilson, *had* been 'one of them'.) Margaret Thatcher never 'handbagged' the Conservative Party (Norton, 1987b: 21–37). She summed up at the beginning of cabinet because she was not certain she would get her way; she never achieved a wholly Thatcherite cabinet or parliamentary party (Norton, 1990: 41–58). As one of her senior cabinet colleagues put it to me, she did not understand parliament (though she thought she did) but she did take it seriously. She would engage with critics.

Blair thus exhibited the characteristics of presidentialism, but on an unprecedented scale. He was detached. As he conceded in his last appearance at Prime Minister's Question Time, he 'never pretended to be a great House of Commons man' (HC Deb., vol. 462, col. 333, 27 June 2007) – reflected in the fact that he promptly announced his resignation from the institution. He had spent less than a year of his parliamentary career as a backbench MP. He was 'executive man' rather than 'parliament man', or rather he was 'single executive man'. Indeed, J.H. Grainger has likened him to Weber's 'ideal type' of independent political leader, a monocrat. 'Policy stems from or is endorsed by the free decision of the inner-determined, value-driven, subjective leader' (Grainger, 2005: 38). He was at the centre of things, more and more appointees were concentrated in Downing Street, and he saw himself as the white knight, charging in to solve problems, rather than leaving it to the relevant ministers, when there was widespread public unease. His style of government was highly personal, as identified in the Butler Report, itself significant in that Lord Butler was a former Cabinet Secretary. The Report noted the informality and relative lack of use of established Cabinet Committee machinery (Butler Report, 2004: paras 605–11); what has come to be termed, in popular parlance, as 'sofa government'. As Naughtie observed, 'The real deals are done elsewhere [than in cabinet], usually in the Prime Minister's study with only three or four people sitting around: and, as often as not, with only two' (Naughtie, 2001: 104). Officials were variously excluded, with no minute kept of what was decided.

What were the consequences of this style of government? My contention is that Blair's lack of grounding, facilitating this particular style, proved a short-term benefit for Blair but a potential long-term problem for the operation of the political system.

It was of benefit to Blair in that he largely got his way. He was, in the words of one Labour MP, 'the most ruthless operator British politics has seen certainly since Mrs Thatcher and probably for much longer than that' (Radice, 2004: 397). He found existing methods frustrating and was willing to ignore or override them. Michael Barber noted that Blair's belief that he could overcome problems through the exercise of personal will was 'at one level ... a strength because it means he takes on intractable issues' (Barber, 2007: 305). By pressing ahead and overriding or ignoring obstacles, he was able to achieve some significant change. What James Barber termed the power situation (Barber, 1972: ch. 1) was generally favourable, at least domestically, certainly during his first two terms of office, so there was little to prevent him in getting his way; in so far as there were problems at home they were truly domestic, affecting relations with his next door neighbour (Naughtie, 2001; Rawnsley, 2001: ch. 9; Peston, 2005: ch. 10; and Campbell, 2007).[2] It was only in the third term that the power situation started to turn against him.

However, his lack of understanding of government also created tensions within the system. His style of government, rather like Edward Heath's (see Norton, 1978), was not sustainable in the long term. The process of government rests on understandings within government. Blair was the first modern Prime Minister who was not a party to those understandings. As a result, there were tensions between the executive and other parts of the political system. He created a remarkable parliamentary situation in which an overall majority in excess of 60 was seen as rendering the Prime Minister vulnerable. He faced unprecedented backbench dissent (Cowley, 2005; www.revolts.co.uk). There was not the mutual respect and interdependence on which the system rested. That was the fundamental problem. The glue, the almost invisible glue, that held the system together started to lose its adhesiveness. Blair left office at a time of unprecedented conflict: there had been clashes before between ministers and the courts, but what was remarkable under Blair was the number of bodies that were involved and the extent of the conflict.

The future

The challenge to his successor, or successors, is to try to restore the ties that bind the system together. Given the flexibility of the system, the relationships can change significantly from one premier to another and they can do so in quite short order, something that was apparent in the transition from Margaret Thatcher to John Major.

What are we to expect of Gordon Brown? There are competing forces at work. On the one hand, Brown wishes to be the opposite of Blair and, as a consequence, to be inclusive. On the other, his natural instinct – certainly his practice as Chancellor – is to be exclusive.

Following the breakdown in the relationship between Brown and Blair, Brown was determined to distance himself from his predecessor. Peston records one senior member of the Labour Party as saying, in 2004, 'The thing which is guaranteed now – which didn't have to be the case – is that, whatever happens, Gordon Brown will not be a Blairite successor to Blair' (Peston, 2005: 326). (The unnamed source went on to say 'Which is madness'.) Brown was determined to be different, not least in terms of his style of government. Brown has some of the grounding that Blair lacked, especially in political activity in general and the Labour Party in particular – and he has more grounding than Blair in parliament and government, though the difference is not that great. Unlike Blair, he lives for politics: 'He lives and breathes it, rarely leaves it' (Peston, 2005: 16; see also Rawnsley, 2001: 146). As soon as he became Prime Minister, he made clear that he wished to revert to cabinet government. In a break from past practice, cabinet began meeting on a Tuesday. Brown also announced changes that reflected thought on constitutional issues. One of his first acts was to publish a Green Paper on *The Governance of Britain*, embodying various proposals to limit the power of the executive (Ministry of Justice, 2007). These included giving new powers to parliament, including the prerogative power to deploy troops abroad, as well as placing the civil service on a statutory footing. The Green Paper was followed by publication of a draft legislative programme (Office of the Leader of the House of Commons, 2007), ahead of the Queen's Speech, giving parliament an opportunity to see and debate the proposals that the government planned to introduce in the next session of parliament. The measures included a Constitutional Reform Bill to give effect to those proposals in the Green Paper that required statutory authorization. It was made clear that the various changes that impinged on the royal prerogative had been cleared with Buckingham Palace.

However, in order to demonstrate that he is not Tony Blair, Brown also has to demonstrate that he is not Gordon Brown. Even before entering government, he 'steamrolled rather than reasoned with critics' (Bower, 2004: 109–10). As Chancellor, he acquired a reputation for taking decisions in isolation, shutting out anyone other than close trusted advisers, and for brooking no opposition in ensuring that decisions were implemented. Early in 2007, former Cabinet Secretary Lord Turnbull referred to Brown's 'sheer Stalinist ruthlessness', a criticism that hit a chord with others who had served in government. Peter Riddell recorded 'I have heard half a dozen other current and even more recently retired permanent secretaries express almost exactly the same doubts about the closed and often ruthless way in which the Chancellor and his inner circle operate' (Riddell, 2007). The question, as Riddell noted, was whether Brown could become more collegial as Prime Minister. He quoted Sir Stephen Wall, a former Downing Street adviser on European affairs: 'Is Gordon Brown capable of operating with the trust and transparency that is necessary for good Cabinet government?'

The answer to Wall's question will determine the form of government during the Brown premiership. If the power situation remains favourable, then it will depend on Brown himself as to whether government is restored as a functioning, inter-related entity or becomes a Blair II centralized powerhouse, where lip service is given to transferring power to others but where the Prime Minister's hands remain firmly holding the reins of power. If he ends up pursuing the latter, then there is the potential to affect the power situation adversely. The nature of the political system allows the Prime Minister to make of the office what he wants, but seeking to concentrate power in Downing Street is to build up trouble that in the long term can prove inimical to good governance.

Notes

1. In the history of the premiership, only two other Prime Ministers – Rockingham and Addington – were appointed without any previous ministerial experience (Englefield, Seaton and White, 1995: 401).
2. The Campbell diaries are revealing, even though much was apparently excluded about the relationship. Note the entry for Saturday, 12 January 2002, p. 602: 'To the Goulds' for dinner. Gail asked whether Philip and I ever had a discussion that did not cover TB [Tony Blair], GB [Gordon Brown], PM [Peter Mandelson] and their varying relationships. The answer is probably not, at least none that lasted more than a minute or two.'

7
A Rebellious Decade: Backbench Rebellions under Tony Blair, 1997–2007

Philip Cowley and Mark Stuart

> Behold, how good and how pleasant it is for brethren to dwell together in unity!
>
> Psalms 133:1

Introduction

Previous Labour leaders used to play down their party's rebellious streak, arguing either that things were not as bad as people thought (probably true) or that some division was a sign of healthy discussion (probably wishful thinking). On becoming Labour leader in 1994, however, Tony Blair's strategy was different: he talked up how divided the Labour Party used to be, in order to talk about how united it had become. As with the creation of so much of New Labour, this involved distorting and exaggerating the historical record. It established a caricature of the past compared to which the present was noticeably more attractive. And it allowed the party's supposed cohesion to be presented as an important part of what made it new, and (just as importantly) what made Labour different from the Conservatives, then in the death throes of the Major government and widely seen by the public as split.

The Prime Minister reinforced that message when Labour backbenchers gathered at Westminster just six days after their landslide election victory in May 1997, telling them they had been elected to support the Labour government, and there should be no indiscipline:

Look at the Tory Party. Pause. Reflect. Then vow never to emulate. Day after day, when in government they had MPs out there, behaving with the indiscipline and thoughtlessness that was reminiscent of us in the early '80s. Where are they now, those great rebels?

His answer: not in parliament.

When the walls came crashing down beneath the tidal wave of change, there was no discrimination between those Tory MPs. They were all swept away, rebels and loyalists alike. Of course, speak your mind. But realize why you are here: you are here because of the Labour Party under which you fought. (Blair, 1997)

Yet even in Opposition, there was plenty of evidence of underlying division within Labour's ranks (Cowley and Norton, with Stuart and Bailey, 1996). The difference between Labour MPs and Conservative MPs prior to the 1997 election – and it was a crucial one – was that whereas Conservative MPs appeared almost suicidally willing to broadcast their differences, even those Labour MPs known to have doubts about the Blairite project had for the most part taken what the *New Statesman* described as 'trappist-like vows', in order to get into government (Richards, 1996). But once in government, things might well be very different. The Parliamentary Labour Party (PLP) had previously never shown a tendency for excessively harmonious relations with the party's leadership, and whilst Tony Blair may have wished for and demanded a disciplined and cohesive parliamentary party – which Prime Minister wouldn't want that? – there was no guarantee that that was what he would get.

Yet amazingly, it was at first what appeared to be happening. Once in government, Labour MPs soon acquired a reputation for bovine loyalty. They were routinely described as lacking backbone and guts, and routinely compared to robots or clones or poodles. As this chapter will show, this was never a fair description – rebellion was more common than people realized, even in the early years of the Blair government – and it became noticeably less accurate as the Blair era progressed. Indeed, by Tony Blair's second parliament, and despite a landslide Commons majority, the Prime Minister struggled to enact key pieces of legislation. As Peter Oborne noted in the *Spectator* in 2004, as the government fought to pass its proposals for the funding of higher education: 'Tony Blair has achieved the impossible. Three years after winning a landslide majority of 160, he is forced to conduct his business as if he were leader of a minority government.' It was, Oborne concluded, 'a failure of party management on a heroic scale' (Oborne, 2004).

This chapter explains that transformation, from accusations of excessive cohesion and leadership dominance to the storms of the later years. It sets out the major revolts of each of the three Blair parliaments, before putting the period in its historical context.

Sporadic trouble, small scale compromises, 1997–2001

Many Labour MPs were already placing a premium on the appearance of unity long before the Prime Minister lectured them in 1997. As one cabinet minister said: '1992 was a watershed. We'd blown it. It got to the soul of the party. If you're in politics, you're in politics to get power. They'd got the message that a divided party is a losing party.'[1] After 18 years in Opposition, Labour MPs began the 1997 parliament desperate not to do anything that might help send the party back to the wilderness; there was a desire amongst some of Labour's new MPs to avoid the appearance of disunity at almost any cost. As one of the newly elected MPs put it in 1997: 'If it's a choice between being seen as clones or being seen as disunited … then I'd choose the clones any day.' So, clones it was. It was at this time that the sheep references became common currency. The reality, though, was more complicated than either Tony Blair desired – or most of the MPs' many critics realized.

The evidence of cohesion was certainly strong. Blair's first government managed something achieved by no other government since that of Wilson's elected in 1966: it lasted the entire parliament without being defeated on a whipped vote in the Commons. Even the Thatcher governments elected with such large majorities in the 1980s had gone down to at least one defeat per parliament. The scariest moment for Blair's whips in the 1997–2001 parliament came when the government's majority fell to 25 at one point in 1999 – but that had been not as a result of a backbench revolt on a key issue, but as a result of a well-organized ambush by the Conservative whips on the Rating (Valuation) Bill.

There were also relatively few rebellions. There were just 96 backbench revolts by Labour MPs between 1997 and 2001. Since party cohesion in Britain began to weaken in the 1960s and 1970s every full-length parliament – bar none – had seen considerably more rebellions. John Major, for example, had watched his Tory MPs rebel on 174 occasions in the preceding parliament.[2] From his new position on the Opposition benches, Major must have looked on wistfully, imagining what his premiership could have been like had his MPs behaved like that. Nor was it just the Major government against which such a level of rebellion looked infrequent. Leaving aside the very short parliaments of 1964–66 and February–October 1974, you have to go back to 1955 to find a full length parliament in which there were fewer backbench revolts by government MPs than the one elected in 1997. That was the era of which a US observer, Sam Beer, wrote that British MPs behaved with a 'Prussian discipline' (Beer, 1969: 350–1).

However, whilst cohesion was high, it was not absolute. The parliament saw Labour MPs break ranks over a wide range of issues, including welfare reform, transport, social security, pensions, freedom of information, criminal justice, House of Lords reform, and student funding. The first major backbench rebellion faced by the Blair government was in many ways the most significant. It came in December 1997 when 47 Labour MPs voted against a cut in lone-parent benefit, with at least 20 abstaining. Although unsuccessful in terms of defeating the government, it was hugely significant in terms of the government's future relationship with its own backbenchers. The rebellion was much larger than anyone had expected, and it made those in government realize that they could not rely on coercion or self-discipline alone to deliver cohesion. As a result, government ministers began to make themselves more available for consultation with concerned MPs. Even if they varied in their willingness to make concessions, almost all ministers were more ready to listen and discuss than they had been previously.

The lone-parent rebellion also resulted in the government facing a significant group of loyal MPs who had very reluctantly voted for the measure (some famously doing so in tears), and felt that the leadership owed them a favour. One MP, who had voted with the government despite grave misgivings, was told by his whip, 'Trust us, it'll get sorted.' Brown responded in his Budget statement in March 1998 by increasing Child Benefit by £2.50 a week above the rate of inflation, the largest ever single increase.[3] Labour backbenchers thus realized both that the sky would not fall in if they voted against the government and that they could achieve policy change if they pressed for it. As one newly elected MP said: 'It gave us a confidence that they are not infallible.'

The government therefore became adept at making concessions in an attempt to win over backbench critics. Even the issue to see the largest revolt of the parliament – over the reform of Incapacity Benefit, when 67 Labour MPs voted against the government in 1999 – found the Social Security Secretary, Alistair Darling, more willing to negotiate and engage with Labour backbenchers than his predecessor, Harriet Harman, had been over lone-parent benefit. But the exemplar of the government's handling of its backbench critics in the 1997 parliament came with the Home Secretary, Jack Straw's deft handling of the controversial Immigration and Asylum Bill during the 1998–99 session. The controversy engendered by the Bill caused some newspapers to talk about the possibility of a government defeat. The *Observer* claimed that the Bill had 'aroused more opposition among backbenchers than any other legislation before Parliament' (McSmith and Wintour, 1999). Straw engaged with the backbench critics of the Bill, and tackled their concerns head-on. Other ministers might have been able to consult and to negotiate, but, commented another MP, 'no-one else is in Jack's league'. Straw's concessions succeeded in placating the rebels without fundamentally altering the shape of the Bill. By the Bill's Third Reading only seven Labour backbenchers voted against the government. One Labour critic of the proposals said despairingly, 'I think that we have reached a pretty pass when, after one minister had consulted and produced some relatively minor concessions, there is dancing within the Parliamentary Labour Party' (HC Deb., 16 June 1999, c.450). Straw was to repeat the tactic – successfully – over the Terrorism Bill, the Freedom of Information Bill, and the Football (Disorder) Bill. In every case, the Home Secretary listened carefully to rebel concerns, engaging with backbenchers.[4] Again, in every case, the concessions granted were relatively minor – but they were enough. One backbench critic viewed such concessions on Bills as amounting to little in reality, and saw Straw as the 'arch exemplar' of giving 'the minimum that they can get away with'.

Conversely, when the government failed to compromise (or, sometimes, where the nature of the issue made compromise difficult), they faced more sizeable rebellions. During the Report stage of the Transport Bill, for example, which allowed for the part-privatization of National Air Traffic Services (NATS), and where compromise was difficult, there were three sizeable rebellions, the two largest of which saw some 46 Labour MPs support the idea that any new company would be made into a not-for-profit organization. A similar pattern occurred over the proposed abolition of trial by jury in so-called 'either way' cases. As with NATS, the nature of the issue left little room for manoeuvre on either side. When the vote on Bob Marshall-Andrews' reasoned amendment was taken at the end of the Second Reading debate, 29 Labour MPs voted against the government. By the Bill's Third Reading, that figure had not changed substantially, with 28 voting against the government.

But for the most part, the government was usually prepared to do deals with its backbenchers. These had the effect of reducing the level of rebellion, dampening down several potentially damaging rebellions and extinguishing several other putative revolts altogether (Cowley and Stuart, 2003). Had the government been as autocratic as was sometimes implied, the number (and size) of rebellions under Blair would have been greater. Had Labour's backbenchers been as feeble as was sometimes implied, there would have been no need for such concessions in the first place.

Moreover, even based on its observable behaviour, it is possible to dismiss some of the wilder claims made about the PLP's behaviour between 1997 and 2001. Compared to the Conservative MPs in the 1950s, for example, the PLP elected in 1997 was almost feral. Labour MPs between 1997 and 2001 rebelled roughly *nine* times more often than did Tory MPs in the 1950s. There were also more rebellions by Labour MPs between 1997 and 2001 than there were against the Attlee government. And although Labour MPs did not rebel very often during Blair's first parliament, when they did, they were likely to do so in significant numbers. The average (mean) size of the revolts between 1997 and 2001 was 15, a figure greater than in all but three post-war parliaments (and greater than in all but two full-length parliaments) (Cowley, 2002).

And as the parliament progressed so the number of backbench rebellions began to increase, as the self-discipline that was so strong at the beginning of the parliament began to wear off. The third session of the parliament, between 1999 and 2000, saw more rebellions than the parliament's first two put together. In part, this was because it was asking a lot for MPs to remain that self-disciplined for that long. But it was also because the imperatives for cohesion appeared to have become less important. As the parliament progressed, it became increasingly clear that the Conservatives were not recovering in the polls, and so rebellion became less risky and far easier.

Rebel early, rebel often, 2001–05

From a very early stage in the second Blair term, it became clear that the PLP was increasingly restless. One whip described the parliamentary party as being 'in the most foul mood' when it reconvened after the election. The parliament's very first session of Prime Minister's Questions saw some hostile questions from Labour backbenchers, as did the first private meeting of the PLP.

It was not that there had been any great turnover in personnel. Only a handful of seats had changed hands in the standstill election of 2001, and so 85 per cent of the Commons membership was the same after the election as before. But Labour MPs were now politically more experienced;

winning a second term had emboldened many, some of whom felt (perhaps erroneously) that they had personally been more responsible for their victory in 2001 than they had been in 1997, when they had come in on Tony Blair's coat-tails. As one of the new intake put it, talking about the 1997 intake of which she was a member:

> A lot of them never expected to win. And some of them had hardly spoken to a Labour MP before. And, as far as Ministers were concerned, they were overwhelmed by them, these important people, especially Secretaries of State. And as for the Prime Minister! But after a while, they got to know that these were ordinary people. They learnt that you wouldn't be burnt to death if you voted against the Government. And that Secretaries of State were ordinary, fallible, people, who can make mistakes. They stopped being overawed by Office.

Many of the new 2001 intake who joined their ranks were also more experienced politically, and were less willing than the 1997 intake had been to take the views of whips and minister as gospel. Early on in the parliament, one senior whip identified the growing ranks of what he called the three 'disses': the perennial dissenters; the dismissed (ex-ministers); and the disappointed (those overlooked for ministerial office) (Benedetto and Hix, 2007). Together, these three groups amounted to around a third of the PLP, or around half of the backbenchers; as the whip put it, they constituted 'combustible material'.

The government whips therefore began the parliament knowing that they faced difficulties with many of their backbenchers. But cushioned by yet another mammoth majority, they did at least think they should be able to withstand most rebellions, and reach the end of the parliament undefeated. They therefore tried an ambitious long-term strategy, in which they hoped to build up good relations with backbenchers during the 2001 parliament and contain the habit of rebellion, so that after the following election – when they expected Labour to have a much smaller majority – they would still be able to govern easily.

This strategy failed utterly. The 2001 parliament saw Labour MPs vote against their whips on 259 separate occasions, more than in any other post-war parliament save that between October 1974 and 1979. But the Wilson/Callaghan government of 1974–79 lasted five years, whereas the second Blair government covered just four. As a percentage of the divisions to occur in the parliament, the period from 2001 to 2005 tops the post-war lists, with Labour backbenchers rebelling in 20.8 per cent of votes, a higher rate of rebellion than in any other parliament since

1945. A total of 218 Labour MPs voted against their whip during the parliament's four years; as one whip put it, the 'threshold of rebellion' was crossed by most Labour MPs.

The most dramatic rebellions came over the decision to go to war in Iraq. The largest revolt on the issue in March 2003 saw 139 Labour MPs vote against their whip, along with some abstentions. This was the largest rebellion by MPs of any governing party – Labour, Conservative or Liberal – on any type of policy for over 150 years. It could easily have been worse. There was a slightly smaller (though still enormous) rebellion in February 2003, when 121 Labour MPs voted against the government; the whips at least succeeded in persuading a dozen Labour backbenchers who voted against the government in February to switch their votes in March.[5] The government won the two votes comfortably, thanks to Conservative support, but at a heavy price, with more than half of their backbenchers defying the whip. Ironically, the minister charged with the task of cutting the size of these rebellions was the new Foreign Secretary, Jack Straw. Straw's usual tactics of what one Labour MP described as 'carefully calibrated concessions' (HC Deb., 21 November 2001, c.354) did not work with Iraq, where there was little or no wriggle room. In an effort to bring round some of the rebels, the Prime Minister let it be known that he would resign if he was defeated over the issue (although since he had Conservative frontbench support, this was always an unrealistic threat).[6] It was the first, but not the last, time he would employ such a tactic.

Iraq aside, extremely large rebellions were also seen over government legislation. The rebellions in 2003 over the introduction of foundation hospitals broke the record for the largest health policy rebellion ever by Labour MPs against their own government. In 2004, the 72 Labour votes against the Second Reading of the Higher Education Bill, the Bill that introduced top-up fees, was precisely double what had until 2001 been the largest education rebellion ever by Labour MPs in government. In the case of both foundation hospitals and top-up fees, Labour MPs also objected to how the policy had been produced, complaining that legislation had been presented from No.10 to the PLP as a *fait accompli*. This became a familiar complaint during the Blair era, with Labour MPs complaining about policy emerging fully-formed out of Downing Street and being dropped onto the PLP, rather than developing out of the party's policy apparatus.

This did not mean that MPs were unable to gain policy concessions once the Bill had been produced, merely that they felt excluded from its genesis. Indeed, the sheer scale of opposition to both foundation hospitals and top-up fees meant that Labour backbenchers were able to gain quite significant concessions from government. Both bills were good examples, yet again, of how the government was prepared to negotiate with its backbenchers in order to get legislation through. To take, as an example, the case of top-up fees, the government compromised right from the initial White Paper to the final Lords amendment stage: pegging the cap on fees to £3,000 per year; restoring grants for the poorest students; establishing a universities access regulator to increase working-class student entrance rates; fixing the cap throughout the next parliament; promising an independent review of fees after three years; increasing maintenance grants substantially; allowing remission of fees for poorer students; promising a debate and a vote in both Houses before the cap on fees could be raised after 2010; and giving a duty, rather than a power, on the Secretary of State for Education and Skills to maintain the cap if a university attempted to raise it in the future.[7] As one MP commented: 'They listened, and then they moved.'

In both cases, the concessions helped the government survive undefeated. The government scraped home by 17 votes on the closest foundation hospitals vote in November 2003, and by an even narrower margin of just five on the Second Reading of the Higher Education Bill in January 2004. This led Simon Carr of the *Independent* to describe the Labour rebels as 'a consistently disappointing lot', adding, 'If they needed six votes to bring the government down, they'd get four. If they needed one, they wouldn't get it. They shrink to fit.' There was an element of truth in this observation, although it could have been applied to every single set of government backbenchers since the Second World War, if not before. Backbench rebellions didn't start fizzling out in 1997. In both cases, however, the government played on backbench fears – and, in some cases, ignorance – about the consequences of defeat, threatening its rebellious backbenchers with victory, predicting dire consequences, including prime ministerial resignations, votes of confidence, and elections, should the government be defeated.

These, though, were just the largest revolts. In the four years after 2001 there were also rebellions over anti-terrorism legislation (repeatedly), Community Health Councils, smacking, asylum and immigration (again, repeatedly), faith schools, living wills, trial by jury, gambling, the firefighters, the Housing Bill, organ donation, the Enterprise Bill, the European constitution, ID cards, and banning incitement to religious hatred. On top of those, there were a multitude of smaller, more isolated, revolts, sometimes consisting of a lone MP, sometimes seeing just a handful of rebels go through the division lobbies in defiance of their whips. 'It's now a rebellion a week', complained a whip mid-way through the parliament – although it was, in fact, more like two a week. This behaviour continued right throughout the parliament. The final sessions of most parliaments pass off without much in the way of dissent among government backbenchers. By contrast, the 2004–05 session saw Labour MPs rebelling in sizeable numbers over six contentious Bills, with the Prevention of Terrorism Bill producing the longest day of parliamentary business since Labour came to power in 1997, the Bill passing between Lords and Commons for a mammoth 28 hours. Because of this extended parliamentary ping-pong, many of the hardcore opponents of the Bill notched up a large number of dissenting votes on the same issues over and over again, as the Bill zipped back and forth between Commons and Lords. Even on the day that the Prime Minister announced the date of the general election, Labour MPs were *still* voting against their government.

Minds were not concentrated, 2005–07

Not that he could have done much about it, but it is now clear that Tony Blair would have been better off had he been able to have his parliamentary majorities in a different order. Mrs Thatcher had a small but workable majority in her first parliament – when MPs' self-discipline is at its tightest – followed by two landslide majorities to cushion her against any tendency to increased rebellion. Tony Blair had his largest majorities first, during which rebellions became commonplace, and then saw the cushion removed.

Once it became clear that Labour would be re-elected for their third term with a smaller majority of 66, the line from Labour HQ was that this smaller majority would help 'concentrate the minds' of Labour MPs. The bloated majorities enjoyed since 1997 had allowed Labour backbenchers to rebel without giving much thought to the consequences. With a smaller majority, so the argument went, Labour MPs would have to exercise more self-discipline. This view was also accepted by many outside observers, who would point out that the government's majority was larger than in most post-war parliaments, and – a comparison Tony Blair himself would use – was larger than that with which Mrs Thatcher had managed between 1979 and 1983.

Such commentators (and the Prime Minister) had forgotten the last time a government found itself re-elected with a much smaller majority. In the days after the 1992 election, most commentators declared that John Major's 21 seat majority was a perfectly workable state of affairs. But they had reckoned without the extent to which the habit of revolt had been widespread within the Conservative parliamentary party during the Thatcher years, when (just as between 1997 and 2005) MPs had been able to rebel relatively freely given the size of the majority. When the majority came down, it did not force Bill Cash, Teddy Taylor et al. to behave better. They had also forgotten how the Labour government of 1974–79 managed (or rather, didn't) with a small, and sometimes non-existent, majority, with self-immolation rather than self-control being the order of the day.

Allowing for defeats and retirements, there were 60 Labour MPs who survived the 2005 election who had rebelled on ten or more occasions between 2001 and 2005. Whilst the smaller majority had the potential to make some of the other, more infrequent, rebels change their behaviour, it was unlikely to stop rebellions by many of these 60. In one of its more prescient passages, a book published in late 2005 noted:

> Still there, for example, are 56 of those who voted against the Government's last Prevention of Terrorism Bill, introduced just before the 2005 election, and easily enough to defeat the Government should they mishandle similar legislation now, even after the recent terrorist attacks. (Cowley, 2005: 246)

And indeed, just as predicted, in mid-November 2005, just six months into the 2005 parliament, the government went down to two defeats during the Report stage of the Terrorism Bill. The government had proposed extending the length of time for which a terrorist suspect could be held without charge from 14 days to 90 days. In two separate votes, Labour MPs limited the extension to 28 days. These were the government's first defeats in the Commons on whipped votes since Labour came to power in 1997; and, with the government losing by 31 and 33 votes, the largest substantive defeats in the Commons since July 1978, when the Callaghan government failed to overturn a Lords amendment on the Wales Bill.[8]

Two more defeats came on 31 January 2006 during the Lords Amendment stage of the Racial and Religious Hatred Bill. Neither of these rebellions – one consisting of 26 MPs, another of 21 – should have been large enough to defeat the government, but the whips had miscalculated, allowing too many Labour MPs to be absent for campaigning in the Dunfermline and West Fife by-election. The embarrassment was made all the worse by the fact that the Prime Minister was present for the first vote but was then allowed to leave the Commons before the second – which was then lost by a majority of just one. The defeats in November 2005 can fairly be described as a failure of political leadership, the government failing to acknowledge the scale of discontent on the backbenches; those in January 2006 were simply a failure of whipping.

No other post-war government with a majority of over 60 in the Commons went down to as many defeats in an entire parliament, let alone merely in its first session. Indeed, John Major's much-derided Tories had suffered just four defeats as a result of backbench dissent on whipped votes in the five years between 1992 and 1997. The third Blair term thus managed to achieve in its first year what it took Major five years, despite having a majority three times the size. In total, the first session of the 2005 parliament saw backbench Labour MPs rebel on 95 occasions, equating to a rebellion in 28 per cent of divisions. That easily eclipsed what had been the most rebellious first session of the post-war era, the 1992–93 session (a rebellion in 23 per cent of divisions) when John Major struggled so terribly with the Maastricht legislation.

The defeats were a wake-up call to the government that they no longer enjoyed the cushion of the landslide majorities of the previous two parliaments. As a result, even greater efforts were made to prevent further defeats, with the government going further in terms of compromising over a number of bills. The exemplar was the government's proposals for welfare reform. In the run-up to the publication of the government's Green Paper on welfare reform, *A New Deal for Welfare: Empowering People to Work* (Department for Work and Pensions, 2006), John Hutton, the Secretary of State for Work and Pensions, responded to opposition from Labour MPs by abandoning plans to extend means-testing for the long-term sick, instead focusing on extra occupational help for claimants. As a result, the White Paper's reception was far more positive than it would otherwise have been, and when the Welfare Reform Bill eventually reached the Commons' Report stage in January 2007, there were only three small rebellions, involving just seven Labour MPs. Hutton's actions had defused what could have been a very serious problem; one of those involved in the process described it as 'a model of how you engage and defuse a potential difficulty'.

Sometimes, however, the concessions were still not enough. This was most obvious with the government's Education White Paper, and the subsequent Education and Inspections Bill in the 2005–06 session. Several leading government backbenchers, including all six members of the PLP's Parliamentary Committee, produced what they termed an 'Alternative White Paper' (AWP), demanding changes to the policy. The government met many (although not all) of the rebels' demands, and the Education and Inspections Bill that followed was significantly changed from the White Paper. It was then further amended prior to Second

Reading, with an expectation amongst Labour MPs that it would be further changed in committee. As a result, just under half of the 91 signatories to the AWP voted against the Bill at its Second Reading.[9] Yet despite this considerable movement from the government, the Bill saw several large backbench revolts (the largest comprising 69 Labour MPs), and the Bill only passed at both Second and Third Reading thanks to support from Opposition MPs.

Sometimes, there was relatively little room for concessions anyway. The government's decision to proceed with the renewal of Trident – another one of those issues on which it was difficult to compromise – produced the largest revolt of Blair's third term, with 95 Labour MPs defying their whips on one vote. As with schools reform, the policy was carried only thanks to the votes of Opposition MPs. But whereas with schools reform there had at least been a desire to get the Bill through just with Labour votes – for it not to be seen as a 'Tory bill' – there was an acceptance from very early on with Trident that this would not be possible. It meant that three of the key policy decisions taken during Tony Blair's premiership, encompassing foreign policy (Iraq), defence (Trident) and domestic policy (schools reform), were only passed thanks to Opposition votes. It was all a long way from the supposed unity that marked New Labour out as distinct.

When the whip was off

Some of the most striking examples of backbench influence during the Blair era came on issues involving unwhipped votes. There was, for example, the blocking in 2001 of the government's attempt to oust Donald Anderson and Gwyneth Dunwoody from the chairmanships of two select committees. On two free votes, the government's position was over-turned, more than 100 Labour MPs going against the known preferences of the whips on both votes (Cowley, 2001). There was also the government's various retreats over House of Lords reform, both at the beginning of the 2001 parliament, where it abandoned the proposals contained in its *Completing the Reform* White Paper (Department for Constitutional Affairs, 2001), and at the beginning of the 2005 parliament, where it dropped plans to let MPs vote using an alternate vote (AV) system to decide their preferred composition for the Lords. In both cases, backbench opposition was fierce, and the government wisely backed down.

The third example – often misunderstood – was the issue of hunting with dogs. Ever since they voted in such overwhelming numbers for

Michael Foster's Private Members' Bill in November 1997, Labour MPs consistently refused to allow their government to wriggle out of a total ban on hunting with dogs. When he was Home Secretary, Jack Straw attended a packed meeting of Labour's backbench committee on Home Affairs, at which nearly all of the 100 or so MPs in attendance made it clear that they wanted to see a total ban. As he left the meeting, Straw was heard to say that he could see no point 'lying in front of a tank'. Every time that the government tried to offer a compromise, or a delay, or some other concession to the hunting lobby, their backbenchers refused to concede the issue. Throughout the 2001 parliament, the government repeatedly attempted to reach some form of compromise, only for Labour backbenchers to refuse to allow them to concede.

This was at its most visible in November 2004, with No.10 attempting to engineer a compromise by indicating that the Prime Minister would support licensed hunting. Yet on a free vote, just 25 Labour MPs supported his preferred option. They included five members of the cabinet plus the minister responsible, Alun Michael, along with two other ministers of state. They were joined by five whips, led by the Chief Whip, Hilary Armstrong.[10] This left just 11 Labour backbenchers. On the other side were six cabinet ministers as part of the broad mass of 297 Labour MPs. The Prime Minister therefore voted along with just 8 per cent of the Labour MPs to have voted. Facing him were the remaining 92 per cent. The authors cannot think of (or find) an occasion in the post-war period when any PM has been so detached from his or her parliamentary party.

A similarly dramatic split came in the 2005 parliament when the government abandoned its 2005 manifesto commitment to allow smoking to continue in pubs that were not serving food – what was described as a 'partial ban' (Labour Party, 2005: 66). Faced both with cabinet splits and overwhelming evidence of backbench hostility, the government then allowed MPs a free vote on two more restrictive options, resulting in the abandonment of a pledge that the government had made to the electorate less than a year before. In itself, this was remarkable. Once more, we cannot think of a comparable event in the last 50 years. Even more remarkable were the divisions the votes revealed within the PLP. Given the chance to stick with the initial 'partial' ban, just 29 Labour MPs (including John Reid, the cabinet minister most closely associated with it) did so. A staggering 91 per cent of Labour MPs to vote – including the Prime Minister – walked into the opposite lobby to the position on which they had fought the election under a year before. The second vote, on private clubs, saw 84 per cent vote against what had been in their manifesto. If nothing else, the votes showed the wisdom of the government having allowed a free vote on the issue.

Both smoking in enclosed public places and foxhunting are now banned because of the power exercised by Labour's backbenchers. Whatever one's views about the policies *per se*, that aspect of the process is striking.

Conclusion

A key criticism of the Blair government was that it had weakened and diminished the role of parliament in British politics (Cowley, 2007). A key part of this thesis of parliamentary decline was the belief that there was an increasing lack of independence amongst backbench MPs – from Roy Hattersley's claim that Labour MPs were 'the most supine Members of Parliament in British history' (Hattersley, 2005) to the belief of the Power Inquiry that the whips 'have enforced party discipline more forcefully and fully than they did in the past' (Power Inquiry, 2005: 133).

Yet the evidence of the Blair decade does not support such an argument. Rather the opposite: there is plenty of evidence that MPs today are more independent-minded and willing to defy their whips now than they used to be. In the 60-plus years of the post-war era – the period for which we have the most reliable data – cohesion was at its highest at Westminster in the 1950s (Norton, 1975). There were two whole sessions in the 1950s during which not a single Conservative MP voted against their whip. Tony Blair's whips would have sold their souls for that sort of discipline.

In total, Labour MPs voted against their whips in 16 per cent of divisions. That compares to a figure of 14 per cent for the Thatcher governments, between 1979 and 1990 – the last time there was a similarly extended period with one Prime Minister in office. During the 11 Conservative years under Mrs Thatcher, Conservative MPs cast a total of 4,259 votes against their party whip. The figure for the Blair era is 6,520, more than 50 per cent higher, despite the Thatcher era being slightly longer.[11]

As this chapter has demonstrated, the Blair decade broke a host of records for backbench rebellion. It saw the largest rebellion for 150 years (on Iraq); the largest ever rebellion during a Labour government on a health issue (foundation hospitals); the largest ever Labour rebellion on an education issue (top-up fees); the largest ever defence-related rebellion to be suffered by a Labour government (on Trident); the equal largest rebellion at Second Reading (also on top-up fees); and the largest rebellion at Third Reading (schools reform). While the 1997–2001 parliament may have seen relatively infrequent rebellion, the 2001–05 parliament saw the highest rate of revolt in the post-war era, and the 2005–07 period saw a rate of defeat without precedent for a government with a majority of over 60. Prior to 1997, one of the Conservatives' 'New Labour, New Danger' adverts had tried to imagine what life would be like under Labour – and included a sentence about a rebellion involving '50 Labour MPs'. There were plenty of occasions during the Blair era when a mere 50 would have been a relief for the whips.

In part, the rise in backbench dissent was merely the inevitable product of being in office continually for ten years – a phenomenon that would be recognized by most previous Prime Ministers. Yet it was also a consequence of the Blair style of government – with Labour MPs growing increasingly irritated by his habit of dropping fully-formed policies on them and expecting their automatic wholehearted support – and of the policies which he put forward. As a result, part of Blair's legacy in terms of party management has been to alienate a wider group in the mainstream of the PLP, who are increasingly concerned about the way that policy is formulated in No.10, something that the new Prime Minister, Gordon Brown will need to address, if he is to avoid similar problems.

Notes

1. This chapter draws on research into the behaviour of the PLP, funded by the Leverhulme Trust and the ESRC. In total, that research involved around 200 interviews with MPs, and any unattributed quotations in this chapter are drawn from those interviews.
2. Indeed, when the Maastricht Bill was undergoing its painful passage through the Commons at the beginning of the 1992 parliament, Major suffered 93 rebellions in that session alone – almost as many in one parliamentary year as Blair suffered in the whole of his first term.
3. Another good example of this phenomenon occurred in November 1999, when the government raised the basic state pension by only 75 pence a week. Such was the furore in the Parliamentary Party and in the wider Labour movement, that Brown, in his pre-Budget statement that November, focused the bulk of his package on giving more money to pensioners.
4. In the case of the Freedom of Information Bill, for example, Straw effectively held a seminar with MPs, re-drafting the Bill while on his feet in the Chamber of the Commons. HC Deb., 4 April 2000, cc.917–34.
5. Eight of the February rebels chose to abstain, while four ended up voting with the government (Cowley, 2005: 124).
6. For a debate on how credible this threat was, see Cowley, 2005: 125–6.
7. The details of the top-up fees concessions can be found in Cowley, 2005: chapter 7; for foundation hospitals, see chapter 6.
8. We say 'substantive' because technically the last time any government was defeated by that much was on 28 March 1979 when a Conservative MP moved a prayer annulling an increase in the price of firearms certificates. Then, only

one Labour MP – Max Madden – rebelled, but the government did not have its troops in place, and the prayer was carried by 115 votes to 26, a majority against the government of 89.

9. A total of 44 (48 per cent of the signatories) voted against the Bill's Second Reading; 34 (37 per cent) voted for the government; whilst another 13 did not vote (with at least five of the 13 being deliberate abstentions).

10. Of these, two were merely acting as tellers to ensure that the business was expedited through the Commons.

11. There were, in absolute terms, slightly more separate backbench revolts by government MPs under Thatcher than Blair (534 to 485) but the Thatcher era was longer, and those revolts that did take place were noticeably smaller.

8
New Labour and the Unions: The Death of Tigmoo?

Eric Shaw

Introduction: A very special relationship?

'For over 80 years', Minkin wrote in his definitive study, the trade union–Labour Party link 'has shaped the structure and, in various ways, the character of the British Left' (Minkin, 1991: xii). Although, as Minkin demonstrated in abundant detail, the link was frequently punctuated by disputes, some of them serious, 'the legitimacy, centrality and naturalness of the relationship were rarely brought into question. It was taken for granted that the unions and the party were organically connected' (Ludlam, Bodah and Coates, 2002: 224). This is no longer the case. Predictions that the organic interlock between Labour and the affiliated unions would disintegrate have proved wide of the mark. Instead, it has persisted and remains a central structural characteristic of the Labour Party, even under the 'New Labour' regime. However, this chapter will suggest, the nature of the link is undergoing some fundamental alterations.

Chris Howell has suggested that the linkage between union movements and social democratic parties was rooted in a system of 'political exchange'. Put in the simplest terms, this argued that the former supplied crucial resources (such as money, organization) to the latter which reciprocated with supportive legislation. Howell contends that the material basis of this exchange is crumbling largely because of deep-rooted structural changes in the nature of capitalism manifested in the reconfiguring of patterns of power and interest. Social democratic parties have been impelled to formulate a new political economy which no longer assigns unions a prominent role. For this reason, the party–union connection is in historical decline (Howell, 2001).

The concept of a 'political exchange' highlights a major element of the party–union relationship in the United Kingdom. This relationship could never have survived a century and, moreover, could never have retained its vitality and its capacity to surmount often grave conflicts unless it was held together by hard considerations of mutual interest. The protection of labour's industrial interests was the 'anvil upon which "labour alliance" forged, it was the most basic and unifying purpose of the Labour party' (Minkin, 1991: 11). Yet, the notion of a political exchange captures only one dimension of the party–union relationship in the UK. That relationship was also, as Minkin observes, 'defined in terms of a common loyalty and a deeply felt commitment to a wider entity and purpose – the labour movement'. The concept of 'the movement' underscored the indissolubility of the party–union. It was 'both a description and an aspiration' (Minkin, 1991: 4). As a description, it referred to the organic institutional entanglement between the party and the affiliated unions. As an aspiration, it referred to shared purpose and engagement in a common struggle. The argument of this chapter is that whilst the party–union link as a strategic alliance will survive and continue to have a substantial effect on the organization and programme of the Labour Party, it is losing its character as a movement. The culture of shared norms, sentiments, ambitions and ideals which nourished the labour alliance is decomposing. 'This great movement of ours' ('Tigmoo' in affectionate short-hand) is vanishing.

The record of the Blair government

The incoming Blair government promised the unions 'fairness not favours'. 'Not favours' meant, on the one hand, that the industrial relations settlement that had emerged from the Conservative years was, in its essentials, to be respected. 'Fairness', on the other, was defined principally in terms of affording employees protection against exploitation and arbitrary management and ending mass unemployment. Labour's 1997 general election manifesto pledged to introduce 'basic minimum rights for the individual at the workplace', to establish a minimum wage, to accord to unions the right to secure recognition by employers and, finally, to revoke the Major government refusal to sign the EU's Social Chapter which extended some protection to employees (Labour Party, 1997).

In relation to full employment, for no failing did Labour so relentlessly condemn the Conservatives than for their policies which consigned huge numbers to the dole queues. Although the scale of joblessness was already beginning to slacken in the final years of Tory rule, it continued to stand at a historically high post-war level. The Blair government committed itself to provide (in a rather cautious and nuanced formulation) 'employment opportunity for all'. The crucial point is that New Labour did not abandon full employment as a prime object of economic policy, but instead pursued it with energy and application.

The results – at least compared to similar-sized EU countries such as Germany and France – have been quite impressive. The percentage of the working age population in paid employment rose from 70.8 per cent in 1997 to 74.7 per cent by the end of 2004, or from 25.7 million to 27.4 million in total (Taylor, 2005: 196). What had appeared to be the intractable problem of large numbers of young jobless was at least partially resolved. Whether its performance is quite so superior to continental laggards as the government claims is a matter of dispute, with recent research by Sheffield Hallam University suggesting that there may be as many as 1.7 million 'hidden jobless' diverted on to other benefits, such as incapacity benefits (Elliott, 2007). But there has been broad agreement on two points: that much effort has been invested in cutting unemployment and that the overall impact of New Labour policies has been positive. It is notable that failure to tackle unemployment has not figured on the unions' charge sheet against the government.

With regard to the regulation of pay and conditions, the Blair government has favoured some degree of re-regulation to protect workers against exploitation in terms of both pay and working conditions whilst maintaining what it was proud to call the 'most lightly-regulated' system in the EU. Thus a priority in its first term was the introduction of a national minimum wage. This was a demand for which (some) unions had fought long and hard and had been incorporated into the party's programme as an iron pledge under the Smith leadership. A Low Pay Commission was set up entrusted with the right to recommend the level of the minimum wage, enacted in April 1999. By June 2007, after a number of upgradings, it stood at £5.35 per hour for adults. It had been calculated that, by 2004, over 1.7 million poorly paid (and mainly part-time) workers had benefited from the minimum wage (Vigor, 2005: 160). Coupled with the various tax credits schemes to supplement low wages, the effect has been to increase significantly the earnings of the lowest income decile (Hamann and Kelly, 2003: 646).

However, the government was less keen to regulate hours of work. In 1999 the annual European Union Labour Force Survey reported that British employees worked some of the longest hours in the EU (Eurostat,

1999). The EU's Working Time Regulations stipulated that workers must not be required normally to work over 48 hours per week. However, ignoring strenuous TUC representations, the Blair government excluded millions of workers from coverage by allowing workers to 'waive' their rights under the regulations (seeking 'derogations') and by exempting a number of occupational categories – greatly diluting the impact of the regulations. As a result, hours worked in the UK remain amongst the highest in the EU (Smith and Morton, 2001: 123; Glyn and Wood, 2001: 63).

In terms of the extension of individual employee rights, 'fairness' was primarily defined by the government in terms of reviving employee rights which, it acknowledged, had been seriously eroded under the Tories. It has enacted a whole battery of individual worker rights including the right to be accompanied by a trade union official during a disciplinary or grievance hearing, whether or not a trade union was recognized; a restoration of the qualifying period for protection against unfair dismissal to 12 months; a very substantial raising of the maximum compensation figure for unfair dismissal; and extended parental rights (Glyn and Wood, 2001: 61; Hamann and Kelly, 2003: 647; Howell, 2004: 9). However, the government has been loath to extend to part-time, temporary and agency workers – who number amongst the most vulnerable and poorly paid groups in the British labour market – the protections and rights enjoyed by workers on permanent, full-time contracts, often blocking and watering-down EU legislation or securing exemptions for UK employers (McKay, 2001: 294; Smith and Morton, 2006: 413; Taylor, 2005: 189).

In relation to the extension of collective employee rights, the Conservative government after 1979 launched a relentless assault on the trade unions with secondary action banned, mandatory strike ballots imposed and unions exposed to legal action if they went on strike without fulfilling complex and detailed statutory procedures (Michie and Wilkinson, 1994: 17). Even before Blair's arrival to the leadership, Labour had largely abandoned its earlier pledges to repeal this legislation. The 1997 general election manifesto stated baldly that 'the key elements of the trade union legislation of the 1980s will stay – on ballots, picketing and industrial action', but it did promise to introduce legislation to allow people to join a union and to facilitate union recognition (Labour Party, 1997).

Intense controversy accompanied the framing of the Blair government's provisions on union recognition and the outcome, as it eventually emerged in the Employment Relations Act, was very much a compromise. For the first time a legal right of employees to trade union representation was established. Two methods of statutory recognition of trade unions by employers for collective bargaining over pay and conditions were introduced. Under the first, a union would be recognized if a majority of those voting *and* at least 40 per cent of those eligible to vote supported it – a (much) higher proportion than those who voted Labour in its three successive triumphs. Under the second, the Central Arbitration Committee could insist on trade union recognition where the union could show it had already recruited a majority of the employees in the proposed bargaining unit (Gennard, 2002: 585; Smith and Morton, 2001: 124).

But on one point the government was adamant: there would be no easing of the tough legislative framework constraining union rights to engage in industrial action. Solidarity action remains banned, legally permissible industrial action is defined very narrowly and balloting procedures required for such action are extraordinarily complex and demanding. The UK legal regime regulating industrial action persists as one of the most restrictive in the EU (McKay, 2001: 297; Glyn and Wood, 2001: 61–2; Towers, 1999: 86–7; Brown, 2000: 302–3).

Attention was also focused upon the question of the two-tier workforce, i.e. the differences in pay and conditions which had arisen when workers were transferred from the public sector to the private sector and when new workers were recruited to carry out jobs previously undertaken in the public sector. The effect of this has been a notable deterioration of conditions in terms of wages, employment status, holidays, pensions and sick pay (Toynbee, 2003: 57–9, 79).

Much to the anguish of the unions, far from reversing the transfer of previously public activities to the private sector, the Labour government accelerated it, especially through the rapid expansion of the private finance initiative (PFI). Unions' efforts (which notched up some victories in Conference votes) to deflect government policy proved unavailing and for this reason they concentrated their efforts on ending the two-tier workforce. They demanded that previously publicly-employed workers be transferred to the private sector and those who moved into jobs formerly in the public sector – as a result of contracting-out and PFI deals – should be guaranteed 'no less favourable' terms and conditions than those still employed by the state. The government initially resisted these pressures but by early 2003 it was evident that if steps were not taken to end the two-tier workforce the party–union relationship would be sorely impaired. At the Warwick conference in July 2004 (formally a meeting of the party's National Policy Forum), the government finally conceded the phasing-out of the two-tier workforce throughout most of the public sector. It was a major union achievement.

The shaping of the party–union relationship

The trajectory of party–union relations can best be understood in terms of the impact of four variables: resources, interests, power, and ideology. Some of these pertain to political and organizational relationships within the Labour Party, others to wider societal relationships. The variables not only directly impact on the party–union connection but interact in complex and unpredictable ways – so predictions about the future have to be treated with caution.

Prior to Blair's leadership, the union role in Conference, the Labour Party's National Executive, the electoral college for electing the leader and deputy-leader and within the candidate selection process had been slimmed down. The union share of the Labour Party Conference vote fell from 90 per cent to 50 per cent, and of the electoral college from 40 per cent to 33 per cent, to be cast by individuals and not *en bloc*. Initially, Tony Blair and the so-called party 'modernizers' toyed with the idea of a divorce between unions and party but 'settled instead for a weakening of the internal decision-making institutions in which the unions play a part, and for a reduction of the union role within those institutions' (Ludlam, Bodah and Coates, 2002: 235). In 1996–97, the 'partnership in Power' proposals introduced sweeping changes in Labour's organization and policy process (Shaw, 2002). The unions lost their majority on the National Executive (from 17 out of 30 to 12 out of 32) and they were given just 30 seats on the new National Policy Forum which (in theory) was to be the key policy determining body. More important in practice was the new Joint Policy Committee upon which there was no union presence by right and which the party leader effectively controlled.

The impact of these changes was substantial, but should not be exaggerated. On the one hand, the unions had forfeited their domination of Conference and the National Executive Committee. But, on the other, the unions had never used their preponderance of votes to assert control over Labour Party policy. The lack of any mechanisms by which Conference could enforce its wishes on a Labour government (or, for that matter, the Parliamentary Labour Party) meant that in practice union 'barons' never could, did, or indeed want, to 'run the party' (as demonstrated conclusively in Minkin, 1991). Furthermore, the fact that the capacity of unions to shape internal party policy-making had diminished did not, in practical terms, matter a great deal because the party itself had effectively lost its capacity (except as an occasional prodder) to shape government policy. So the loss of union vote in the party's deliberative arenas did not translate into a commensurate shrinkage of influence, for that influence was, in practice, much less than it might seem to be.

On the question of the resources of the Labour Party, there can be no dispute that, for most of its existence, the party has been heavily reliant on union finance without which it could never have sustained a mass organization. On the other hand, as Minkin demonstrated, union money was not customarily used as a weapon to badger the party. Indeed, 'there were and remain unwritten prohibitions against open threats of financial sanctions' (Minkin, 1991: 626). Nevertheless, party reliance on union money did create a relationship of dependency and it was with the object of lessening that dependency, as well as with finding the means of meeting the ever greater expenses that the 'professionalization' of party campaigning and communication imposed, that sustained efforts were made to tap alternative sources of finance. The main alternatives were much increased state funding, a more ample subscription income from an expanded membership base, and private donations from wealthy benefactors. The first was potentially the most lucrative but was thwarted by a most distinct public reluctance to accede to it. The second option – building a mass membership – initially seemed encouraging. In the early years of the Blair leadership, Labour's individual membership rose impressively, to reach a peak of around 400,000 in 1997. Unfortunately it then began to tumble and at an accelerating rate. By 2007 it was estimated to have shrivelled to a dismal 180,000, the lowest level since the 1920s. Mass membership had proved 'a passing fantasy' (McIlroy, 2007: 1). It was via the third option, private donations, that new income was to most abundantly flow. Labour had always had a small number of wealthy well-wishers (e.g. Lord Haskins of Northern Foods), but after Blair's accession to the leadership and then Labour's arrival to power, their numbers grew rapidly and their munificence too. The proportion of the party's income which derived from the trade unions fell from around two-thirds in 1992, to 40 per cent by 1997 and then to 33 per cent in 2001 (Leopold, 2006: 193). Sadly, however, New Labour was now to be hoist by its own petard.

'Tory sleaze' – the exchange of money for political favours – had proved an appealing election slogan and Labour promised to introduce laws to clear up the Augustan stable of party finances. The fact that the Blair leadership almost immediately displayed an impressive willingness to accept large donations from businessmen, some of less than impeccable virtue, with the assumption furthermore of favours, produced much unfavourable publicity which lent added urgency to legislative action. The Political Parties, Elections and Referendums Act 2000 stipulated that a list of all donations to political parties above £200 had to be submitted to an Electoral Commission and published, and the source of all national donations over £5,000 had to be declared (Leopold, 2006: 193). This meant open season for the Tory press to publish the names of Labour's most lavish benefactors – and any titles, favours or other benefits which, coincidentally or not, these benefactors had received from a grateful government. Not all of this publicity was appreciated and the copious amounts of money which had begun to flow in New Labour's direction from rich men eager to part with their money began to dry up.

But all was not lost since it transpired there was a loophole in the legislation. If potential donors provided 'loans' (ostensibly on a 'commercial' basis) rather than grants then their names need not be published. Unhelpful publicity would be avoided and generosity could be properly rewarded, protected from the prying eyes of the media. It was estimated that over £20 million flowed into New Labour's coffers as a result of these secret 'loans' – as revealed when the press disclosed that the Prime Minister had recommended lenders for peerages. The outcome was extreme embarrassment when what proved to be a long-running (and still not concluded) police investigation was launched and Tony Blair was himself interviewed by detectives and some of his key aides arrested. An Electoral Administration Act was hurriedly passed in 2006 requiring that loans be reported in the same way as donations (McIlroy, 2007: 4). Not entirely unexpectedly, 'the supply of large individual and corporate donations dwindled' (Leopold, 2006: 193). The upshot was that, a mass membership having proved a mirage and with the largesse of the rich rapidly ebbing, the party remained heavily reliant on the unions.

In fact, it was becoming evident that this dependence extended beyond direct financial assistance. In successive elections affiliated unions had played a key role in mobilizing support for the party through providing personnel and organizational support as well as hard cash. Under the aegis of the umbrella body, the Trade Union and Labour Party Liaison Organization, they established phone banks, spearheaded voter registration drives, organized a cadre of workers to carry out constituency campaigning and appointed trade union coordinators in all of Labour's key seats. Research indicated that this had a significant impact on Labour's vote share, and indeed was 'central to Labour's retention of almost all of its 146 key seats in 2001' (Ludlam and Taylor, 2003: 734). Furthermore, by 2001, and even more so by 2005, it was becoming evident that the number of activists willing to volunteer their services in staffing grassroots constituency electioneering was falling rapidly. This rapid depletion in the number of party workers rendered the party more – not less – reliant upon the help (especially manpower) the unions could supply.

The problem, as Labour entered its second term, was not so much its undue reliance on union cash, but that some of the cash might disappear as a result of a rash of left-wing victories in union polls, including in the largest unions: Dave Prentis in Unison, Derek Simpson in Amicus, and Tony Woodley in the TGWU. The latter two unions merged to former the biggest union in the UK, Unite, in 2006. These, and other leaders in smaller unions, represented quite a spread of opinion but they all shared a deepening disenchantment with key New Labour policies, including the expansion of the role of the private sector and the establishment of foundation trust hospitals in the NHS, tardiness in ending the two-tier workforce, the rapid expansion of the private finance initiative, the retention of a highly flexible labour market, the preference for means-testing rather than universality in pension provision, the failure to take effective measures to reduce steep inequalities in the distribution of income and wealth, and a general partiality towards business.

Increasingly, the left-wing leaders of the big unions concerted their political interventions in an effort to reclaim the Labour Party. After a long period when the Labour Party Conference seemed to have lapsed into docility, the unions secured the passage of motions criticizing major government policies including on pensions, foundation hospitals, PFI and commercial involvement in the NHS. The government simply shrugged-off these defeats. Seasoned union leaders were, of course, well aware that adverse conference votes would have minimal impact on the government. However, what if they retaliated by reducing the supply of money? In 2003 the transport union RMT, the communications union CWU, GMB, and Unison all cut funding to the party. Some of the funds thus saved were used to finance union campaigns *against* government policies, notably marketization and commercialization in the public sector (Leopold, 2006: 195). Two small unions (RMT and FBU) which had bruising industrial encounters with the government (in the case of the FBU, a bitter and prolonged strike by the fire-fighters) disaffiliated from the party.

However, these turned out to be isolated instances of dissent. The slicing back of funds was intended primarily as a warning shot rather than harbinger of deeper cuts in the future. Mainstream left-of-centre leaders in the big unions remained unflinching adherents of the party–union link. Derek Simpson, the left-wing leader of the engineering union Amicus, bluntly told his conference that, 'if anyone believes

[that] anyone apart from the Labour government will do anything for us, you're in the wrong meeting, you're in the wrong organization' (quoted in Ludlam and Taylor, 2003: 739). Indeed, the unions continued liberally to fund the party. McIlroy estimated on the basis of the Electoral Commission's figures, that they provided some 65 per cent of outright donations to the party. Despite the tough talking of recent years, the unions collectively dispensed some £56 million to the Labour Party between 2001 and 2006. Indeed, 'AMICUS alone gave the party more than £8 million, the TGWU more than £7 million, USDAW nearly £6 million and UNISON more than £10 million' (McIlroy, 2007: 8).

There was no direct bartering, no formal *quid pro quos* between money and policy. Yet awareness of the party's continued dependence on the unions for financial and organizational assistance inevitably contributed to a state of mind more receptive to policy concessions to the unions, of the type detailed above. Sensitivity to union representations always increased as elections neared, and this was exemplified by the Warwick Agreement in July 2004. This consisted of a series of pledges for legislative action in a third Labour term (to be incorporated into the party's 2005 general election manifesto), including policy proposals affecting pension provision, the work–life balance, redundancy pay, the implementation of EU directives and an extension of the two-tier workforce agreements to the whole of the public sector (Heery, 2005: 11).

The unions and New Labour's political economy

'The strength and content of party–union ties', Howell has suggested, are 'ultimately dependent upon a kind of bargain, or a base of overlapping material interest, which in turn is heavily influenced by structural economic factors' (Howell, 2001: 12). How governments construe material interests – and their implications for hammering out policy – varies according to a range of factors including circumstance, external pressures, ideology and so forth. During the post-war generation, though Britain faltered in its efforts to develop stable corporatist institutions on the North European model, successive Labour administrations continued to rely on trade unions to contain inflationary pressures, regulate industrial strife and improve Britain's poor productivity. The unions were not simply another set of pressure groups: they were essential partners in the economic and social governance of the country.

By 1997 the Keynesian propositions that had underpinned this form of economic management were out of fashion. In the intervening years there had been 'a transformation of the assumptions and institutions of economic policy-making which had dominated the previous 30 years' (Annersely and Gamble, 2004: 145). New Labour had no desire to resurrect Keynesian regulation and the economic role of the state was now more modestly understood as to create the conditions to allow market forces to work more effectively. Price stability was seen as an overriding economic goal, but crucially was now to be secured not by incomes policies or social contracts, but by a combination of transferring control over monetary policy to the Bank of England, and maintaining a deregulated labour market where wage levels could be held in check by market forces. Brown and his advisers were convinced that the abatement of trade union power in the 1980s had been a major factor in productivity improvements. The waning of collective bargaining had rendered significantly higher levels of employment compatible with price stability: stronger unions spelt fewer jobs (Charlwood, 2004: 386). Indeed, an insistent Treasury theme was that the UK's 'decentralised and relatively weak collective bargaining system' had given the country a sharp competitive edge (Coats, 2005: 30).

From this perspective it was easy to see how the needs of business gelled with those of the economy and the country as a whole. High profits supplied the fuel which corporations needed to expand output, acquire new markets, create jobs, and thereby generate the tax revenues that could be used to rebuild Britain's public infrastructure. Conversely, the typical claims made by unions – for higher wages, greater employment security, and more elaborate schemes for employee protection – seemed more likely to jeopardize than promote national prosperity. Indeed, partnership with business – and not the unions – was, according to Tony Blair, 'a founding principle of New Labour and it will not change' (*Guardian*, 6 November 2001). This means not only that New Labour is hostile to the unions but also that it envisaged only a restricted role for them. 'For sure', Brendan Barber, TUC General Secretary observed, New Labour ministers 'recognise our right to exist, and a citizen's right to join. They can see that individuals may benefit from belonging to a union ... But this is not the same as recognizing that unions, and the collective bargaining and right to effective representation that we pursue, are in general a force for good' (Barber, 2003). Furthermore, Blair himself (and many of his closest advisers) had a somewhat jaundiced view of the unions and the role they had played both in the party and the country at large. Indeed, 'He was unwilling to risk losing business support for New Labour by trying to reinstate what would have been widely seen as a discredited model of corporatism' (Coats, 2005: 29). In effect, the New Labour 'modernisation project' 'deliberately sought to develop a positive and intimate relationship with business and a more arms-length and unsentimental one with trade unions' (Taylor, 2001a: 246).

In relation to the exercise of political power, no less important was the fact that the trade unions were in no position to compel the government to take a more benign view of them. Power relationships have an impact on governments, independent of interests, ideologies and even the search for electoral advantage. Power constellations structure 'actors' perceptions of a realistic and legitimate range of debate ... and of their own capacity to shape policy in accordance with their preferences, and therefore their political strategies' (Huber and Stephens, 2001: 323). Writing originally in the 1950s, Crosland pointed out that full employment and the growth in union density, cohesion and organizational capacity 'by transposing at once the interests, and therefore the attitudes, of the two sides, has dramatically altered the balance of power at every level of labour relations' (Crosland, 1964: 12). This balance of power was now being reversed. Union membership (and density) reached its peak in 1979 when it stood at 13.2 million. In the subsequent two decades it plummeted, falling to barely 7 million when the Blair government came to power in 1997. By the time Blair left office, it stood at a little below 7.5 million, equivalent to a union density figure of 29 per cent. Equally, the proportion of the workforce whose pay was set by collective bargaining had already halved from around 70 per cent to 35 per cent (Metcalf, 2004: 4).

Furthermore, trade unionism in Britain operates in a chilly and inhospitable climate. A whole range of economic changes have undermined union bargaining power ranging from the collapse of employment in former strongholds such as mining, ship-building and automobiles, the shift in employment from larger to smaller units of production, from manufacturing industry to the service sector and from areas where traditions of trade unionism were strong to those where they were weak. All these trends have hampered recruitment and attenuated the sentiments of solidarity and common interest which are the bases of effective union organization (Charlwood, 2004: 393). 'It is a sad fact', one former TUC official concluded, 'that we have a relatively weak trade union movement in the UK' (Coats, 2005: 29). Irrespective of their goals, Labour governments in the 1960s and the 1970s felt they had little option in key areas of policy, but to try to hammer out agreed positions in collaboration with the unions. The Blair government neither had the disposition nor has felt constrained to do so.

This is not to say that (as during the Conservative years) unions have been kept out in the cold. The advice and comments of trade unions were sought as a matter of routine on a whole host of questions. The government provided large sums of money to help fund union training and educational efforts. The TUC and senior trade unionists 'now had ready access to ministers and their involvement in the Government's proliferating Task Forces afforded another opportunity to influence its thinking' (Undy, 2002: 643). Tripartite institutions have revived. Thus trade unions have significant representation on new bodies such as the Low Pay Commission, the Central Arbitration Committee, the national Skills Alliance and the Sector Skills Councils as well as older organizations, such as the Health and Safety Executive and the Advisory, Conciliation and Arbitration Service (Nash, 2006: 10; Coats, 2005: 32). But there are firm limits to the role of trade unions within the policy process. The extensive consultation of unions by government which is an established part of the institutional landscape in much of Western Europe is generally lacking. Moreover, 'There is no general social pact in New Labour's Britain and no standing machinery of social partnership' (Heery, 2005: 9). Unions, from the New Labour perspective, were seen to represent but 'one pressure group among many, with no special claim on government attention, sympathy or support' (Ludlam, Bodah and Coates, 2002: 229).

New Labour's unitary frame of reference

There was something profoundly inimical to trade unionism at the heart of New Labour. For New Labour's principal political strategist, Philip Gould, 'trade union domination' had been a major bar hindering Labour's 'modernization' and a major cause of its bleak electoral performance since the 1970s (Gould, 1998: 19). In the past the party–union relationship had been defined 'in terms of a common loyalty and a deeply felt commitment to a wider entity and purpose – the Labour Movement' (Minkin, 1991: 4). The metaphor 'movement' connoted not only a permanent alliance, rooted in shared interests, between the 'industrial and political wings. Indeed, what constituted labour as a *movement* was the belief that each struggle was, or could be, linked into a larger social purpose' (Hinton, 1983: viii). That purpose did not take the form of an explicit ideological statement, even of a vision of a new society. Rather it reflected the sense that 'the movement' represented 'us' – the 'common' people, 'ordinary working men and women' – against them – the elites, the establishment, the men of power, property and privilege. The object was not to transform the existing social order but to secure for labour a recognized, legitimate and secure place within it. Its ethos was a cautious one, 'an ethos of resistance, not of attack; of the objects of history, not of the subjects'.

Rather 'it existed to protect "us" against the injustices perpetrated by "them", not to enable "us" to join "them", and still less to replace "them" by "us"' (Marquand, 1991: 21–2).

For New Labour the mentality of 'us' and 'them' is antiquated. As Blair told delegates to the Labour Party Conference prior to taking office: 'forget the past. No more bosses versus workers. You are on the same side. The same team' (Blair, 1996c). In effect, New Labour adheres to a broadly unitary frame of reference, which discerns no structured conflicts of interest over the distribution of material resources, status or power, either at workplace or at societal level between capital and labour, employers and employees. It views the social order as fundamentally unified and regards both capital and labour as stakeholders in a common enterprise, social partners for whom collaboration is the most rational arrangement. Different claims inevitably have to be juggled and reconciled but the assumption, that if one 'side' benefits then the other suffers, was to fundamentally misunderstand the nature of the employment relationship and the realities of a modern economy. The essential role of the unions within industry was no longer seen as 'to correct an imbalance of power in the workplace, but to create a context in which the productivity and creativity of workers is properly harnessed for the good of the firm' (Howell, 2004: 14).

From such a perspective the notion of the party and unions as combined in a movement, bound together in a 'shared historical project' which sought to elevate the power and status of 'workers by hand and by brain' was archaic. Economic success in an increasingly competitive global economy demanded that the needs of business trump those of the trade unions (Taylor, 2005: 191). Industry and finance were viewed as (what may be called) public interest organizations with the right to act as partners in the economic governance of the country. The unions, in contrast, were awarded a secondary status as pressure groups whose demands were sectional since their interests did not objectively align and indeed were frequently at odds with the common economic welfare, as now defined. As TUC General Secretary John Monks put it, trade unions were often regarded 'as embarrassing elderly relatives at a family get-together' (Sylvester, 1999).

Conclusion

For Howell, the union–party relationship was, in its essentials, a system of political exchange: money, votes, mobilizing assistance in exchange for legislative advances. It was buttressed by a social democratic 'industrial relations project' which conferred upon the unions a positive and substantial role in the political economy. At the end of the Blair decade, for the party, the gains flowing from the exchange are problematic and the industrial relations project has collapsed: it is this, above all, 'which explains why contemporary social democracy is in the process of divorcing itself from organized labour' (Howell, 2001: 9).

This analysis contains more than a grain of truth but it unduly conflates two aspects of the party–union relationship, which we can call the pragmatic and the normative. The pragmatic grounds which sustain the party–union connection remain quite strong – despite New Labour's desire (for electoral reasons) to keep the unions at arm's length, despite the many policy rifts between the two, despite even the unions' drift to the Left. From the unions' perspective, whatever the disappointments, New Labour *has* delivered on a whole range of issues. These include the National Minimum Wage, the enactment of union recognition procedures, the enhancement of individual employee rights, the ending (for the most part) of EU opt-outs, the efforts poured into eradicating mass unemployment, the major boost to public spending and the phasing out of the two-tier workforce. From the Labour Party's perspective, the unions remain a ready supplier of funds, personnel and campaign mobilization efforts. Ironically, given New Labour's hopes, in some ways its dependence has intensified as other sources of help have dried up: membership is in free fall, constituency organization is falling rapidly into disrepair and donations from benefactors are rapidly tapering off. Without the unions, party organization and constituency campaigning would probably be falling apart.

This, of course, helps explain the readiness of the government to make a battery of concessions at the Warwick Agreement in the run-up to the 2005 general election. By the same token, the predominantly Left-leaning leadership in the major unions has no desire to detach themselves from the Labour Party. As pragmatic, realistic and seasoned political operators they are fully aware that, in the present set-up, the only available political vehicle for the advancement of union interests is the Labour Party. The Conservative electoral revival is likely to intensify that attachment. David Cameron may be seeking to distance his party from its Thatcherite legacy but the terrible gashes inflicted on the unions in the long Tory reign will need far more time to heal before union leaders will be able to contemplate another Conservative government with anything other than deep apprehension and alarm.

But, if it is highly premature to pronounce the end of the party–union connection, its normative (as against pragmatic) aspect is rapidly fading. There is now little sense of shared social purpose, of engagement in a common project. The notion of the labour movement – 'this great movement of ours' – as the ultimate repository of loyalty and solidarity is evaporating, scarcely even surviving as a rhetorical device. The era of 'the labour movement' is quietly drawing to a close. 'Tigmoo' may soon be as dead as a dodo.

9
New Labour and the European Union

Jim Buller

Introduction

How should New Labour's policy towards the European Union be assessed? Because the criteria we employ to evaluate this record will affect the conclusions we reach, it is important that an explicit discussion of these benchmarks is provided. One popular approach in the more general literature on the Labour Party is to judge its achievements against a broader statement of its principles, ideals or values. When it comes to New Labour, academics have sought to gauge its actions in terms of its ability to forge a 'third way' or moderate social-democratic programme. Applied to the sphere of foreign affairs, we would expect such a policy to start from the position that globalization has radically altered the nature of state sovereignty in the twenty-first century. Consequently, any moderate social-democratic diplomacy should work with the grain of this structural context, while simultaneously trying to develop initiatives designed to ameliorate the adverse consequences of interdependence. We might add that a 'Third Way' foreign policy represents a repudiation of crude *realpolitik* and a commitment to internationalism as a way of addressing some of the problems traditionally resolved at the nation state level (Giddens, 2006, 2007; Deighton, 2001; Vickers, 2000; see also Williams, 2005: 15–31).

If the United Kingdom is now a member of a new international community in which states are mutually dependent on each other, and where the national objectives are often realized through intergovernmental collaboration, the Third Way is clearly pro-European in its stance. It differs from Old Labour, where a commitment to state solutions to domestic problems often conflicted with membership of the EU in the post-war period. It can also be distinguished from the Thatcher and Major governments, which were often criticized by pro-Europeans for continually squandering influence within this supranational organization through a policy of negative isolationism. Borrowing from these 'Third Way' writings, the Blair government has indeed promised to reassert the UK's leadership role in the EU by adopting a more cooperative stance, helping to construct alliances with its partners and forge joint solutions to common problems. Through this energetic diplomacy abroad, New Labour has also sought to reverse the longstanding trend of Euro-scepticism at home by demonstrating the benefits to be had by active engagement with the UK's continental partners. Indeed, Blair has gone further: Britain is uniquely placed to play a 'pivotal' role between the US and the EU in a world where regional blocs are rapidly becoming the organizational units of global politics (Wallace, 2005a: 55). In short, if New Labour is to be judged in terms of its ability to forge a 'Third Way' in foreign affairs, then its actions should be compared to these rhetorical promises.

However, to what extent is it realistic to expect foreign or European policy to be shaped by principles, ideals or values? It can certainly be argued that in the past, Labour's broader ideological position has had little impact on outcomes in this area. Rather, since 1945, one can point to an elite consensus in Whitehall which has displayed an obsession with maintaining the UK's great power status, a preoccupation with maintaining a 'special' relationship with the United States as a means to this broader end, and a consistent ambiguity towards Europe as a policy sphere. In particular, since the early 1960s, Labour has: rejected membership of the EU arguing that it conflicted with one thousand years of English and British history (1961–67); sought membership of this supranational organization for the UK (1967–70); renounced the Heath government's successful terms of membership (1971–74); sought to re-negotiate these self-same terms and put them to a referendum of the British people (1974–75); promised to withdraw from the EU (1980–83); and increasingly championed the EU as an organization compatible with the revisionist social-democratic project being pursued within the Labour Party under the leaderships of Kinnock, Smith and Blair (1988–97). To conclude, if party ideas have played a peripheral role in the conduct of foreign and European policy since 1945, how realistic is it to expect them to 'drive' decision-making after 1997? If not, how fair is it to judge the behaviour of the Blair government against such rhetorical statements when they may only be deployed for the purposes of ideological 'window dressing'?

Even if we accept that after 1997 New Labour was sincere in its discursive commitment to inject 'Third Way' ideals into the conduct of diplomacy at the international level, the autonomy that human agents enjoy to realize such principles is likely to be constrained by broader structural forces. If anything, structural constraints in the area of foreign policy are more significant than they are at the domestic level. Whitehall has no jurisdiction over foreign governments. Powerful international lobbies, multinational companies and global organizations can be just as difficult to control. Finally, (where politicians are concerned) external diplomacy will be influenced by electoral considerations. Successful initiatives in the international sphere, such as the resolution of conflict, can have positive political spin-offs at home. That said, opportunities for conflict resolution are usually quite rare and difficult to predict. A more pertinent consideration for party leaders in office will be to ensure that external developments do not impact adversely on domestic politics. This has certainly been a feature of past UK and EU relations, with the experience of the Major government providing a powerful reminder of how this issue can upset party political fortunes.

In short, to argue that ministers should only be judged on their ability to translate general ideas or values into practice runs the risk of 'abstracting' Labour's performance from the everyday constraints and challenges of office (Taylor, 2001). It follows that an appraisal of the Blair government's record must avoid separating the actions of ministers from the structural context surrounding them. Some politicians will be fortunate enough to inherit a benign structural environment, which provides opportunities for the realization of policy objectives. Others will have little choice but to 'muddle through' in difficult circumstances. To complicate matters further, the properties of these structures will sometimes be mediated by perception, and these interpretations may exercise a causal effect on behaviour that is independent of material reality. A brief account of the structural context facing British foreign policy-makers is therefore necessary before we assess the performance of the Blair government.

Structural context

Since 1945, the UK has been a status quo power that has broadly benefited from the bipolar structure of international relations which developed after the Second World War. Put more accurately, the Cold War helped Whitehall to disguise the reality of British economic and political decline, a tactic which was often thought to contribute to domestic political tranquillity. To this end, ministers (as noted above) cultivated a 'special' relationship with the US which provided them with a status and prestige (not to mention nuclear capability) unrivalled in Western Europe at this time. In contrast, after 1990, Whitehall was faced with a global environment which was more fluid and uncertain than at any time during the post-war period. The collapse of communism in central and Eastern Europe left what many western leaders began to perceive as a security vacuum in this area. The reunification of Germany heightened this anxiety, as many EU governments became concerned that its partner would rekindle an old preference for *ostpolitik*. The EU responded by intensifying the process of European integration as a way of containing this potential German power. The centrepiece of this strategy in the early 1990s was a new three stage plan to create a Single Currency, as embodied in the Maastricht Treaty. The Thatcher and Major governments rejected these moves, yet at the same time appeared powerless to prevent them. It was this combination of events at the European level that was in large part responsible for the growing divisions in the Conservative Party in the first half of the 1990s.

If developments at the external level produced a number of awkward consequences for British party elites, they impacted on domestic politics in such a way as to tighten the constraints on action at that level. Public opinion towards the European project in the UK has always been equivocal at best, although there is some evidence that attitudes warmed to the European Union in the 1980s. From the early 1990s, the electorate returned to its more suspicious stance, reinforced by a British press that had become increasingly Euro-sceptical. The key event in this context appears to have been the ERM crisis of September 1992. Newspapers such as *The Times* and *The Telegraph*, which up until this point had provided broadly balanced coverage of EU issues, now criticized the absence of a government apology for 'wasting' billions of pounds of taxpayers' money defending sterling in the face of currency speculation (Seldon, 1997: 121–6). Gradually, the Conservative Party began to reflect this developing Euro-sceptical climate. Backbench revolts against the leadership became more commonplace. One could point to the case of the 'whipless wonders': eight Tory MPs who defined a three-line whip on the vote on the EU budget. At the 1997 election, approximately 200 Tory MPs opposed the leadership's 'wait and see' line on the euro, preferring a stronger euro-sceptical stance on the issue (Buller, 1999). After 1997, the rise of the UK Independence Party and its capture of three seats at the European Parliament elections in 1999, confirmed this trend. The introduction of any pro-European initiative in this domestic climate was going to be a tricky, perilous process.

However, by the mid-1990s parallel but countervailing forces were beginning to emerge from the ruins of the Cold War, which had much more ambiguous prospects for the European project and the UK's place within it. The most important of these developments was enlargement. Free from the shackles of Communist rule, a number of countries in central and Eastern Europe began to lodge applications for membership in the anticipation of receiving a number of economic and political benefits. Although EU treaties and declarations contained a long-term pledge to overcome the 'unnatural' division of the European continent, the initial response of member states to this enlargement pressure was one of ambivalence. Leaving aside the wide differences in economic and political development that existed between member states and the applicants from Eastern Europe, it was clear that a doubling of the size of the EU in just over a decade was bound to pose significant challenges to existing institutions and policies (Friis and Murphy, 1999). Some commentators also predicted that many of these new entrants would be both 'Atlanticist' and 'intergovernmental' in outlook (Zielonka, 2004). By the end of the 1990s, these changes were beginning to present new opportunities for British statecraft.

The politics of depoliticization: the Blair government and the EU, 1997–2001

It will be argued below that the Blair government's policy towards the EU in its first term was largely a success story. On the one hand, ministers were able to take advantage of the increasingly favourable European situation noted above to play a more active and constructive role within the EU than their Conservative predecessors. Indeed, through the tactic of crafting a range of ad hoc alliances with different countries over separate issues, Britain has arguably moved closer than ever to the centre of gravity in this supranational organization. Where structural constraints were tighter (as they were at the domestic level) the Blair government preferred to accept their logic. In particular, New Labour's promise to reverse the tide of Euro-sceptical public opinion remained unfulfilled. There was no better example of this outcome than the Single Currency issue, where the Treasury in particular favoured depoliticization over a policy of active engagement with the electorate. This tactic may not have reflected the subtleties of 'Third Way' pro-Europeanism, but bearing in mind the experience of the Major government, it was great domestic politics.

Faced with the structural context noted above, the first point to note about the response of the Blair government is that it interpreted these structures as an opportunity to make a 'fresh start' in British diplomacy. In what was to become a common theme of statecraft in this sphere, ministers singled out supply-side economic policy as an area where they could play a leadership role. A manifesto pledge to reverse Britain's opt-out from the Social Chapter was expedited quickly. More ambitiously, ministers began to articulate a Third Way between an Anglo-Saxon emphasis on labour market flexibility and the well-trained, but sometimes highly protected workforce that existed in many European countries. By reducing the burden of 'red tape' on businesses, reforming the dependency culture of welfare and enhancing the employability of those excluded from society, EU economies could also partake in the sort of job creation record that Britain was now experiencing (Brown, 1997d; Blair, 1998a, 1998b). In these early discussions, this 'Third Way' message did not go down well with Jospin, the French Prime Minister at this time and leader of the Socialist government. Moreover, after initially flirting with the idea of a 'neue mitte', Schröder dropped such a narrative when it was perceived to be politically unpopular in Germany. Unperturbed, Blair ploughed on, signing bilateral agreements with the notably more right-wing governments of Berlusconi (Italy) and Anzar (Spain). These efforts seemed to bear fruit at the Lisbon Summit, at which member states promised to transform Europe into the most competitive and dynamic economy in the world by 2010.

This tendency towards bilateral initiatives could also be witnessed in the area of European foreign and defence policy. Shortly before the Amsterdam European Council in June 1997, the UK delegation had resisted Franco-German plans to merge the Western European Union (WEU) with the EU. Now Labour accepted the idea of scrapping the former as a way of augmenting the latter's defence capability. The WEU's military role would be transferred to NATO, thus strengthening the European pillar of this organization. Conversely, the WEU's political role would be folded into the EU, thereby enhancing the authority of the new position of 'high representative' which was also created at Amsterdam. There appear to be two reasons for this change in policy. Having been disappointed at the failure of the employment policy initiative to provide a springboard for Blair's leadership ambitions within the EU, ministers identified foreign and security policy as an alternative route to this broader strategic objective. Second, the Americans themselves indicated that attempts to strengthen the EU's military capacity might have beneficial spin-offs for the cohesion of NATO. These efforts seemed to pay off in December

1998, when Blair and Chirac signed the St Malo agreement to develop Europe's out of area defence potential. Twelve months later, the Helsinki European Council (1999) agreed to set up a 60,000-strong 'rapid reaction force' (RRF) designed to engage in future peacekeeping and humanitarian missions in which NATO (i.e. the Americans) did not want to participate (Howorth, 2004; Williams, 2005: 56–74).

As noted above, this constructive diplomacy was assisted by other structural developments that were taking place within the EU at this time. As far back as the mid-1990s, the prospect of enlargement to the north and east began to create a new set of fault-lines between large and small states, especially over a range of institutional questions. On the one side, the big states (including Britain) began to complain about their level of representation within the Council of Ministers. As they saw it, enlargement was likely to substantially increase the number of small states in the EU, and with it the prospect that smaller countries would combine together to outvote the bigger states on legislation decided by Qualified Majority Voting (QMV). In response, the bigger states demanded extra votes in the Council of Ministers, as well as a demographic criterion that would take the population size of each country into account before a decision was made. These proposals caused general anxiety in the capitals of the smaller states, especially when they were accompanied by suggestions for reform of the Commission. France led the way in warning that an enlarged Commission of 25 states would be over-bureaucratic and unworkable and called on the EU to review whether permanent representation for each government at Brussels was now desirable. Small states opposed these assertions, viewing their permanent representation on the Commission as insurance against domination by the large states.

The first official attempt to resolve these questions was the Amsterdam European Council. However, the contentious nature of these issues, as well as the fact that enlargement was still a relatively distant prospect, meant that little progress was made at this time. Instead, the main institutional innovation of the Amsterdam Treaty was the 'enhanced cooperation' procedure. Here, a range of flexibility clauses were inserted into EU law allowing a group of member states to pool sovereignty at a faster rate than their counterparts (Stubb, 2000). A second attempt to find a solution to these disputes was attempted at the Nice European Council (December 2000), although the passing of time had not healed the divisions noted above. For example, Germany demanded more votes than France in the Council of Ministers to reflect its population growth after reunification. Paris rejected this request, a rebuff which was one of the factors contributing to the absence of the usual pre-joint summit letter. Some commentators speculated that a new era in EU diplomacy was dawning, arguing that the Franco-German 'motor' was no longer up to the task of driving integration in the twenty-first century (Barber, 2000; Graham and Groom, 2000).

At the same time, British statecraft continued to benefit from this more 'open' intergovernmental environment. At Nice, Blair and Cook successfully negotiated a rise in the UK's voting weight in the Council of Ministers to 29 (in line with France, Germany and Italy). They also supported the new 'triple majority' procedure for reaching decisions under the qualified majority vote. Under these reforms, a policy could only be passed if it received: (a) a qualified majority of at least 72 per cent of all votes cast; (b) an absolute majority of all member states; (c) a qualified majority of 62 per cent of the EU's population (subject to a specific request by a member state). At the same time, London remained relaxed about the prospect of losing one Commissioner under the 'deferred ceiling model'. This agreement gave each member state one representative at Brussels until the pressures of enlargement rendered this arrangement impractical. Finally, Blair and Cook safeguarded the British veto on taxation, social security and border issues (Foreign and Commonwealth Act, 2001). For once, the UK was not seen as the 'awkward partner' in Europe. Most post-summit commentary instead focused on France's heavy-handed use of the chair and its more general anxiety about losing its pre-eminent position within the EU (Beach, 2005: 145–75).

During the late 1980s and the first half of the 1990s, it was probably the prospect of EMU as much as any other issue that caused the damaging divisions within the Major government. It is perhaps not surprising then that the key feature of New Labour's policy on the euro in the first term was to depoliticize it and keep it off the parliamentary agenda. The Treasury has attempted to realize this objective by cloaking any decision on Single Currency membership in dry and esoteric economic language. While the Blair government maintained there was no overriding political or constitutional barrier to the adoption of the euro (and so no reason to debate it), this policy must be clearly and unambiguously in the interests of the British economy. These interests were measured by five economic tests.

1. Are business cycles and economic structures compatible so that we and others could live comfortably with euro interest rates on a permanent basis?
2. If problems emerge, is there sufficient flexibility to deal with them?
3. Would joining EMU create better conditions for firms making long-term decisions to invest in Britain?

4. What impact would entry into EMU have on the competitive position of the UK's financial services industry, particularly the City's wholesale markets?
5. In summary, will joining EMU promote higher growth, stability and a lasting increase in jobs? (HM Treasury, 2003b: 1)

A number of commentators have noted that the wording of these tests is so flexible and ambiguous that any judgement might be accommodated by them. This of course is precisely the point. The language is technical enough to be off-putting to anybody who does not happen to be a specialist in the economics of optimum currency areas, while at the same time ensuring that the Treasury retains ultimate ownership of any decision. In the first six months of office, the Treasury did conduct an assessment of whether sterling should join the euro zone in 1999. Only one of the five tests (financial services) was met and the whole issue was shelved.

Looked at from the perspective of New Labour's broader aspirations to reassert Britain's leadership role in Europe, the Blair government's policy on the euro in its first term, was a failure: a judgement that pro-EU commentators were quick to wheel out. However, viewed against the description of the broader structural context noted above, (and not forgetting the Labour Party was out of office for 18 years) this non-decision was understandable. We have already noted the drift to a more Euro-sceptical mood in British politics in the 1990s. A positive decision in the area might not only open up divisions within the Labour Party, but also give the Conservatives an issue that they could potentially make significant political capital out of. In other words, faced with a straight choice between doctrinal consistency and electoral expediency in this area, the primacy of domestic politics triumphed. By the end of the first term, Brown's speeches on the EU had become noticeably more downbeat: his dislike of ECOFIN meetings the subject of much speculation amongst journalists. By the 2001 election, he had also made little effort to hide his disapproval of non-binding recommendations issued by the European Commission asserting that his public spending plans and forecasts were in breach of EU obligations in the Growth and Stability Pact.

The politics of continuity: the Blair government, 2001–07

If the Blair government's policy towards the EU was aided by a relatively benign structural environment in the second half of the 1990s, external shocks at the turn of the century suddenly posed more difficult challenges for British diplomats. In this context, the key developments took place outside the EU: the terrorist attacks on the Twin Towers and the Pentagon on September 11, 2001 and the response of the United States to this tragedy. In particular, a new mood of unilateralism within the Bush administration threatened to bring America into continued and public conflict with the EU in a way that had not been the case before 2001. Bush's 'axis of evil' speech during the hunt for Osama Bin Laden in Afghanistan seemed to mark the advent of a critical juncture. In future, the US would not necessarily wait to deter emerging threats to its security, but eliminate them before they got the chance to develop (White House, 2002). Such a doctrine clearly had awkward implications for Labour's promise that the UK would command a pivotal role between the US and the EU.

Blair's decision to support the US invasion of Iraq in 2003 confirmed the challenges that these structural developments posed for such bridge-building aspirations. Relations with France in particular hit rock bottom at this time. Blair's strenuous efforts to get the Bush administration to support a second UN Security Council Resolution to authorize war cut little ice with Chirac, who threatened to use his veto if any such vote took place. Responding to a report from Hans Blix and his team in February 2003 calling for more time to verify the existence of weapons of mass destruction in Iraq, France and Germany (backed by Russia) tabled a proposal to treble the number of inspectors as an alternative to war. Moreover, after a particularly divisive European Council meeting in Brussels (March 2003) Belgium chaired an impromptu summit with Paris and Berlin, which called for the creation of a European military planning 'nucleus' in Tervuren (Wallace, 2005b). Some commentators perceived this initiative as a direct challenge to the authority of NATO. In the face of this European activity, Bush and Blair cut an increasingly isolated and defiant image on the world stage.

Interestingly, the fallout within the EU from Blair's controversial decision to side with Washington appears to have dissipated surprisingly quickly, although the adverse domestic fallout from this policy has been much slower to evaporate. While as already noted the invasion of Iraq led to divisions between Britain and the Franco-German alliance, it also created significant splits within the EU itself. As well as receiving support from Italy and Spain, many of the prospective member states from central and Eastern Europe backed the UK's stance, confirming the suspected Atlanticist bias of these countries. By December 2003 (less than a year after the Iraq invasion), Chirac, Schröder and Blair agreed to meet together to discuss common approaches to the Constitutional

Treaty being negotiated at the time (see below). Moreover, in recent years the same three countries have taken the lead within the EU in trying to persuade Iran to halt its uranium enrichment programme (with little apparent success). It should be noted that there is no constitutional provision for such action. Under EU rules, the usual practice is for the Troika (the EU High Representative on Foreign Policy; the External relations Commissioner; and the President of the European Council) to respond to any pressing issues (Smith, 2005). These episodes are perhaps evidence that the changing pattern of intergovernmental politics noted above, continues to favour the UK.

However, perhaps the most significant aspect of this whole episode was the apparent ease with which Blair was prepared to act in a way that undermined New Labour's rhetoric of acting as a 'bridge' between Europe and the US. One could point to the meeting at Bush's ranch in Crawford, Texas in April 2002, where Blair agreed in private to support military action without even consulting his EU partners. In return Blair hoped to get Washington to agree that (a) any planning for war be in concert with a broader push for progress in the Middle East; (b) that all efforts be made to assemble the largest possible coalition against Saddam; and (c) that any final decision be pursued through the UN. While the Bush administration paid lip service to all these points, the fact that Blair failed to state them explicitly as preconditions in return for his backing, meant that any chance of British influence was diminished from that point onwards (Seldon, 2004: 567–80). More generally, this episode emphasized the Labour Party leadership's longstanding preference for close relations with the US in the foreign policy sphere. Giddens may be correct to point out that globalization has radically re-shaped the international environment inhabited by member states (Giddens, 2006). We could add that the decline of the Cold War has enhanced the kaleidoscope quality of this external world. But Iraq demonstrates once again how elite political preferences have '... so effortlessly transcended all of these changes' (Gamble quoted in Baker and Sherrington, 2004: 363). The continuity of British foreign policy in this respect is quite striking.

Another example of continuity in the Blair government's relations with the EU was its policy towards the euro after 2001. It was argued above that New Labour's approach to handling the Single Currency issue in the first term was to depoliticize it for domestic political reasons. Precisely the same strategy was followed in the second term. The key event in this context was a second Treasury assessment on the prospects of euro membership, published in June 2003. The final report took a year and a half to complete and was accompanied by 18 background studies, running to 2,000 pages of tightly argued economic analysis. While nobody could question the seriousness with which the Treasury approached its task, the sheer size of this document guaranteed that it would only be read by specialists. The cabinet itself was given just two weeks to digest the content before a final pronouncement was made. For all its comprehensiveness, the 2003 assessment came to largely the same conclusions as had been reached in 1997. It was difficult not to take the view that the whole affair had been deliberately drawn out so as to turn the public off the issue. The irony of course was that the Treasury had been pushed into this second assessment by Blair, who promised (without consulting Brown) in the run-up to the 2001 election that it would take place. Blair initially hoped that he would be able to persuade the Chancellor to 'fix' the assessment in favour of joining, but was sadly disappointed (see Buller and Gamble, 2008).

If the Bush administration's policy of unilateralism in response to 9/11 served to complicate the Blair government's EU diplomacy, a second unwelcome development for the Blair government at the external level was the announcement in 2002 of a Convention on the Future of Europe. The purpose of this Convention was to review once again those institutional questions that had generated so much intergovernmental friction in the 1990s. The Convention deliberated from the end of February 2002, eventually producing a draft EU constitution which was debated by member states at the Thessaloniki European Council in June 2003 (Magnette and Nicolaidis, 2004; Norman, 2005). After another year of negotiations, the Constitution was finally agreed and signed at the Brussels European Council in June 2004 (the key highlights of which have been analysed in Duff, 2005; Church and Phinnemore, 2006).

It is true that the Blair government was initially opposed to the idea of an EU constitution (Straw, 2002). Such a text threatened to revive a number of the old Euro-sceptical arguments that had caused so many domestic political problems for the Major government. However, once it became apparent that momentum for a constitutional document could not be reversed, the UK delegation played an active role in trying to shape discussions in ways that were commensurate with British interests. It proposed changes that were eventually made to both the Presidency of the Council of Ministers and the European Council (Duff, 2005: 22, 85). It backed suggestions giving national parliaments a formal role in EU decision-making for the first time. At the end of negotiations, Blair was once again able to claim that the UK had protected its so-called 'red-lines'. Unanimity in the areas of taxation, social security and EU budgetary arrangements had been preserved, while a veto over judicial matters was maintained. Despite the fact that the Charter of Fundamental Social Rights was now to be incorporated into EU law, the British delegation worked hard to get inserted a form of wording that ensured it could never be utilized to overturn Britain's industrial relations legislation (Foreign and Commonwealth Office, 2004). It should be noted that British business organizations still display some concern that, as and when the Charter achieves binding effect, the European Court of Justice will exploit the text to develop a body of case law that undermines Britain's flexible labour market. Overall, however, it was generally considered that Blair was one of the big 'winners' at Brussels. This was certainly the verdict of both *Le Monde* and *Le Figaro* at the time (Bremner and Boyers, 2004).

It follows then that Blair's unexpected decision to grant the British public a referendum on the EU constitution was curious, especially when it seemed to go against New Labour's longstanding preference for depoliticizing European matters. It appears that such a move was heavily influenced by Jack Straw (Foreign Secretary) who warned Blair that his refusal to countenance a plebiscite was damaging morale on the Labour backbenches. In this context, the best tactic was to make virtue out of necessity, while at the same time stealing some of the Tories' political thunder just before the elections to the European Parliament. It may also have been the case that Blair genuinely believed his powers of persuasion would help win such a vote. There was certainly a perception in No.10 that British Euro-scepticism was grounded in ignorance rather than any deep-seated phobia towards the EU. As and when the government made a recommendation in support of the Constitution, accompanied by a publicity drive, such a development would boost the 'yes' campaign (see for example, Blitz, 2004; Binzer Hobolt and Riseborough, 2005). It should be said that few commentators were convinced by these arguments and the general consensus was that Blair had made a big mistake and would lose the vote. If this judgement looked plausible, Blair was lucky: the French and Dutch publics saved him from having to fulfil his promise when they both rejected the Constitution in referendums in 2005.

Since 2005, the Labour leadership's preference for depoliticization appears to have reasserted itself. Both Blair and Brown (since he became Prime Minister) have used the ongoing re-negotiation of the EU constitution as the main reason for dropping the Labour Party's commitment to provide a referendum. They have argued that the UK's 'red lines' continue to remain unbreached, while its opt-outs from the Charter of Fundamental Rights and criminal law have been retained. At the same time, ministers have asserted that the new text is significantly different from the one agreed in 2004, thus rendering null and void Blair's earlier promise of a plebiscite. The formal title has changed from 'constitution' to 'constitutional treaty' to 'amending treaty', and mention of the EU flag, anthem and motto were initially stripped out, but latterly reinserted at the last minute. It remains to be seen whether such a depoliticization tactic will work. At the time of writing, increasing numbers on both sides of the House of Commons question the credibility of these arguments. So much so that Ian Davidson, leader of Labour's campaign for a referendum, has predicted that 120 of the party's MPs will vote against the leadership's line on this issue (BBC News, 2007).

Conclusion

What conclusions can we draw about New Labour's European policy since 1997? Perhaps the first comment to make is that it has largely been successful, especially if our normative judgement takes account of the institutional constraints on political action in this area. The Blair government has, by and large, played a constructive role in EU negotiations over a range of difficult issues. The UK has moved closer to the centre of influence within this supranational organization, partly through the forging of a range of bilateral alliances with different countries over different issues. Finally, the Labour leadership has kept difficult European questions off the domestic agenda, especially the euro, which has always contained the potential to disrupt British politics. In this activity, the Blair government has been lucky in the sense that enlargement has bequeathed to it a more benign structural environment at the European level. Even so, when the divisions and chaos of the Major years are remembered, this depoliticization of the European question must go down as a significant achievement.

Second, viewed in a broader context, it is the continuity of policy that is the most striking in this sphere. Of course, one can point to Blair's more cooperative style and his more *communautaire* tone as evidence of a break with the past. Indeed, Blair may very well be the most pro-European Prime Minister that the UK has had since Edward Heath. But as noted above, when European commitments have clashed with the crude realities of electoral politics, the latter has won out (a trait which has a long pedigree in this area). In some ways, the opposite conclusion can be drawn about the 'American connection'. Despite the disappearance of the Cold War, the decline of bipolarity and the new world of globalization, the UK's penchant for a 'special' relationship with the US remains a permanent fixture of British diplomacy. Yet this policy continuity has yielded adverse domestic political consequences for the Labour leadership. Indeed, it is somewhat ironic that Anglo-American relations have replaced Europe as the major dividing line in British politics.

10
Blair's Liberal Interventionism

Raymond Plant

Right up to the close of his premiership Tony Blair insisted that he was a liberal interventionist in foreign policy and that this commitment had guided the various military actions which he had ordered as Prime Minister or which he had coordinated with others either in NATO, the UN or the 'coalition of the willing' in relation to Iraq. Given that the Iraq invasion overshadowed virtually everything about his government in the latter period of his time in office and that the invasion of Iraq and its consequences almost certainly foreshortened his time in office, and given that his historical reputation is, to say the least, going to be highly coloured if not dominated by Iraq, it is important both to understand the moral and political case for liberal interventionism and to see how well it fits into Blair's 'Third Way' approach to politics. There is no doubt that Blair took the elaboration of the case for liberal interventionism very seriously and he made substantial speeches on the theme, including the definitive speech in Chicago on 'The Doctrine of the International Community' (Stelzer, 2004). However, it is equally clear that these speeches fall a long way short of a convincing normative case for the position on which his foreign policy rested. Therefore my aim in this chapter will be to set out as strongly as I can the case for liberal interventionism – as it is found in the literature of political theory and international relations as well as by Blair and Jonathan Powell (his former Chief of Staff) who has also written about these matters (Powell, 2007) – to address the critical response that there has been to that case and to see how both the positive case and its critique fit into Tony Blair's own account of the position that he espoused and how far criticism of liberal interventionism applies to his version of it.

I begin with a brief sketch of the liberal interventionist position which Blair has espoused. This will not be detailed at the moment but will become so when we consider his actual response and indeed possible responses to critics of his position. Tony Blair clearly links his view of foreign policy to the fact of globalization – a very general but central theme in his account of 'Third Way' politics. Globalization has created a situation in which economic changes affect all parts of the world even though, of course, a specific site will be the basis of the set of circumstances causing the ripple effect around the globe – think only of the sub-prime mortgage crisis in the USA and its effect on the global banking system. So, to quote Blair's own speech on 'The Doctrine of the International Community':

> 'Many of our domestic problems are caused on the other side of the world. Financial instability in Asia destroys jobs in Chicago and in my own constituency in County Durham. Poverty in the Caribbean means more drugs on the streets of Washington and London. Conflict in the Balkans causes more refugees in Germany and in the US.' (Stelzer, 2004: 107)

For Blair, globalization has profound effects for the politics of international relations as well as for the economy. It leads to a rethinking of what the national interest is when our interests can be changed or at least challenged by remote changes in other parts of the world. It is a matter of what Professor W.J.M. Mackenzie very presciently saw many years ago as the world 'political ecology' – where disturbances can have profound effects on societies which are not close either geographically, culturally, ethnically or in religious terms to the original site of the disturbance. To use Mackenzie's own example, racial or religious tensions in the Punjab may have a direct effect on the streets of London. For Blair, what Mackenzie called political ecology leads to a doctrine of international community: 'Just as within domestic politics, the notion of community – the belief that partnership and cooperation are essential to advance self interest – is coming into its own; so it needs to find its own international echo' (Stelzer, 2004: 108).

We have to cooperate in order to achieve not only common goals but also self interested ones in the international sphere as we have to do in terms of communities within the nation state. We can achieve more in terms of our self interest as a nation by acting cooperatively and in concert with others than we can achieve in an isolated manner. Isolation is a false mark of sovereignty because if sovereignty means, among other things, pursuing the national interests of a sovereign state this now needs to be done in cooperation just because of the degree of global interdependency as the result of greater economic globalization. Operating through cross-national bodies, the UN, the EU, NATO, and *ad hoc* arrangements like 'coalitions of the willing' are now indispensable to the achievement of national purposes and interests. Hence the doctrine of the international community rests as Tony Blair insists on this clear sighted way of enhancing the ability of a nation state like Britain to pursue its national interest by cooperation with others. The parallel with Blair's supposed communitarianism in domestic politics is clear as the quotation pointing this out given above shows.

However, what is left under-explored in this position is that while Blair thought that the idea of community in domestic policy underpinned ideas about duty and responsibility and what we owe to one another – as well as the idea that we enhance our own interests through cooperation rather than by unilateral action – this does not feature all that much in this version of the international community. It is one thing to say that the current interconnectedness of the world gives states incentives to cooperate and indeed be concerned about what happens in somewhat remote locations because of their spill-over effects. For example, a concern with Kosovo being based on the potential refugee problem in parts of Europe and the USA and to have this concern as a matter of national self interest if the situation is sufficiently acute. It is another issue altogether to invoke the idea of an international community in moral terms to justify intervention on moral ground. For example, in terms of protecting human rights from either genocide or other forms of violence against individuals and groups as was taking place in Kosovo. This requires a much thicker sense of international community in the same way as grounding duties and responsibilities in the national community depends on more than just noticing that we can often advance our own interests in cooperation with others.

What needs to be grounded for a moralized form of interventionism which Blair eventually came to espouse is, first of all, the centrality of human rights to the idea of a shared international morality which an international community has to embody if it is to be *more* than a cooperative vehicle for advancing self interest and that this doctrine of rights has in turn to do two things. The first is to ground a *right* to intervention and secondly it has to have the capability of justifying a *duty* to intervene to protect rights. This is essential if some of Blair's observations on intervention are to be seen as morally coherent. In arguing, as he did, that we would be morally culpable not to have intervened in Kosovo or in Iraq, that we would have blood on our hands if we had not intervened, presupposes a prior duty to intervene in respect of which we are culpable if we do not follow through on that duty. We cannot be culpable for not doing something unless we *ought* to have done that thing, or to put it another way, had a duty to do it. This moral case is absolutely crucial because one cannot just say that we are culpable for not relieving suffering wherever in the world we find it unless we have a prior duty to do that. Unless we can establish what our duties are, this doctrine of culpability means that states can be held responsible for all the harm they are currently not preventing. This, it might be argued, is an irrational moral position because it can never be implemented and its aims can never be achieved – a point that Tony Blair himself accepts in his 'Doctrine of the International Community'.

In order to be clear about where the responsibilities of states lie and to fix the extent of their culpability it is necessary to set out what our antecedent obligations in fact are. There is no way that the doctrine of international community as set out by Blair in this speech is rich enough to ground obligations of this sort. In order to ground this duty we need to have quite a strong doctrine about human rights and their protection and a sense that the international community is put under an obligation by the existence of these rights to protect them. The point here is that it is not just the national state that has an obligation to protect the human rights of its members but that states more generally have an obligation to protect the rights of members of national states when a national state is either intentionally infringing them or is inadvertently or negligently allowing them to be infringed. This has to be seen as a positive duty. States generally might claim that they are respecting the human rights of individuals in all other states because they are doing nothing to infringe them. The position needed to ground intervention has to be very much stronger. It has to be the view that states have a duty not just to respect the rights of those in other states by forbearing from interference of their own with such rights but also that they have a positive duty to protect such rights when they are infringed by the government of the right holders or where they are infringed by the actions of a third party state. Even then this may not ground as much as interventionists want as we have to be able not only to establish a right to intervene but possibly also a duty to do so. It certainly has to be the latter if we are to be held to be culpable for not intervening – the blood on our hands argument.

So one initial issue is whether Tony Blair's own account of the doctrine of the International Community can in fact justify the invocation of such duties and the claim that we are morally negligent if we do not respond to the call of such duties. The question will also arise as to how this thicker account of international community would relate the thinner account of community as a basis for achieving self interest. There has to be a relationship between the two because in fact even assuming that we do have a positive duty to protect the rights of others in other states we are not going to discharge the duty to protect rights in every case and the reason for that is very likely to be that it is not in our interest to do so. This is a point which Blair recognizes in the Chicago speech and I will discuss it more fully below.

The argument about the moral basis for intervention also has to assume that the claims embodied in human rights claims are in some sense commonly shared across states even if we do not want to get into the question as to whether they are objective and absolute sorts of claims. The reason for this is that given that a doctrine of human rights is going to provide the shared moral ground for the basis of an international community in the thick sense then it has to be assumed that such values are given and shared. That is to say it is at least a practical challenge to moral relativism. Defenders of moral relativism might want to make two sorts of claims here. The first is that such rights are in fact morally specific and are in fact embodiments of the values of Western liberalism. Therefore, an intervention justified on the grounds of human rights would in fact be interventions based on Western as opposed to shared and universal values. So, for example, there have been arguments about Asian values and how these in the strongest version of the argument can be seen as alternatives to Western rights or alternatively can be seen as a moral basis for the *interpretation* of the specific moral requirements of rights in a particular society with a specific culture and set of traditions. This is a more modest variation of this argument. It could be argued from this perspective that it may be the case that at the most general level the rights set out in the UN Charter, for example, are shared across the international spectrum since accepting those rights is part of UN membership.

Nevertheless, there can be wide and important differences about the interpretation of those rights in specific circumstances. Rights to, for example, life and liberty will always have to be subject to interpretation and these interpretations are going to reflect the traditions and values of the states within which they are interpreted. There is no way of avoiding this divergence of interpretation since the rights are couched in the most general terms and there has to be in all cases a process of interpretation and it is at this point that moral relativism may again arise in that there is no definitive interpretation of what these rights mean in specific cases.

This is a matter of local interpretation against the background of the moral traditions of particular societies and ways of life.

There is a second issue here and that again focuses upon what, in my own view, quite wrongly has come to be seen as an ideological division over rights. The Western view, so it is argued, is that the rights which provide a shared moral basis for an international community are in fact civil and political rights. These rights are real or genuine. They can form the basis of an international morality (much as natural law did before the Reformation) and as such can provide the moral basis for intervention when these rights are egregiously infringed by a state in relation to its own citizens. However, there is also the view that social, economic and cultural rights are equally rights and should be taken into account when judging the moral basis of an international community. Hence, on this view, if a state is infringing economic rights or cultural rights in an egregious and obvious manner then this ought to be as much a matter of concern for the international community as civil and political rights. In the period of the Cold War this difference of view on rights was a matter of ideological division between the West and the Soviet Union and China. The West would insist that only civil and political rights were in fact genuine rights whereas the Soviet Union and others would insist that social and economic rights should have priority over civil and political rights. The imperative to meet the physical needs of people took priority, so it was claimed over their liberties as protected by civil and political rights. The point to make at this stage of the argument though is that given that both sorts of rights are recognized by the UN there is no *a priori* reason for refusing to allow that social, economic and cultural rights could be regarded as part of the shared moral basis of the international community. A refusal to recognize this might actually exacerbate the case for saying that rights are intrinsically enmeshed in the relativism controversy since one part of the world accepts one set of rights, another part of the world gives priority to another set of rights. This can do nothing but harm to the claim that a set of rights can in fact provide the basis for a sense of international community in a thicker sense than just a mechanism for facilitating the pursuit of self interest.

It might be argued that these are arcane and irrelevant philosophical points, but this is surely not the case because invoking human rights as a basis for intervention is in fact a challenge to the fact of state sovereignty and the norm of non-intervention which has gone along with that. If a centrally important norm of international politics – that of non-intervention – is going to be abridged in favour of arguments about the centrality of human rights then there has to be a pretty clear understanding of what rights are, when they are being neglected or wilfully misinterpreted and perhaps even more importantly the difference between a third party state respecting the rights of citizens in another state by not engaging in any action that would infringe them, that is to say respect via forbearance and the positive protection of such rights by military intervention. The challenge of the human rights agenda is to what might be called the Westphalian system of independent sovereign states and a shared norm of non-intervention, a point which both Blair and Jonathan Powell accept. So we need to explore this issue in more detail.

Therefore the doctrinal basis of liberal interventionism has both a positive side in terms of having a basis in human rights and the defence of human dignity and worth reflected or embodied in those rights, and a negative side in a *critique* of the Westphalian system (as it has come to be called) of state sovereignty along with the norm of non-intervention.

It is usually held that the Treaty of Westphalia which concluded the Thirty Years War in 1648 heralded the emergence of the full blown idea of state sovereignty – that there was no political or legal power higher than that of the state to which the state had to defer. In Mediaeval times the Roman Catholic Church had at least theoretically and sometimes with practical effect tried to claim a moral and political authority which transcended that of individual states, autonomously governing cities, dukedoms etc. It also claimed to represent the authority of natural law which transcended the positive law of individual communities and to which positive law should cohere. Natural law provided a shared moral and political set of objective values and principles which should be drawn upon in the governance and legal systems of particular states so that states which failed to match up to natural law principles could be regarded as defective in particular ways which could sanction the intervention of a righteous ruler. This changed quite fundamentally with the Treaty of Westphalia which embodies the principle of *cuius regio eius religio*, that each state should follow the religion of its ruler. This recognition of religious pluralism, as we would now say, dealt a fatal blow to any future ambitions that the papacy may have had towards moral and political hegemony and at the same time to natural law as well – in so far as it was thought to need some kind of common religious underpinning. Similarly the historic doctrine of natural law was also being undermined by either philosophical critiques or reinterpretations – as for example in the case of Thomas Hobbes. Alongside the emerging doctrine of state sovereignty there also developed a norm of non-intervention except in self defence. Indeed this norm is part of the UN Charter with again the exception being self defence and protection against genocide. It is also possible to intervene in other well defined circumstances under Chapter 7 Resolutions.

It is easy to see why such a norm was attractive to emerging sovereign states. It certainly constrained their own power, but at the same time it did embody several desirable things. First of all the equality of states in terms of their mutually recognized sovereignty. So in this context size, population and military might did not give large states a *de jure* right to intervene, conquer, or reduce to vassal status weaker or smaller states. So there was a strong incentive for smaller states to seek to maintain the norm of non-intervention as a condition of their self determination and their equality with larger states. In addition, the norm of non-intervention apart from the obvious case of self defence and later genocide did not require resources of arms and/or treasure to fulfil. As a doctrine or norm requiring that states abstain from intervention the doctrine embodied a costless duty which could always be performed. Forbearance does not require resources. As such, this norm could become a genuine rule of international politics just because it required inaction rather than action except in the case of self defence or similar kinds of threats – which in turn could be demonstrated to be real, egregious and palpable. So the rule could be clear, costless and observable and exceptions to it were to be regarded as empirically establishable.

This is not so easily the case with an interventionist policy. A view that other states have a right and possibly even a duty to intervene to protect rights makes this a positive rule which will involve costs and political calculation about when those costs are worth bearing. It is also the case that the basis of intervention in terms of human rights is going to be more controversial than a norm of non-intervention just because of disagreement about what rights require in terms of their protection and which rights are to take priority in terms of their potential demands on the international community.

In this respect it is quite unlike the norm of non-intervention as the norm did not make any strong moral requirements. Each state could have its own moral and religious culture so there was no requirement for there to be some form of common international morality to sustain the international system other than the self interest which all states would have in terms of seeking to sustain their own sovereignty and thereby adherence to the norm of non-intervention.

This point of view can lead to a kind of moral relativism too. Although the Westphalian system presupposed in 1648 that European rulers would be Christian, with their differences being of a denominational sort, the way the state system has developed and the idea that states have their own religious, cultural, familial and educational traditions, for example, can easily lead to the view that moral principles are relative to such traditions and have meaning and force only in so far as they are embodied within them. As we have seen, this can influence understandings of the nature and scope of rights and their interpretation.

Such relativism also reinforces the idea that intervention is wrong because it is an intervention in another state with its own traditions, values, and ways of life justified in terms of the potentially very different values and traditions of the intervening state. So, for example, critics of interventionism might argue that Western countries are prone to justify interventions in terms of what may be seen as Western values, such as human rights or democracy, which may not be at the centre of the concerns of other societies with different traditions, religions, cultures and ways of life.

Because there is on this view no shared morality or at least no shared interpretation of what morality demands, an international system which allowed intervention to be morally driven would be at the least very unpredictable and, at the worst, anarchical. It would be impossible to know when moral concern was thought to be sufficient to justify intervention, whereas the appeal to self interest embodied in the doctrine of sovereignty made the international system stable and, in a sense, calculable. States would have some sense of when they might provoke another state to seek to use power to protect its own interests and sovereignty and one would not therefore have to rely on potential vague and controversial substantial moral norms to uphold the international system. Self interest, state sovereignty and the norm of non-intervention would do this job without the need for more substantial and controversial moral norms. The important point here is that unlike the norm of non-intervention – except in the case of self defence and genocide both of which are demonstrable and palpable – there could not be a set of rules to provide a basis for liberal interventionism in foreign policy. The norm of non-intervention can always be met because it is straightforward and costless. A positive interventionist norm cannot be rule governed in the same way. A liberal interventionist foreign policy might well deal a death blow on this view to a system of clear international law.

Realists, as a school in the international relations community – academic, diplomatic and political – share many of the assumptions of what I have just described, although there are some divergences. Realists agree about the centrality of state sovereignty; they agree also about seeing the international system as largely being about the self interest of states and they see this self interest as being projected by power; they argue that international relations is governed by power and interests rather than a morality which goes beyond self interest. However, in practice there is divergence over the norm of non-intervention and over respecting the equality of states and counting weak states (i.e. in terms of size and power) as being on a par with strong states.

On this view, states can intervene in another state when they perceive that state to be a threat to their vital interests in a way that goes beyond self defence (for example, President George Bush Sr's intervention in Panama to arrest General Noriega – threatening the vital interest of the USA in terms of the drugs trade). This links also to the realist view that the rough equality of states doctrine under the broad Westphalian system neglects to recognize the driving force of internal politics, namely interests protected and projected by power. If a smaller state is acting in a way that is perceived to threaten the interests of the larger state then, on a realist basis, one could not expect the larger and more powerful state to feel ultimately constrained by the moral recognition of the rough equality of states. This also links to the issue of morality in another way too. The interests in question for the realist may well have a strong moral dimension. Protecting the interests of a state is likely to mean protecting and projecting its way of life around the world because from that state's point of view this way of life is valuable to it – indeed essential to it. It is what makes its interests important to it.

So it marks a difference with the earlier position in that many realists may want to say that it is perfectly reasonable for a state to pursue the protection of its way of life and values as one of its essential interests and not to be held back from doing so by an acceptance of moral relativism. Realists are not necessarily relativists. I mean in their fundamental views they could hardly be so in that it is central to their position that a state acts in its own self interest – which is not a relativist position. Of course, what a state might regard as being in its interests may well differ from state to state and this may well be informed by widely divergent moral considerations, but underlying those potential differences lies a common thread – namely the pursuit of self interest.

Therefore, the realist position is not opposed to interventionism. What it is opposed to is the moralizing of that interventionist position. For the realist what are crucial are power and interests. Moralizing these whether in terms of the language of human rights or human dignity in terms of an ethical foreign policy is a fundamental error partly because it produces a disingenuous position and also because it is one that cannot be carried through on a consistent basis – something crucial to the idea that a position is morally grounded rather than one based on interests.

It has to be accepted on the realist view that basing a foreign policy on self interest will produce different responses in different circumstances. The same will be true in practice for liberal interventionism but this is less acceptable if the position is supposed to be a morally informed one – if it is morally legitimate or required to intervene *here* why not *there* where the situation is similar? On a realist view there is a clear answer to this question: it is not in our interests to do so; on a moralized view it is much more difficult to make this argument.

Some of these critical views are also to be found in conservative critiques of liberal interventionism; although it has to be stressed of course that many liberal interventionists are neo conservatives. Indeed Tony Blair's speech on 'The Doctrine of the International Community' was republished in a book defending neo-conservative ideas in foreign policy. In so far as they are however, they have put considerable distance between themselves and some classical conservative doctrines, as we shall see. It is also true to say that elements of this critique are also to be found in the writings of communitarian thinkers whose stance is anything but conservative – for example Michael Walzer (Walzer, 1980). And indeed, Mr Blair has often been regarded as a communitarian.

The conservative position is partly an epistemological one: that we do not in fact know enough about the culture, values and ways of life of another state to be able to intervene with confidence. An interventionist foreign policy assumes a level of knowledge and understanding which is unlikely to be available and yet which particularly in the post-intervention period might be utterly crucial to the successful conclusion of the intervention. Most conservative thinkers have been opposed to large scale initiatives whether in domestic or in foreign policy just because of the fragmentary and dispersed nature of knowledge which cannot be brought together to serve a particular large scale political project. The canonical form of this argument was stated by Edmund Burke in *Reflections on the Revolution in France* and in more recent times particularly in relationship to economic planning by Friedrich von Hayek. This lack of knowledge and our inherent inability to coordinate it also means that large scale political projects are full of unintended consequences. This is a particularly acute problem in war – which intervention usually involves – just because all the conventions about the reciprocal behaviour of states have broken down. It is even more difficult than usual to calculate and predict the reactions not just of a government but of the population with their values and traditions to foreign incursion.

One of the more tragic aspects of this is the unintended killing of the innocents which is almost certain to happen. This is not only morally problematic in itself but again leads to unintended consequences because the reaction of the local population to the killing of the innocent will not be able to be predicted.

Other conservative and communitarian criticisms of interventionism in foreign policy are first of all that other ways of life and values have value in themselves, in some sense just because they exist and are valued at least by significant portions of the population. There is, as Michael Walzer puts it, a degree of fit between the population and its cultural, religious and political values. To see intervention as purely a political act which can say topple a regime while leaving the rest of the culture untouched is, on this view, a very naïve approach which fails to understand the close and even organic links between a political order and the wider culture. Even if cultural change is not part of the aim of the intervention, as is often the case, the idea that one can invade another country and leave its culture – in the broadest sense – intact is very fanciful. This organicist view about the deep interpenetration of politics and the culture more generally is a pretty standard conservative and communitarian position. Liberal interventionists are prone to deny it. For example, Fernando Teson in his article in defence of liberal interventionism calls it the 'Hegel myth' (Teson, 1997).

In addition, there are cultural questions to be addressed to the intervening state in the view of conservatives. This particularly focuses on the moral engagement of the population with the issues at stake in the proposed intervention. Usually, states that are intervened in are quite a long way off geographically and possibly even further off psychically and culturally. So beyond the issue of self defence and perhaps genocide, will a government committed to an interventionist foreign policy in fact be able to mobilize its population in favour of intervening in a country on the basis of a set of considerations which are much less palpable and obvious as self defence and Genocide?

Such considerations which are going to be used to justify the expenditure of blood and treasure may well appear to be rather abstract to a rather apolitical population in the state contemplating intervention. So famously, and tragically, Neville Chamberlain made a peace with Hitler over Czechoslovakia because it was a 'far away country about which we know nothing'. In the view of the conservative critic of interventionism this kind of moral distance will prove a crucial inhibiting factor in mobilizing populations, and this is why politicians who wish to create a mood for intervention are likely to have to justify what they are proposing to do in terms of the palpable motives of self defence and genocide even if the reasons for going to war are much more complex than that.

What from a conservative perspective is unlikely to mobilize populations in favour of intervention is a concern with the denial of human rights. This is so for several reasons. Following Burke's lead in *Reflections on the French Revolution* most conservatives see the idea of *human* rights as being rather abstract. They are allegedly claims that we hold in virtue of our humanity rather than say as Englishmen or Frenchmen. The idea of humanity is on this view wholly abstract – it is arrived at by abstracting an account of what it is to be a human being from all the specific forms of identity which they otherwise have: religious, political, cultural, ethnic etc. In the view of the critic of interventionism this is far too abstract a basis for founding a foreign policy stance. People respond to the needs and situations of others in terms of the *specific identities* that they have, not in terms of abstract ideas. Thus in the nineteenth century interventions were often undertaken, for example, in Greece in defence of the Christians in 1820; in Lebanon to defend the Maronite Christians in the 1860s; and later in the century in the Balkans, to protect beleaguered Christian communities. It was a Christian country like the UK intervening in the interests of people whose identity we shared in, at least in this religious respect. This is not the case with human rights on this view. Today we neither share identity – other than an abstract human identity – nor propinquity with many of those who might be on an agenda for intervention.

There is a further issue about human rights violations as a basis for intervention in the following way. To justify interventions on the claimed basis of the shared international morality of human rights so that their blatant violation is always wrong and a *prima facie* ground for intervention will turn out to be morally deceptive because like cases cannot and will not be treated in like manner. In this respect, as I indicated earlier, the conservative position is rather similar to the realist one. We may intervene in Iraq or Kosovo because of rights violations – but we shall not be doing so in Burma or China in relation to Tibet.

Yet if rights justify intervention and if indeed we have a duty to intervene based on rights is not this claim morally seamless? After all it is often thought that rights are categorical claims so that a failure to protect them is always wrong. Yet in practice this claim cannot be universalized because of the facts in the world about power and the distribution of military forces. So rights, on this view, moralize the issue in a way that cannot be sustained. It invokes a claimed rights-base and categorical common morality that grounds obligations, but one which cannot in fact be carried through in a categorical and universalizable way – in stark contrast to the norm of non-intervention which can always be satisfied. So on this view, utilitarian considerations will have to kick in quite early on to control the duties that could spiral out of control if we assume that rights can ground an obligation to intervene. These utilitarian considerations will typically reflect two interdependent things: first of all, that however clear the moral position may be in relation to Burma we shall not be intervening in Burma because it is not in our interests to do so; and secondly, the population of the intervening state would not in fact support an intervention justified on moral grounds unless some interest could be demonstrated to be at stake. We cannot, on this common realist/ conservative view, get away from basic interests, the facts of power, and the conditions necessary for political mobilization.

This brings us back to the purity of the motive for intervention. On this view our motives will always be mixed. Even though we may ground our intervention in terms of rights, why are we choosing to intervene *here* rather than *there* where the rights violations seem to be equally egregious? Answering this question will bring into play a wider range of motives than purely rights based ones, and these are bound to be broadly of a utilitarian character and embody political calculation of power and interests as much as anything else. So in the case of Iraq, the justification for war vacillated between regime change because of human rights violations and security threats to neighbours and to weapons of mass destruction – as well as, for some neo-cons, wider geopolitical considerations about the future shape of the Middle East.

This brings us to another issue at stake between the liberal interventionists and conservative and realist critics. If liberal interventionism rests upon the idea of protecting basic human rights then it will not do just to intervene militarily to change a political regime. It will be also necessary either to engage directly in building up new political and civil structures which will respect rights, or alternatively to facilitate this by other means. This has to be a central aim of policy if the overall aim is the protection of rights because military action and regime change are in themselves highly unlikely to secure this end. If this is not seen as part of the end because as was said by administration officials in the USA over Iraq 'we don't do nation building', then this can be regarded as being utterly irresponsible if the aim of the intervention was regime change in favour of the protection of rights. To fail to engage in the task of building up political and civil institutions to protect rights would be a blatant example of willing the end, namely the protection of and respect for rights, while not willing the means, namely the institution building to achieve this.

Both Tony Blair and Jonathan Powell have seen the point here. In his Chicago speech Blair said explicitly that 'In the past we talked too much of exit strategies. But having made a commitment we cannot simply walk away once the fight is over' (Stelzer, 2004: 112). Powell is very forthright in his speech made long after the invasion of Iraq: 'We need to be better prepared for the aftermath of intervention. We weren't properly prepared in Kosovo, in Afghanistan or in Iraq. It is no good saying as Donald Rumsfeld did that We don't do nation building. That is exactly what we do need to be able to do' (Powell, 2007).

Nevertheless, for the conservative and for some communitarians particularly, such a moral goal which is more coherent than just intervention without institution building is fraught with difficulty and danger for reasons that I have already set out to do with the nature of knowledge and more particularly to do with the interpenetration of politics and the wider culture. In terms of knowledge we do not know enough to be able to take a lead in rebuilding the civil and political institutions of another country, particularly when its religion and culture may be very different from our own, and we certainly will hardly understand the delicate balances which exist between politics, religion and the wider culture. So the critique here is two-fold. Interventionism without institution building is morally disingenuous, but institution building in a society which is geographically and psychically not close to us and our own sense of identity and what matters in life is always going to be very difficult, if not impossible, and full of unintended consequences which may well be tragic. Indeed, for many of these critics, this is exactly what has happened in Iraq.

These arguments, taken together, form the basis of the critique of liberal interventionism. I now want to look at what might be a Blairite response. Some of this has to be speculative since Tony Blair never really confronted these issues in detail. However, I believe that these speculations can have some degree of basis in some of his more general positions but I do think that his commitment to liberal interventionism does point to many ambiguities and indeed possible contradictions in his overall ideological position.

First of all let us take the norm of non-intervention and the sovereignty of states. In his Chicago speech he makes two points in relation to the norm of non-intervention. The first is that:

'Non interference has long been considered an important principle of international order. And it is not one that we would want to jettison too readily. One state should not feel it has the right to change the political system of another or foment subversion or seize pieces of territory to which it feels it should have some claim. But the principle of non interference must be qualified in important respects.' (Stelzer, 2004: 112)

Jonathan Powell in his *Observer* article of 18 November 2007 explicitly links the norm of non-intervention to the Peace of Westphalia and he draws a number of conclusions. The first is that he is unhappy about its moral base – it was used, he argues, as a basis for doing nothing about the Hungarian uprising or the Prague spring, although he does accept that it made some sense in a nuclear-backed standoff. It also meant in his view that after 1648 states would not go to war over ideas and values; they would go to war over self defence and succession and even territory but not in pursuit of the spread of ideas. It is not now a credible policy because with globalization the world is a much smaller place and the impact of domestic policies of states can be felt and pose threats way beyond borders. So the norm of non-intervention has to be modified in this new era. The question is how this modification is to be spelled out and on what grounds it is to be justified.

There is a radical philosophical view which, for example, Fernando Teson takes to be at the basis of the kind of liberal interventionism that he defends, and that is that states and state sovereignty have only instrumental value (Teson, 1997). The central moral issue is the rights of individuals and their protection. States, when they are operating well, are the best way of securing individual rights, but the legitimacy of the state and its claim to protection through the norm of non-interference rests upon whether or not it secures and protects the rights of its citizens. On this basis there is a justification for intervention if a state is not satisfying this basic condition of legitimacy. The state itself has no moral standing independent of whether it protects the rights of citizens. This does not mean that intervention is justified or required in every state with a less than perfect human rights record. There can be decent states which fall below an optimal standard of rights protection but do not fall below some kind of threshold level of decency. This point is taken from Rawls' arguments in his writings on *The Law of Peoples* (Rawls, 1999). In a sense Blair makes a similar point in his Chicago speech when he says that 'There are many regimes that are undemocratic and engaged in barbarous acts.

If we wanted to right every wrong we see in the modern world then we would do little else than intervene in the affairs of other countries. We would not be able to cope' (Stelzer, 2004: 112).

However, there cannot be a kind of algorithm which will determine the boundary between a fully legitimate state and a decent state on the one hand or a decent state and one that falls below that level on the other. This has to be a matter of political judgement. This is crucial since in the latter context the question of whether to intervene or not intervene is going to be a contested matter. The more obvious language in the political context in which this argument is couched is that of failing states, and this is language frequently used by Blair but he has never set out the criteria in terms of which failure is to be established. Teson does this in a very clear way and it certainly provides a firm basis for a liberal form of interventionism and it may well be that such a doctrine can only make sense of the basis of such a view of the legitimacy of the state as the protector of rights. However, neither Powell nor Blair has gone anything like as far as this in their accounts of liberal interventionism. So as a political rather than a philosophical doctrine we are going to have to deal with rather vague ideas about failing states.

This is a problem however, because Jonathan Powell argues that having modified the norm of non-intervention for the reasons that he has given we still need to have a rule-governed international framework:

We need a rules based system. As other big countries rise to be superpowers they will have very different value systems from us. So it is in the US interest as it is in the interest of medium sized powers like the UK, to have the rule of law applied internationally as it is domestically. (Powell, 2007)

In a sense this is an echo of Blair's Chicago speech when he says: 'The most pressing foreign policy problem we face is to identify the circumstances in which we should get actively involved in other people's conflicts ... So how do we decide when and whether to intervene?' (Stelzer, 2004: 112).

The problem is, as Blair has already said and Powell echoes this, we are not going to intervene even when there are egregious human rights violations in Burma to use Powell's example. Critics have pointed out that interventionism as a positive act is always costly and we may not want to bear the cost, because we may not be able to mobilize home populations in the cause. In addition, because our interests will be differently engaged in different places we are likely to have highly differentiated responses to circumstances. It is difficult to see how this can be fitted into the rule governed framework which both Blair and Powell say they want to see. The obvious basis is a value driven one with human rights at the centre of this as would befit liberal interventionism.

However, in his article Jonathan Powell rather undermines what may well be his view. On the liberal view, rights are at the heart of interventionism because they are part of a common moral currency. They are not just the values of Western liberalism. They are in fact universal moral demands and should not be seen as Western because to do so would be to commit the genetic fallacy, as Teson makes clear. Rights can have a universal salience even if they did first emerge in the West. The origins of a conception have no direct bearing on the validity and objectivity of that view. So, on this basis, along with a rejection of moral relativism human rights could provide the foundation stones for a set of rules for intervention. However, in the earlier passage quoted from Powell he makes it clear that part of the need for a new set of rules is that new superpowers will arise whose values are very different from our own. So the implication is that the rules cannot be based on universal values in these circumstances; but then what will they be based upon?

Secondly he goes on to argue that the values underlying interventionism are essentially 'our' values – presumably he means those of the West and that these values in fact coincide with our interests. That is to say Western interests are best served by the set of values on which we would rely to justify interventionism. Now this may be a very honest assessment, but to say that rights and democracy are our values and indeed serve our interests is not a very secure basis for convincing the rest of the world that what we need is a set of rules given the downplaying of the previous rule of non-interventionism. If the rest of the world see these rules as a programme for projecting Western values and Western interests they are highly unlikely to agree to a new set of rules if, as Powell says, the new superpowers will have very different values from our own. So it does seem in this respect at least that liberal interventionism cannot, pace the attempts of thinkers like Teson, be seen as having some kind of universal validity and salience.

It does look as though liberal interventionism as a political doctrine, at least as interpreted by Blair and Powell, is in the end just a more expansive form of realism in international relations about the projection and protection of interests together with the thinner or weaker doctrine of international community which I identified earlier, namely that we can project and protect our interests best in partnership with others. It may be, as Powell says, that these interests actually coincide with our values in many respects. That may be true, but it is not then really a position which we could expect to provide a firm basis for the new set of rules accommodating interventionism and a move from the norm of non-intervention which Blair and Powell argue that they want.

11
Blair's Record on Defence: A Strategic Analysis

David Lonsdale

Introduction

The record of Blair's period in office makes it inevitable that defence figures significantly in our perception of his time as Prime Minister. From operation Desert Fox in 1998, to the ongoing war in Iraq, Blair has revealed a propensity to use military force as a tool of policy. Whilst there has been much analysis concerning the implications for his relationship with his own party, little has been written from a Strategic Studies perspective. This work seeks to rectify this gap in the literature. In doing so the following chapter will present a dispassionate analysis of how effectively Blair has used military force to achieve his policy objectives. There is no other way a strategic analyst should judge the former Prime Minister. Such an approach is not only correct from a conceptual perspective, but is also in line with the standards set by the Blair government itself. The 1998 *Strategic Defence Review* differentiated itself from the reviews of the previous Conservative governments by claiming that foreign policy goals would drive defence policy. Indeed, the review opens with a section entitled 'A Strategic Approach to Defence'.

The chapter will begin by briefly defining the nature of strategy, and in particular the challenges faced by those who engage in it. From here, the work will then assess Blair's conduct of strategy on a number of operations and issues: Kosovo, the 'war on terror' (including Afghanistan and the fight against domestic terrorism), Iraq, and finally the issue of Trident replacement. It will be argued that although Blair has something of a mixed record as a strategist, on balance he has performed reasonably well in the face of substantial obstacles and challenges.

The complexity of strategy

At the heart of strategy is the notion that military force is a tool of policy (Clausewitz, 1993). In this sense strategy can be thought of as the bridge over which these two different worlds interact (Gray, 1990). Alternatively, Eliot Cohen describes the relationship as being characterized by an unequal dialogue. Both sides (political and military) need to communicate and discuss what is required to achieve the desired policy objectives, and just as importantly what is possible. However, the dialogue lacks equity because ultimately military force must serve the ends of policy (Cohen, 2002). Thus strategy can be defined as *the art of using military force against an intelligent foe (or foes) towards the attainment of policy objectives*. The relationship between policy and military force is the first cause of complexity for those engaged in strategy. The political and military worlds exhibit significant differences: they have very different cultures; operate within different concepts of time; define results and success differently; and may have differing attitudes towards secrecy and openness. Perhaps most importantly, although the military is a much more flexible instrument than some would believe, it is still fundamentally a violent, blunt instrument (Lonsdale, 2007). To use such an instrument for political objectives, increasingly in the glare of the global media, is an art, and not one that often is pleasing to the senses. The modern strategist must somehow achieve his policy objectives whilst operating within the restrictions of prevailing norms and values, but at the same time respecting the nature of war. That nature is unchanging and can be characterized as violent, chaotic, uncertain, and competitive.

Beyond the problems associated with the interaction between policy and war, the strategist faces many others. Strategy is a multidimensional activity. Modern Strategic Studies has identified as many as 17 dimensions that influence the performance of the strategist. Depending upon the context some of these dimensions will be more significant than others. However, a degree of competence must be achieved in all of them if success is desired (Gray, 1999). War also has a polymorphous character, meaning that it can take many forms. Indeed, Tony Blair has had to deal with the rich and varied range of warfare. He has used British forces in small-scale operations against irregulars in Africa, fought large-scale regular warfare in Iraq (in the first phase of the war), engaged in peacekeeping operations, and had to deal with the question of the future of Britain's nuclear weapons. The challenge posed by the polymorphous character of war relates to both war preparation and conduct. Those with responsibility for force composition and training must ideally create and train forces that can cope with the entire gamut of tasks that may be demanded of them. However, this is rarely achieved because certain tasks require very different forces and approaches. And, since the future is uncertain, there is no guarantee that the preparations made will be appropriate for the coming challenges. In addition, wars do not always neatly fit into one category. As Vietnam and Iraq demonstrate, a war can exhibit characteristics from across the spectrum of warfare, or may change character quite rapidly.

In addition to the above, the Prussian general and theorist Carl von Clausewitz identified that war is permeated by 'friction'. Put simply, friction is a term that encompasses the many things that impede performance in the field of strategy. These include bad weather, inadequacies in intelligence, or equipment failure. In Clausewitz's own words friction is 'the only concept that more or less corresponds to the factors that distinguish real war from war on paper' (Clausewitz, 1993: 138). Certain aspects of friction emanate from interaction with the enemy. Edward Luttwak incorporates this into his notion of the paradoxical logic of strategy. Whilst we endeavour to fight a war as efficiently as possible, by definition the enemy will attempt to offset our strengths, and if successful will inevitably make our task harder and more complex (Luttwak, 1987). This point is no better illustrated than in the following comment by Confederate General George Pickett when asked why the Confederates lost at Gettysburg: 'I think the Union Army had something to do with it' (DiNardo and Hughes, 1995: 76). Thus, when judging Blair's strategic conduct we must bear in mind that he is not entirely the master of his own destiny. This is true not only in terms of interaction with the enemy, but also with allies.

Taken together, the above challenges make strategy, especially in the context of a modern liberal and democratic state, an inherently difficult activity to control. There are many factors that impede the strategist from achieving his goals. With these thoughts in mind we are better placed to judge Tony Blair's record on strategy.

Kosovo

Before the Kosovo conflict, Tony Blair had already used military force in operation Desert Fox against Iraq in 1998 to degrade its Weapons of Mass Destruction capabilities. This first attempt at strategy was very limited in nature and so will not be discussed in any detail. However, the one thing that both Desert Fox and Kosovo have in common is Bill Clinton. In both instances Blair had to deal with the fact that the major coalition military power was under the control of a cautious President. This factor is particularly evident in Kosovo, to the extent that for much of the conflict Clinton's concerns reduced the strategic options available to NATO. Nonetheless, despite this and other factors yet to be discussed, both NATO, and Blair in particular, came away with a qualified victory: meaning that they achieved their primary objectives.

The caution of the NATO leadership (emanating at least partially from both Blair and Clinton) to a large degree dictated their chosen strategy: a coercive campaign of graduated escalation conducted exclusively from the air. Such a strategy is aimed at breaking the will of the enemy through the infliction of pain, so that they accede to your demands. However it is extremely difficult to accurately judge the level of punishment required to alter the behaviour of the target. The Clinton administration reveals this in its naively optimistic assessment at the beginning of the war that only a few days of bombing would coerce Milosevic to halt the military campaign in Kosovo (Lambeth, 2001; Daalder and O'Hanlon, 2000). In fact, the air campaign lasted 78 days. In addition, a campaign of graduated escalation, which slowly increases the range of targets and intensity of the bombing, merely provides the enemy with time to adjust themselves to the pain inflicted. Nonetheless, despite its inadequacies, a coercive air campaign is a tempting option for leaders who require results at minimum costs. However, NATO's chosen strategy was particularly inappropriate for the objectives sought. Until the Serbian leadership was coerced it could continue the campaign of ethnic cleansing, which was conducted by small units of infantry. Such units are difficult to target from the air. This point is illustrated by the fact that at least 10,000 Kosovo Albanians died during the NATO air campaign (Lambeth, 2001: 225).

Not only was an air power coercive campaign inappropriate for the policy objectives sought, it was severely undermined by the publicly announced decision to rule out the use of ground troops. Both Blair and Clinton made public statements outlining this aspect of their strategy. This flies in the face of the advice proffered by the strategic theorist J.C. Wylie, who warns that the danger of having only one plan is that the enemy may discern and counter it (Wylie, 1967: 71). During the Kosovo conflict, NATO not only had just one plan initially, they also saved the enemy the trouble of identifying it. Such an approach causes some rather obvious problems in the interactive environment of strategy. In Kosovo, this meant that the air campaign against Serbian forces in the province was subject to effective countermeasures. A lack of NATO ground forces meant that Serbian paramilitary units could remain dispersed, which in turn made them less vulnerable to air power. In addition, the inherent caution of the NATO leadership imposed further restrictions on the air campaign. Fear of pilot losses compelled NATO aircraft to fly above 15,000 feet in order to avoid Serbian air defences. This inevitably compromised the ability of the pilots to strike their ground targets. This problem was compounded by a severe sensitivity to civilian casualties, which compelled pilots to ensure visual identification of targets before bombing. Taken together, this meant that many sorties ended without weapons release, and also made the bombing campaign much more vulnerable to countermeasures. During the campaign the Serbs made effective use of decoys and deception, which resulted in NATO aircraft either failing to hit their targets or striking dummy targets instead. Again, the absence of ground troops exacerbated these problems. With ground troops in place, many of the Serbian deception techniques would have been unusable or discovered. Indeed, NATO bombing sorties became much more effective towards the end of the war, when Kosovo Liberation Army units began to engage Serbian forces in greater numbers. This forced the Serbs to concentrate their numbers and operate more in the open.

Kosovo was not a particularly encouraging first outing for NATO as a military alliance. Aside from the caution of the main NATO leaders, the effectiveness of the military campaign was also compromised by the unwieldy alliance structure. Decisions were made on the basis of a unanimity principle, and thus the campaign moved at a slow pace. It has been concluded that NATO never actually formulated a strategy as such. Instead, due to the difficulties of achieving a strategic consensus within the alliance, the military campaign focused on targeting issues, and not on the bigger questions of strategy (Lambeth, 2001). The experience of operating within NATO in Kosovo had a direct impact on how the United States operated in Afghanistan in 2001, when it initially ignored the alliance during the early stages of the campaign.

Despite the many difficulties highlighted above, NATO did achieve its primary objectives. The ethnic cleansing was eventually halted, Serb forces withdrew, and the Kosovo Albanian refugees returned to their homes. Some of the credit for this positive outcome must go to Tony Blair. After his initial reluctance to commit ground forces, Blair eventually worked hard to persuade President Clinton that such an option must be seriously, and publicly contemplated (Kampfner, 2004: 57). In this respect he seems to have shown a more developed grasp of strategy, and its central component of interaction with the enemy. The increasing discussion of deploying ground troops seems to have had an impact on Milosevic. Other factors that played a part in the Serbian decision were the withdrawal of Russian support for its traditional ally, the increasing shift in the NATO air campaign to economic and infrastructure targets in Serbia itself, and the will of NATO not to relent (Lambeth, 2001). In the end, NATO's campaign did coerce the Serbians. However, again to Blair's credit, it took the presence of NATO ground forces to provide security and reassure the Albanians that they could return to Kosovo.

The war on terror

Whereas some in 'Old Europe' seem to underestimate the significance of the terrorist attacks of 9/11, this is not the case with Tony Blair. From the outset, Blair seems to have appreciated the level of threat posed by Al Qaeda and its associates. Whilst it is certainly possible that the threat from Islamist terrorism can be overplayed, it does represent the most clear and present danger to British national security. When we consider the term 'war on terror', strictly speaking, it is a misnomer. Terrorism is simply a form of war, and therefore cannot have war waged against it. Thus, despite the grand pronouncements, it is safe to assume that the war on terror is rather a war against Islamist terrorist organizations; with Al Qaeda as the most prominent. Although seemingly amorphous, Al Qaeda does have a hierarchical structure and can be said to exist as an organization with common ideals and purpose. Its main functions appear to be to act as an organizing body, supporting, funding and training individuals and groups around the world who share its core beliefs (Gunaratna, 2002).

Al Qaeda has a hierarchy and assets, both of which can be targeted. In this sense, by attacking its training facilities and killing or capturing its key commanders the threat posed by Al Qaeda can be reduced. However, it is unlikely that the threat from Islamist terrorism will ever by eradicated. This is not necessarily a problem from a strategic perspective. Strategy is about achieving policy objectives, not necessarily defeating an opponent in an absolute physical sense. Thus, announcements calling for the eradication of terrorism can be regarded as unrealistic. In reality, policy objectives may be met when terrorism against western targets is minimized to acceptable levels of violence. How this is strictly defined is open to debate.

Before assessing the efficacy of Tony Blair's policy on the war on terror, it is useful to discuss how terrorism should be confronted from a strategic perspective. This will give us analytical criteria by which to judge performance. Much thinking on counterterrorism is curiously light on discussion of strategy. Instead, emphasis is placed upon eradicating the social and political causes of terrorism, intelligence, and dealing with it as a law and order issue (Home Office, 2006). Whilst important, these aspects should not alone define our response to terrorism. Terrorism must be seen as a strategic problem. As noted, terrorism is a form of war, which simply means that a terrorist actor is using military force to achieve some policy objective. In this respect the label of war on terror is useful for its inclusion of the term 'war'. Harry G. Summers is correct in his criticism of US policy during Vietnam. By not declaring the operations in Vietnam as a war, the US restricted its options and, perhaps more importantly, did not adequately prepare the public for the conflict to come and the associated sacrifices (Summers, 1982). Thus, since terrorism uses physical force, this element of a terrorist strategy must be countered as much as their social and political support base must be undermined. What we must dispense with is the notion that killing terrorists merely increases recruitment to their cause. Colin Gray is correct to note that would-be foot soldiers of terrorist organizations can be deterred if they think they will die for little gain (Gray, 2003: 34). Indeed, evidence from Vietnam indicates that military defeats for the communist guerrillas seriously depressed recruiting and led to an increase of defections to the South Vietnamese government forces (Record and Terrill, 2004: 24). Inflicting a sense of military defeat on terrorist organizations can contribute to this effect. Another vital ingredient of counterterrorism is intelligence. Since terrorists employ irregular tactics and formations, intelligence operations are very much at the heart of attempts to counter their activities. Finally, it must be recognized that counterterrorism campaigns are usually very protracted in their nature.

On the basis of the above analysis, Tony Blair's handling of the war on terror can be mostly praised from a strategic perspective. Blair has worked to promote a lasting solution to the Israel–Palestine question, and thus sought to remove one of the prime motivations for Islamist terrorist recruitment (Kampfner, 2004). On the domestic front, Blair appears to realize that the powers of the police and intelligence agencies required upgrading to deal with the new level of threat. This new threat emanates from the tactic of the suicide bomber and the nature of the targets. The IRA could certainly be ruthless, but in many respects they conducted a limited campaign in terms of targets and operations. Their tactics were well understood and their targets usually well chosen, often with the desire to minimize civilian casualties. In addition, because their operatives sought to survive any attack, they could be more easily deterred from a particular operation through the fear of death or capture. Suicide bombers operate in a more permissive tactical manner. Thus, prevention of an attack is more challenging and time urgent. Prevention requires accurate and timely intelligence, and the will to act. However, as the London bombings of 7/7 revealed, the intelligence services are overstretched; they simply have too many potential targets to track. Thus, a controversial element of the government's anti-terrorism approach has been detention without trial. This may be necessary to either extract intelligence from suspected terrorists, or to physically prevent them from engaging in acts of terror. Such an approach has been controversial in relation to civil liberties and human rights. Whilst such concerns may need airing, the nature of this particular war may require us as a society to be flexible on these issues. Tony Blair seems to understand this.

The first major military action following 9/11 was the invasion of Afghanistan. Blair revealed an eagerness to fight alongside the Americans in Afghanistan, to show solidarity and to help strengthen the special relationship (Kampfner, 2004: 129). Thanks to its allies in the Taliban government, Al Qaeda had established extensive terrorist training camps in the country. It has been estimated that tens of thousands of terrorist recruits had visited the camps. These included those who conducted the 9/11 attacks (9/11 Commission, 2004: 67 and 155). Thus, Afghanistan was as close to a home base as Al Qaeda would ever have. In this sense, the invasion had a number of beneficial outcomes. It disrupted Al Qaeda's training activities in the country, and thereby disrupted current and future operations. In addition, key individuals within the organization have been killed or captured. In general terms, the invasion depleted the enemy's capabilities. Also, enemy combatants captured in theatre could provide intelligence vital to combating terrorism. As an added bonus, the Taliban has been removed from power, and the social and political rebuilding of Afghanistan has begun.

It can be concluded that the strategic rationale for invading Afghanistan was sound. However, although the campaign was generally successful, it did suffer from some deficiencies. Once again, the United States was initially reluctant to deploy large numbers of ground forces. Instead, the so-called 'Afghan Model' was adopted. Under this arrangement coalition air power supported Northern Alliance forces on the ground. This support was facilitated by the insertion of coalition special forces and intelligence service personnel. There was some logic to this approach. In many respects it played to the strengths of the different participants.

The coalition possessed large amounts of accurate firepower, and the Northern Alliance forces possessed local knowledge of the terrain and had experience of fighting the Taliban and Al Qaeda. However, the problem with this arrangement became apparent during the battle at Tora Bora. Significant elements of the enemy had been isolated in this mountain cave complex, including the prized asset of Osama Bin Laden. However, despite intense fighting, it is believed that Bin Laden and his key lieutenants escaped. It appears that Bin Laden had escaped because the Northern Alliance forces on the ground did not push their attack sufficiently vigorously (Biddle, 2002; Kampfner, 2004: 147). Had the coalition taken more of the burden of the ground offensive, Tora Bora may have produced even more dramatic results. As it was, the enemy still suffered considerable casualties.

Almost six years after the invasion of Afghanistan, Taliban and Al Qaeda forces are still engaged in fighting with British and coalition forces. This fact has led to some sensationalist headlines and comment. For example, the *Mail on Sunday* declared on a front page spread that Afghanistan had become Britain's Vietnam (Nicol, 2006). Despite such ill-informed comment, Afghanistan can be regarded as an ongoing qualified success. As already noted, Al Qaeda's operations and capabilities have been dealt a serious blow. In addition, the Taliban have been removed from power, and Afghanistan has made some progress towards a more tolerant, prosperous and liberal society (Evans, 2006). What Afghanistan teaches us is the requirement for patience in the war on terror. Relatively quick victories, easily identifiable on a map, will not define the long war against Al Qaeda and its affiliates. Indeed, fighting may continue for many years in the country. However, if we regard the war in Afghanistan as the initial phase of the war against Al Qaeda, then the significant reduction in the enemy's capabilities may be regarded as success enough. Tony Blair's main mistake may have been to make ambitious pronounce-ments regarding the future development of the country (Kampfner, 2004: 149). As a conviction politician, he may sometimes ignore the fact that strategy is about prudence and realistic goals. After all, strategy is the art of the possible (Murray and Grimsley, 1994: 22).

Generally speaking, Tony Blair has shown great political courage in relation to Afghanistan. He certainly did not shy away from the operation in the first instance, and despite political pressure at home, has continued to increase British forces and operations when required. Afghanistan is far from a done deal. Nonetheless, in the first real response to 9/11 western forces dealt a serious blow to the main enemy.

Iraq

Despite the ongoing difficulties in Iraq, Tony Blair's support for the invasion may prove prudent in the long run. However, regardless of the validity of his initial decision, and even with the situation in Iraq seemingly as intractable as ever, it would be catastrophic to cut and run; victory (in the sense of achieving the policy objectives) is essential. Iraq has become a key theatre in the war on terror. Undoubtedly, mistakes were made in Iraq before and during the war. Tony Blair's initial mistake was to place too much emphasis on Iraq's Weapons of Mass Destruction (WMD) as the prime motivation for the invasion. Beyond this mistake, the most damaging strategic error was a lack of detailed planning for the post-war environment. This mistake has been intensified by further decisions during the war itself, many of which once again emanate from an overly cautious approach, which itself is a product of western democratic perceptions of war.

It is fair to assume that Saddam Hussein's regime continued to harbour WMD aspirations. Saddam had shown a distinct determination to acquire WMD and a reasonable degree of efficacy at outwitting the United Nations inspection and sanction regimes (Murray and Scales, 2003: 32–8). Thus, although his ambitions could have been contained for some time without military action, only military action and regime change could bring this issue to a conclusion. Nonetheless, in 2003 his WMD programme could not be considered a clear and present danger, and there were bigger concerns that should have been given priority. In addition, despite attempts to link him with Al Qaeda, there is little evidence to suggest that he had any real operational connections with Bin Laden and his associates (9/11 Commission, 2004: 66).

Much has been written on the intelligence aspect of the build-up to the Iraq war. The Butler Report suggests that there was no direct attempt by the Blair government to influence the findings of the intelligence community. Nonetheless, the government dossier on Iraq's WMD (which was produced by the Joint Intelligence Committee), did not contain important caveats concerning the certitude of its assessments. For example, the famous '45 minutes' claim was not incorrect, but its context was neither explained nor understood. Iraq probably did have the ability to deploy WMD within that timeframe, but only of a battlefield variety (Butler Report, 2004: 139). The problem facing Blair at the time was a distinct absence of reliable intelligence on Iraq's WMD programme. As a result, too much credence was given to human sources associated with the Iraqi National Congress, an exiled group who had obvious motivations to support an overthrow of Saddam's regime. We can conclude that Blair's main motivation for war was based on uncertain, questionable intelligence. Perhaps he placed too much credence on this intelligence because of the mistakes made before 9/11. Although there was never any detailed intelligence regarding the 9/11 attacks, both the United States and Britain were aware that something big was being planned. In the event, neither country effectively used the available intelligence to its full potential. As a result, Blair may have overcompensated in the run-up to Iraq. In fact Blair stated: 'I for one do not want it on my conscience that we knew of the threat, saw it coming and did nothing' (Kampfner, 2004: 113, 199).

Aside from his concerns regarding Iraq's WMD programme, there may have been other motivating factors behind Blair's decision to support the invasion. Two likely candidates are his desire to maintain a close transatlantic relationship, and a desire to support the legitimacy of the United Nations. On the issue of WMD Iraq had constantly been guilty of evading the UN. Blair may have seen this as undermining the significance of, what he perceived as, an important international organization. Whatever his main motivations, Blair became party to a long-held plan of some within the Bush administration to invade Iraq (Kampfner, 2004: 25).

Despite the questionable intelligence basis for the invasion, Blair still may have been correct to fight alongside the US. With the current state of the European security and defence posture, the US is still the only power that can realistically defend western security interests against substantial threats (Gray, 2004). This is not to say that the US is equally capable in every situation. However, no other country has anything close to its capabilities in power projection. It is therefore essential that Britain maintains a close strategic alliance with the US. It has been a longstanding aim of enemies of the West to decouple the US from its European allies. Alliances, like marriages, require maintenance and sacrifices. At times you may have to fight unwanted wars in order to ensure that your ally will be there when you really need them. Iraq was not an essential war for Britain. However, we may be glad of US capabilities in a future that could be characterized by more aggressive and powerful states such as Iran or China. Geopolitics is a long game.

Although Blair's decision to fight alongside the US may have been prudent, the outcome of the war could potentially have been substantially better had different decisions been taken. Much attention has been given to the inadequate planning for the post-war environment. Whilst more preparation in the political and social aspects of control may have aided the stability of post-Saddam Iraq, it was in the realms of power that the real mistakes were made. Put simply, neither the US nor Britain understood how to exert power, nor its significance. The Iraqi population had shown enormous respect for Saddam's brutal form of power. In this respect Ralph Peters is correct when he laments the lack of power displayed by the coalition in the early stages of the post-war period: 'in the weeks immediately following the toppling of the regime, crucial portions of the population never really felt America's power' (Peters, 2004: 31). This is not to suggest that coalition forces needed to replicate Saddam's methods. Rather, it is to note that authority must be established through the presence of adequate forces, and the willingness to punish those who transgress against the ruling authority. To coin a phrase, the people do not have to like you, as long as they respect you. It is in this respect that Tony Blair's strategic weaknesses are most evident. Blair's idealism may lead him to believe that with positive engagement people can be persuaded to take the correct path (Kampfner, 2004: 183). Blair perhaps underestimated the role coercion plays in international politics and strategy.

Another folly of the coalition was to quickly hand power back to the Iraqis. This decision may have been based on some misconceived commitment to concepts of freedom and legitimacy for the invasion. However, in a country as potentially divisive as Iraq, a political system should have been designed and enforced by the coalition. Although this may fly in the face of notions of self-determination, its value is evident in the success of Germany and Japan after the Second World War. Instead, the coalition is now suffering a similar fate as in South Vietnam, where the US had to deal with a complex political environment and an unreliable government.

In Blair's defence, in Iraq he was very much at the mercy of the US and its approach. The failure of the US to deploy sufficient forces to ensure control was beyond the control of Blair, and yet he had to deal with the results. It also seems that Blair was himself surprised at the lack of planning by the US for post-war reconstruction (Kampfner, 2004). Also, Tony Blair was handicapped by the fact that most modern defence establishments and strategic commentators work from a flawed understanding of counterinsurgency (COIN) theory. In addition, western ethical and legal codes restrict his freedom as a strategist. Modern doctrine on COIN is largely based upon seminal works such as Thompson's *Defeating Communist Insurgency*, which was constructed from his experiences and observations in Malaya and Vietnam (Thompson, 1966). In particular, modern COIN practitioners place great emphasis on issues of popularity and legitimacy in the eyes of the local inhabitants. Whilst there is some value in these aspects of COIN doctrine, the so-called 'hearts and minds' approach, it is important not to neglect the less palatable aspects of strategy. For example, the defeat of the insurgency in Malaya took 12 years, and involved some fairly draconian methods such as curfews, the mass forced relocation of 400,000 people, detention without trial, and execution for possession of firearms or explosives. In addition, the insurgents were subjected to a protracted war of attrition, during which their numbers were slowly eroded, at the cost of 500 British deaths. In summary, rather than being a competition in popularity, COIN is rather a competition in authority. Steven Metz is compelling when he claims that 'it is less an assessment of a preferred future that drives insurgents or insurgent supporters than an assessment of who will prevail – the insurgents or the regime' (Millen and Metz, 2004: 5). Blair, like many in the modern political establishment, does not have a full grasp of the role played by power in international politics. Even if he did, it is not clear that he would have the will or freedom to exercise it effectively.

To Blair's credit he has stood his ground quite well, despite the growing levels of criticism over his Iraq policy. This is crucial because war is a battle of wills. The insurgents and their Iranian allies are perfectly aware of this. As in Vietnam, the insurgents cannot prevail whilst coalition forces remain in sufficient numbers. Thus, their main strategic objective is to increase pressure on western decision-makers until they feel compelled to withdraw their troops. On both the war on terror and the insurgency in Iraq, Blair seems to be aware of this essential strategic truth. The main negative geopolitical outcome of Iraq is that it may have distracted the West from more urgent security issues, such as Iran and the wider war on terror. It may have dulled our appetite for aggressive military adventures at a time when countries such as Iran need a robust response.

In summary, we can conclude that Iraq is a war that did not need fighting; certainly not in 2003. However, from the perspective of maintaining our alliance with the US, Blair was, on balance, correct to commit British troops alongside American forces. Perhaps the greatest error was, and is, the manner in which the war has been fought and the mistakes made in relation to the political organization and control of post-Saddam Iraq. In this respect the West appears a reluctant conqueror. This is rather like only half committing yourself to a tackle in football or rugby; you are more likely to get injured as a result. Let us hope that we are not so badly injured in Iraq that we have to miss the next match.

Trident replacement

The decision to replace Britain's Trident nuclear fleet was controversial, but from a strategic perspective should be welcomed, albeit with some reservations. After a period of consultation the Blair government decided to replace the Trident submarine fleet at a cost of £15–20 billion. In addition, Britain will work with the US to extend the life of the missiles themselves until 2042. The Blair government seems to have chosen a fairly prudent option. However, a more imaginative strategic approach may have produced an even more credible and useful nuclear capability for Britain.

The Trident decision was made on the basis of a balanced assessment of the current and possible future strategic environment. The Defence White Paper correctly identified the uncertain nature of the future, and also noted worrying trends in nuclear proliferation (Ministry of Defence, 2006). The White Paper identified a range of potential threats, from terrorist and rogue state possession of WMD, to the potential re-emergence of a major state-based nuclear threat. Thus, the threat rationale for Trident is well made. The Blair government also showed a reasonably solid grasp of the concept of escalation dominance. Quite correctly, one of the justifications given for Trident is that it largely prevents another actor from escalating conflict to a point, in capability terms, which Britain could not match. Also worthy of praise is the fact that the government explicitly does not discuss the conditions under which Trident would be used. Yet, it does not rule out first use. This is to be welcomed as it suggests that the government may regard Trident as a fairly flexible instrument of strategy; not restricted merely to a second strike capability in the face of a WMD attack on Britain. In support of this, the government also notes that the yields of the warheads can be adjusted, which increases the flexibility of the weapon system. Finally, there is recognition of the advantages for NATO of Britain and France retaining independent nuclear forces. This complicates the calculations of potential enemies by giving the alliance three centres of nuclear decision-making.

Thus, the case for retaining a British nuclear capability is well made on strategic grounds. What about the choice of weapon system? For a country such as Britain Trident is indeed the prudent choice. As the White Paper recognizes, a Submarine Launched Ballistic Missile (SLBM) offers a robust system that has global range, is less vulnerable to pre-emptive strikes, and is less likely to be intercepted in flight. However, there are some concerns with the government's choice and arguments. Firstly, the government has put all of its eggs in one delivery basket. Whilst

Trident is one of the least vulnerable weapon systems, its invulnerability cannot be taken for granted. Since strategy is an activity conducted against intelligent foes, the development of a countermeasure is always possible. Thus, there is strategic sense in diversifying your means of delivery to include land-based ICBMs and air-delivered systems. Britain is the only declared nuclear state to have rejected the triad approach to delivery systems. During the 1990s Britain gave up its land-based missiles, nuclear artillery and the RAF's free-fall nuclear bombs.

The White Paper also declares that Britain has opted for the minimum level of destructive capability required to achieve its nuclear deterrence objectives. This is a curious statement from a strategic perspective, which may actually be intended for domestic political purposes and/or to strengthen the largely defunct non-proliferation regime. Trident, even with the government's 20 per cent reduction in warheads, is an extremely destructive weapon system. Each submarine can carry 16 D5 missiles, with each D5 carrying up to 12 warheads, with each warhead having a yield of up to approximately 100 kilotons. As a point of reference it should be noted that the bomb dropped on Hiroshima had a yield of only 13 kilotons. Therefore, from a technological perspective the notion of minimum destruction looks problematic. The message the government seems to be sending out is that Britain is a responsible, perhaps even reluctant, member of the nuclear club. This latter point creates perhaps the most worrying aspects of the government's nuclear policy. By stressing a minimum destructive capability, the government may undermine the credibility of its deterrent threat. A reluctant nuclear power may not go to brink when needed.

Alternatively, one could regard the emphasis on a minimum destructive capability as actually enhancing deterrence, as the weapons appear more useable. By reducing the power of your weapon systems you may be able to avoid the dilemma of surrender or armageddon. However, the 'more useable' argument would have more credence if the government had opted for a more flexible range of nuclear capabilities. Such an option could have included warheads with much smaller yields and more varied delivery methods. The ultimate manifestation of this is the current discussion in the US of so-called 'mini-nukes'. Such weapons have more varied use, including, for example, destroying a time-urgent terrorist biological weapons target. In such a case nuclear weapons give you a much higher probability of an assured kill. Alternatively, so-called battlefield nuclear weapons represent a more credible response to the small-scale use of WMD against British forces on overseas operations. In this respect, smaller nuclear weapons could be used *in extremis* in support of British forces in action. Unfortunately, in a response to the House of Commons Defence Committee, the Defence Secretary Des Browne appeared to rule out such a role for Britain's nuclear weapons when he declared that they 'are not intended, nor are they designed, for military use during conflict' (HCDC, 2007: 32). This statement not only reveals that the government may in fact perceive deterrence as the only role for its nuclear forces, but also reveals a distinct misunderstanding of strategy. Does the Defence Secretary not regard nuclear weapons as a military instrument?

Finally, what is also missing from the government's White Paper is any recognition of a warfighting doctrine for Britain's nuclear weapons. A warfighting stance adds credibility to deterrence by accepting that these weapons may have to be used in anger, and thus doctrine is produced to fight and win a war involving nuclear weapons. It would be unreasonable to expect detailed discussion of such a doctrine in a White Paper, but some recognition would diminish the sense of a reluctant, self-deterring nuclear power evident in Blair's nuclear strategy. In fact, beyond the basic notion of deterrence, there is little evidence of a carefully constructed nuclear strategy at all.

Conclusion

Like any leader using military force to achieve policy objectives, Tony Blair had to deal with the many complexities of strategy. In particular, he had to balance the requirement to operate in harmony with the nature of war with the restrictions of domestic politics and prevailing western norms and values. Did he succeed as a strategist in this respect? His record is somewhat mixed. There have been some notable successes, as in Sierra Leone, Kosovo (eventually), and Afghanistan. However, although he showed courage in Iraq, the war was badly handled from a strategic perspective. In defence of Blair, many of the key mistakes were made by the Bush administration, and therefore somewhat beyond his control. On Trident replacement, Blair took the easier, if prudent option. Nonetheless, under Blair Britain appeared as a reluctant nuclear power without any clear nuclear strategy.

In order to deal with the complexities of strategy Clausewitz notes that amongst the key characteristics of a great strategist are moral courage and determination. Despite moments of weakness, as in the early days of Kosovo, at times Blair showed substantial courage. For example, in Sierra Leone limited British forces engaged in a number of high risk operations to help stabilize the former colony. Blair also demonstrated courage by maintaining his position in the war on terror and Iraq, despite significant levels of criticism. This courage may be partially based on Blair's reasonably astute understanding of the nature of the threat environment facing Britain. Blair also seems to have learned, and understood, one of the key truths of strategy: that war is a battle of wills. Above all else, what is clear is that a guiding principle for Blair appears to have been the maintenance of the transatlantic relationship. This led him into Iraq, but will hopefully pay dividends in the future should western security be severely challenged again.

12
Conclusion

Simon Lee

A clear sense of national purpose?

In a speech to mark the commemoration of the fiftieth anniversary of the Labour Party's historic 1945 general election landslide, Tony Blair claimed the task confronting his party in July 1995 was 'nothing less than national renewal'. This in turn would require 'economic renewal, social renewal and political renewal' (Blair, 1995, cited in Blair, 1996d: 20). For New Labour to once more become '"the people's party"' capable of leading 'a governing consensus', it would have to learn the three key lessons of 1945. These were the need for 'a clear sense of national purpose'; the need 'to win the battle of ideas'; and the need 'to mobilise all people of progressive mind around a party always outward-looking, seeking new supporters and members' (ibid.: 13).

When Tony Blair stood down as Prime Minister some dozen years later, New Labour had delivered an unprecedented three consecutive general election victories. It had also delivered an unprecedented decade of unbroken economic growth. Both British politics and British society had changed dramatically during the ten years of New Labour. However, there was little evidence of a clear sense of national purpose, or of the mobilization of all those of a progressive mind. Most damagingly, there was little evidence that New Labour had won the battle of ideas. If anything, British politics appears stranded on the ideological common ground first identified and occupied by the Conservative Party, under the leadership of Margaret Thatcher and the inspiration of Sir Keith Joseph in the late 1970s (Lee, 2007: 220–5). Therefore, this chapter concludes our study of ten years of New Labour by exploring the legacy of the

Blair governments, the inheritance of the Brown government, and the prospects for the Labour Party to deliver an historic fourth consecutive general election victory.

One of the consistent themes of many of the major speeches delivered by Tony Blair and Gordon Brown during the decade of New Labour government was their desire to forge a partnership between the public and the private sectors for the purpose of national renewal. Thus, for example, when Brown identified the modernization of the British economy as the new mission for the Treasury, he spoke of the need for 'a new national purpose based on an end to short-termism and an understanding of the need to take a long term view, government, industry and the financial community' (Brown, 1999). Unfortunately, Brown's final Budget report as Chancellor of the Exchequer documented how industry had failed to rally to his patriotic call for investment for the long term.

Despite a decade of low interest rates (by the UK's historic standards), business investment contributed only 0.25 per cent to GDP growth between 2000 and 2005, compared to 0.75 per cent from government investment, and 2 per cent from private consumption (HM Treasury, 2007a: 254). Indeed, total business investment had actually fallen by 4.7 per cent during 2006, having risen by only 3.25 per cent during 2006 (Office for National Statistics, 2007h: 4). Rather than investing for the long term at home, UK investors have continued to prefer overseas investment or speculative trading. By the end of the third quarter of 2006, UK companies' stock of investment abroad, at £760 billion, was a third larger than the £566 billion invested by foreign companies in the UK, contributing net earnings equivalent to 3.5 per cent of GDP (HM Treasury, 2007a: 262). The City of London's financial markets have continued to develop innovative and highly profitable ways of trading all forms of financial products and commodities, frequently on the most short-term basis. Those highly competitive markets have rarely justified Brown's portrayal of them as a 'financial community'.

Far from reflecting a sense of national purpose, the economic legacy of ten years of New Labour has reflected the dependence of the Brown Boom, and its underlying British model of political economy (see Chapter 2), upon economic growth led by rising public expenditure (financed by higher taxes and borrowing), and private consumption and house price inflation, financed by rising private debt and imprudence. By the end of November 2007, total UK personal debt had reached £1,400 billion, a 9.5 per cent increase on the previous 12 months, which included £223 billion of consumer credit, or £4,700 per average UK adult. This also meant that average household debt in the UK had risen to £8,956 (excluding mortgages), but £56,324 when mortgages are included. Consequently, during the past 12 months, a record £94.5 billion in interest charges was incurred, equivalent to an average annual household debt repayment of £3,794 (Credit Action, 2007: 1).

New Labour's British model of political economy was founded upon the fatal conceit that, by forging a public–private partnership which harnessed the vast financial resources, organizational flair and capacity for innovation of dynamic corporations and successful entrepreneurs, the Blair governments' policies would be able 'not only to support but positively enhance markets'. However, New Labour has not been able to deliver its claim that 'markets are a powerful means of advancing the public interest' (Balls, Grice and O'Donnell, 2004: 18). The Northern Rock crisis, and the Brown government's provision of guarantees for retail deposits and unsecured obligations in the wholesale money market, has demonstrated that the private and public interest do not always coincide, and that it is not possible for the taxpayer to transfer the responsibility for the consequences of irresponsible risk-taking onto the shoulder of private shareholders.

Towards the end of Brown's tenure as Chancellor, both he and Ed Balls, in the latter's capacity as Economic Secretary to the Treasury, championed both the City of London as an exemplar of the opportunities for the UK to benefit from globalization, and the City's new risk-based regulatory structure as an exemplar of best practice (Brown, 2007a; Balls, 2007). Six months later, the reality of New Labour's attempts to harness the private sector in a partnership to advance the national purpose has been laid bare. Private sector interests have taken risks in the mortgage market, but the taxpayer has been left to rescue the lamest of sub-prime lame ducks. Loans and guarantees have been extended on a scale never witnessed in the bailout of Rolls-Royce and British Leyland during the 1970s, and British Steel and BL during the 1980s. A leaked memorandum from the chief global economist at Goldman Sachs, one of the City's leading investment banks and a key adviser to the Treasury over the disposal of Northern Rock, stated that 'the "Northern Rock" factor has badly dented the UK's reputation for being the world's pre-eminent financial centre' (Porter and Winnett, 2008). When added to the £25 billion of borrowing from the Bank of England by Northern Rock, the guarantees given to lenders and investors have extended the UK taxpayers' exposure to around £55 billion or £1,825 per taxpayer (*Daily Telegraph*, 2007). Markets, after all, may not be a powerful means of advancing the public interest.

For a decade, New Labour maintained a clear opinion poll lead over the Conservative Party in relation to questions of economic competence.

There is mounting evidence that the Northern Rock crisis may have dented further a reputation for competence that was on the wane before Brown's departure from the Treasury. In December 2006, when he delivered his final Pre-Budget Report, public opinion had been equally divided over Brown in the Ipsos MORI satisfaction index between 42 per cent who were satisfied with the Chancellor's performance and 42 per cent who were dissatisfied. By April 2007, public opinion had deteriorated into an overall 13 per cent net dissatisfaction, with only 32 per cent satisfied and 45 per cent dissatisfied. The overall public Economic Optimism Index (EOI), which had been prominently positive during New Labour's early months in office (and as high as plus 19 per cent in June 1997), turned negative in February 2000, and never again returned to net optimism. Indeed, by the time of Brown's promotion to the role of Prime Minister, the EOI was registering a minus 20 per cent rating, and had soared to a near record minus 39 per cent by November 2007, as the Northern Rock crisis deepened (Ipsos MORI, 2007).

New Labour's reputation for economic competence has been further undermined in relation to Northern Rock, by the revelation from the Governor of the Bank of England that the Bank and the Treasury had come to 'the very clear understanding that we had no adequate tools for dealing with a failing bank', at a meeting in 'late 2006' (Treasury Committee, 2007: Q1632). This meeting had been attended by Ed Balls, but nothing had been done to remedy the deficiency before the onset of the Northern Rock crisis nine months later. The taxpayers' £55 billion of loans and guarantees to Northern Rock investors and creditors has also meant that, if the bank has to be fully nationalized by the Brown government, or partially nationalized through the conversion of loan facilities into bonds, the government's rule that national debt will not exceed 40 per cent of GDP is liable to be broken.

At the end of November 2007, public sector net debt had risen to £519.4 billion (equivalent to 36.7 per cent of GDP), up from £487.6 billion (or 36.4 per cent) a year earlier (Office for National Statistics, 2007i: 4). The addition of up to £55 billion of Northern Rock debt, albeit possibly only on a short-term basis, would push the national debt beyond 40 per cent. Northern Rock has become a political symbol and an economic metaphor for the wider legacy of private debt and imprudence that had built up during the later years of the Brown Boom. Most damagingly for New Labour's tarnished legacy of economic competence, for the first time in a decade the Conservative Party has begun to enjoy a consistent lead in opinion surveys. For example, in an end-of-year YouGov survey for *The Sunday Times*, 31 per cent of respondents indicated they most trusted

David Cameron and George Osborne to raise their and their family's living standards, compared to only 26 per cent who most trusted Gordon Brown and Alistair Darling (YouGov, 2007). Moreover, in a subsequent YouGov survey, 54 per cent of respondents were either quite worried or very worried that the global credit crunch would make them poorer, while 54 per cent admitted that their bills had risen faster than their income during 2007 (YouGov, 2008). Following the worst December retail sales for 13 years, the worst outlook for employment for ten years, and with the gloomiest prospects for property prices since November 1992, Gordon Brown warned the British people that 2008 would bring 'global financial turbulence' (Watt, 2007). In itself, this warning was the most telling evidence that, following a decade of continuous economic growth, New Labour's British model of political economy had not succeeded either in its ambition to lock in macroeconomic stability and fiscal prudence, or to rally a public–private partnership to the cause of national renewal.

Triumphant in the battle of ideas?

After a decade in office, and despite its three consecutive general election victories, New Labour can be no more certain that it has won the battle of ideas in British politics. When he originally set out his vision of the Third Way, Tony Blair portrayed his vision as a modernized social democracy that would reconcile and unite 'the two great streams of left-of-centre thought – democratic socialism and liberalism – whose divorce this century did so much to weaken progressive politics across the West' (Blair, 1998d: 1). In practice, rather than reconciling liberalism with democratic socialism, the latter has been abandoned. Just as Thatcherism's Second Way of British modernization abandoned One Nation Toryism, in order to move British politics from the middle ground of the post-war social democratic First Way of British modernization to the common ground of market liberalism and an asset-owning popular capitalism, so too has New Labour abandoned Old Labour's commitments to nationalization and the redistribution of income and wealth in order to occupy and contest the political common ground (Lee, 2007: 43–65).

The great strength of Blair's Third Way vision for New Labour was that it delivered electoral success. The great weakness of this vision was that it required the Labour Party to occupy ideological territory defined by its political opponents. Where Old Labour had campaigned traditionally on behalf of working people to identify the economic and social inequalities arising from capitalism, New Labour's occupation of the common ground has seen it embrace and subsequently advocate the moral and material benefits of the market order. The importance of this seismic shift in British politics over two political generations has been demonstrated by the positions adopted by Blair's successor as Prime Minister and his principal rivals.

Gordon Brown has recognized that the key ideological battle before the next general election will be to convince the electorate that he, rather than David Cameron or Nick Clegg, is the most authentic voice of liberalism. Such has been Brown's conversion to liberalism that, during the decade of New Labour government, he never once made a major speech on democratic socialism or that tradition of ideas within the history of the Labour Party (Lee, 2007). On the contrary, Brown has used major set-piece speeches, such as the inaugural Donald Dewar Memorial Lecture, to identify himself with the liberalism of Adam Smith (Brown, 2006d). On other occasions, Brown has acknowledged his intellectual debt to thinkers such as Jonathan Sachs and James Q. Wilson – the latter a major inspiration for neo-conservatism (Brown, 2004c). The measures undertaken by Brown and the Treasury to engineer 'a private sector solution' (HM Treasury, 2008) to a financial market failure, and thereby to avoid a full nationalization of Northern Rock, have demonstrated Brown's determination to distance his government from the Labour Party's democratic socialist heritage once and for all.

For his part, David Cameron has claimed that New Labour's ideological and policy shifts under Tony Blair have meant that the key challenge confronting the Conservative Party under Cameron's leadership is to come to terms with its victory in the battle of ideas. Indeed, the Conservative Party's previous problems 'arose from the triumph of our ideas', and the party's failure to recognize that it was the natural successor to Tony Blair and New Labour. For Cameron, 'Social justice and economic efficiency' are the common ground of British politics (Cameron, 2006d). From his perspective, the task for the Conservative Party is 'to deliver the radical reform that Labour are temperamentally and politically incapable of' (Cameron, 2005a). Consequently, the key ideological and political contest, in the marginal constituencies of Middle England where the next general election will be decided, will be between Gordon Brown's sympathetic liberalism, on the one hand, and David Cameron's liberal conservatism, on the other.

The degree of ideological and policy convergence between the two party leaders is evident on a range of domestic and foreign policies. For example, on economic policy, the 2007 Comprehensive Spending Review has confirmed that New Labour is committed to the same principle of 'sharing the proceeds of economic growth between lower taxed and well-funded public services' (Osborne, 2007) as Cameron's Conservatives. On public services reform in England, Cameron shares the same commitment to further market-based reform (Cameron, 2005a) as Brown's own agenda for the personalization of services through 'greater choice, greater competition, greater contestability ... [and] a coming together with the third sector and social enterprise' (Brown, 2007b). On foreign policy, both Brown and Cameron are committed to a foreign policy, rooted in the national interest, which accords primacy to the transatlantic 'special relationship' over that with the European Union. Indeed, the deep Euro-scepticism shared by both party leaders, and their desire to turn the EU outwards to face the competitive challenge posed by the United States, China and India, has been reflected in the similarity of Brown's vision of a 'Global Europe' (Brown, 2005c) and Cameron's vision of a '3G Europe' (Cameron, 2007b). Because of this degree of convergence, the next general election is likely to become a question of which leader and political party is deemed by the electorate to be the most competent to deliver, especially on the economy, law and order, and public services. At that juncture, the fact that New Labour will have been in office for three terms will be both its greatest asset, given the mixture of inexperienced youth and failed former Conservative Party leaders in the shadow cabinet, and its greatest weakness. As in 1979 and 1997, the electorate might simply decide that it is time for a change.

The progressive dilemma resolved?

When New Labour campaigned in the spring of 1997, Tony Blair promised 'a new politics' in which New Labour would be 'the political arm of none other than the British people as a whole' (Labour Party, 1997: 2). New Labour's mission in politics would be 'to rebuild this bond of trust between government and the people' (ibid.: 4). As part of its contract with the British people, New Labour would 'clean up politics, decentralize political power throughout the United Kingdom and put the funding of political parties on a proper and accountable basis' (ibid.: 5). This promise to clean up politics included, amongst other measures, commitments to a staged process of reform 'to make the House of Lords more democratic and representative', and 'a referendum on the voting system for the House of Commons' (ibid.: 32–3). Tony Blair set out with the ambition for his political party 'to mobilise all people of a progressive mind' (Blair, 1995, cited in Blair, 1996d: 13), and for it to attract new and additional members. However, New Labour's failure to restore trust to British politics, by not delivering on its manifesto commitments to clean up politics, has prevented it from mobilizing 'all people of progressive mind' and thereby resolving the progressive dilemma in British politics (Marquand, 1991).

The final months of Tony Blair's tenure as Prime Minister were discoloured by the furore surrounding the 'cash-for-honours' scandal. Indeed, Blair's premature departure from office, rather than honouring his pledge to serve a full third term as Prime Minister, was accelerated by the political humiliation arising not only from his twice being interviewed by police at Number 10 over the 'cash-for-honours' allegations, but also from the arrest and re-arrest of Lord Levy, the Labour Party's chief fundraiser, the arrest of Ruth Turner, Downing Street's Director of Government Relations, and the questioning of Jack McConnell, Scotland's First Minister and John McTernan, Downing Street's Director of Political Operations. Despite the decision of the Crown Prosecution Service not to charge anyone, Gordon Brown entered Number 10 having reiterated New Labour's promise of 'a new kind of politics in this country', with 'a new style of government in the future' (Brown, 2007c). However, within the first six months of the Brown government, the Labour Party had been rocked by sleaze surrounding undeclared and illegal donations to the party by businessman David Abrahams, and then police investigations into a donation to Wendy Alexander, the leader of the Scottish Labour Party, by Paul Green, a Jersey-based businessman. This demonstrated how difficult it would be for Gordon Brown to deliver his promised 'new politics' in practice. Most embarrassingly of all, Peter Hain, the Secretary of State for Works and Pensions, admitted the failure to declare no fewer than 17 donations, worth £103,155, given in support of his unsuccessful bid for the deputy leadership of the Labour Party (Wintour, 2008).

The reappearance of sleaze so early in the tenure of the Brown government has readily demonstrated the difficulty that Gordon Brown and the Labour Party will face in giving renewed momentum to the New Labour project after a decade in office, especially against the backdrop of a likely recession and rapidly deteriorating public finances. Despite its three consecutive general election victories, the fact remains that New Labour has experienced a significant loss in support and membership. In May 2005, Labour polled 9.6 million votes, 35.2 per cent of the popular vote, and won 355 of the 646 seats contested. However, this was not only the lowest share of the vote ever recorded by a victorious political party at a UK general election, but also equivalent to only 21.6 per cent of the electorate, itself a record low figure for a victorious party (Mellows-Facer, 2006: 8, 13). This meant that New Labour had haemorrhaged no fewer than 4 million votes since May 1997, a fall of 8 per cent in its share of the popular vote (Yonwin, 2005: 10).

One of the greatest failures of New Labour's political reforms has been the failure to renew the Labour Party itself. By the end of December 2006, the party's membership had fallen to 182,370, down from 198,026 in 2005 (Labour Party, 2007: 5), and less than half the membership when Tony Blair had taken office, and sought to double membership under New Labour. If membership was to continue to decline annually by 27,000, the average annual decline since 2000, the Labour Party would have no members at all by 2013 (BBC, 2006). At the same time, the party's finances were equally troubled, registering net liabilities (including pension liabilities) of £24.86 million at the end of 2006 (Labour Party, 2007: 10). The Labour Party's parlous financial position and declining membership has increased its dependency upon large donations from rich individuals and the trade unions. However, as the 'cash-for-honours' and subsequent party funding scandals have shown, there may not be an alternative to a fully elected House of Lords and more generous state funding for political parties, if New Labour is ever to restore its heavily tarnished reputation.

As the authors of this volume have shown, what the ten years of New Labour have demonstrated is how difficult it is for any UK government to deliver lasting political, economic and social renewal, irrespective of the size of its parliamentary majority, the weakness and frequent disarray of the principal Opposition parties, and the state's willingness to engage in legislative hyperactivity and a top-down permanent revolution of public services reform. However, in a sense this should not come as any great surprise to the seasoned student of modern British politics. After all, after 18 years of privatization, market liberalization and deregulation, the Thatcher and Major governments remained thwarted in their project to roll back the frontiers of the state, a fact both openly acknowledged by Margaret Thatcher herself (Thatcher, 1996) and confirmed by the Treasury's statistics on long-term trends in public expenditure (HM Treasury, 2007b: 49).

Thatcherism delivered a British modernization project which kept the Conservative Party in office for a political generation, only for an ungrateful electorate to banish it into political exile for the next. At the next general election, after more than a decade of New Labour, Gordon Brown's most earnest hope must be that the Labour Party does not suffer a similar fate at the hands of an increasingly demanding and fickle electorate.

References and Further Reading

Students new to the subject may want to read the publications marked with an asterisk*.

9/11 Commission (2004) National Commission on Terrorist Attacks upon the United States, *The 9/11 Commission Report* (Washington, DC: Government Printing Office). www.911commission.gov/report/index.htm.

Anderson, P. (1992) *English Questions* (London: Verso).

Annersely, C. and A. Gamble (2004) 'Economic and Welfare Policy' in S. Ludlam and M. Smith (eds), *Governing as New Labour* (Basingstoke: Palgrave Macmillan).

APACS (2007) 'Record number of transactions on plastic cards over festive season', APACS press release, 2 January (London: Association of Payment Clearing Systems).

Astle, J., D. Laws, P. Marshall and A. Murray (eds) (2006) *Britain After Blair: A Liberal Agenda* (London: Profile Books).

Bacon, R. and W. Eltis (1978) *Britain's Economic Problem: Too Few Producers*, 2nd edn (London: Macmillan).

Baker, D. and P. Sherrington (2004) 'Britain and Europe: Europe and/or America?', *Parliamentary Affairs*, 57(2): 347–65.

Balls, E. (1998) 'Open Macroeconomics in an Open Economy', *Scottish Journal of Political Economy*, 45(2): 113–32.

—— (2001) 'Delivering Economic Stability', Inaugural Oxford Business Alumni Lecture, Merchant Taylors' Hall, London, 12 June.

—— (2004) 'Stability, Growth and UK Fiscal Policy', Inaugural Ken Dixon Lecture, Department of Economics, University of York, 23 January.

—— (2006a) 'The City as the Global Finance Centre: Risk and Opportunities', speech at Bloomberg, City of London, 14 June.

—— (2006b) 'Britain's Next Decade', The Fabian Lecture, 1 November.

—— (2007) Speech at the FSA Principles-based Regulation Conference, London, 23 April.

Balls, E. and G. O'Donnell (eds) (2002) *Reforming Britain's Economic and Financial Policy: Towards Greater Economic Stability* (Basingstoke: Palgrave Macmillan).

Balls, E., J. Grice and G. O'Donnell (eds) (2004) *Microeconomic Reform in Britain: Delivering Opportunities for All* (Basingstoke: Palgrave Macmillan).

Barber, B. (2003) 'New deal or no deal', Address to the Unions 21 10th anniversary conference, 8 March (London: Trades Union Congress).

Barber, J. (1972) *The Presidential Character* (Englewood Cliffs, NJ: Prentice-Hall).

Barber, L. (2000) 'Late Nights in Nice', *Financial Times,* 9/10 December.

Barber, M. (2007) *Instruction to Deliver* (London: Politico's).

BBC (2006) 'Labour "facing membership crisis"', *BBC News*, 26 December. Available online: www.news.bbc.co.uk/1/hi/uk_politics/6209399.stm.

—— (2007) '120 Labour MPs "may back EU vote"', *BBC News*, 28 August.

Beach, D. (2005) *The Dynamics of European Integration: Why and When EU Institutions Matter* (Basingstoke: Palgrave Macmillan).

Beckett, F. and D. Hencke (2004) *The Blairs and their Court* (London: Aurum Press).

*Beech, M. (2006) *The Political Philosophy of New Labour* (London and New York: I.B. Tauris).

Beer, S. (1969) *Modern British Politics* (London: Faber and Faber).

Beetham, D. (ed.) (1994) *Defining and Measuring Democracy* (London: Sage).

Bekhradria, B. (2007) *Demand for Higher Education to 2020 and Beyond* (Oxford: Higher Education Policy Institute). www.hepi.ac.uk/pubdetail. asp?ID=234&DOC=reports.

Benedetto, G. and S. Hix (2007) 'The Rejected, the Ejected, and the Dejected: Explaining Government Rebels in the 2001–2005 British House of Commons', *Comparative Political Studies*, 40: 755–81.

Bennister, M. (2007) 'Tony Blair and John Howard: Comparative Predominance and "Institution Stretch" in the UK and Australia', *British Journal of Politics and International Relations*, 7: 2–19.

Biddle, S. (2002) *Afghanistan and the Future of Warfare: Implications for Army and Defense Policy* (Carlisle, PA: Strategic Studies Institute).

Binzer Hobolt, S. and P. Riseborough (2005) 'How to Win the UK Referendum on the European Constitution', *Political Quarterly*, 76(2): 241–52.

Black, D. (1958) *Theory of Committees and Elections* (Cambridge: Cambridge University Press).

Blair, T. (1994) *Change and National Renewal: Leadership Election Statement 1994* (London: Blair Campaign).

—— (1995) Let Us Face the Future: The 1945 Anniversary Lecture (London: Fabian Society).

—— (1996a) *New Britain: My Vision of a Young Country* (London: Fourth Estate).

—— (1996b) John Smith Memorial Lecture, London, February.

—— (1996c) Speech to the Annual Labour Party Conference, Bournemouth, 3 October.

—— (1996d) 'The Radical Coalition', speech at a Fabian Society commemoration of the fiftieth anniversary of the 1945 general election, 5 July 1945, in T. Blair, *New Britain: My Vision of a Young Country* (London: Fourth Estate).

—— (1997) Speech to the Parliamentary Labour Party, Church House, London, 7 May.

—— (1998a) 'A Modern Britain in a Modern Europe', speech to the Annual Friends of Nieuwspoort Dinner, the Ridderzall, the Hague, Netherlands, 20 January (London: Foreign and Commonwealth Office).

—— (1998b) 'The Third Way', speech to the French National Assembly, 24 March (London: Foreign and Commonwealth Office).

—— (1998c) 'The Five Clear Principles of the Centre-Left', speech in Washington DC, 6 February, reported in the *Guardian* 7 February.

—— (1998d) *The Third Way: New Politics for the New Century* (London: The Fabian Society).

—— (2004) 'The Doctrine of the International Community' in I. Stelzer (ed.) *Neo-Conservatism* (London: Atlantic Books).

Blanden, J., Gregg, P. and Machin, S. (2005) 'Intergenerational Mobility in Europe and North America', Centre for Economic Performance, London School of Economics, http://cep.lse.ac.uk/about/news/IntergenerationalMobility.pdf.

Blitz, J. (2004) 'Blair's Short Term Pain For Long Term Gain', *Financial Times*, 19 April.

Bower, T. (2004) *Gordon Brown* (London: HarperCollins).

Bremner, C. and R. Boyers (2004) 'France and Germany Paint Britain as Villain', *The Times*, 21 June.

Brown, George (1971) *In My Way* (Harmondsworth: Penguin).

Brown, Gordon (1995) *Fair is Efficient: A Socialist Agenda for Fairness*, Fabian Pamphlet 563 (London: Fabian Society).

—— (1997a) 'Statement from the Chancellor on the central economic objectives of the Government', HM Treasury press release, 6 May (London: HM Treasury).

—— (1997b) Speech at the Lord Mayor's Dinner, Mansion House, London, 12 June.

—— (1997c) 'Exploiting the British Genius – The Key to Long-Term Economic Success', speech to the Confederation of British Industry, 20 May.

—— (1997d) 'No Quick Fix On Jobs', *Financial Times*, 17 November.

—— (1998) Speech to the Confederation of British Industry President's Dinner, London, 22 April.

—— (1999) 'Modernizing the British Economy: The New Mission for the Treasury', lecture to the Institute for Fiscal Studies, 27 May.

—— (2003) 'A Modern Agenda for Prosperity and Social Reform', speech to Social Market Foundation, Cass Business School, 3 February. www.hm-treasury.gov.uk/newsroom_and_speeches/press/2003/press_12_03.cfm.

—— (2004a) 'Foreword', to E. Balls, J. Grice and G. O'Donnell (eds), *Microeconomic Reform in Britain: Delivering Opportunities for All* (Basingstoke: Palgrave Macmillan).

—— (2004b) *Budget Statement*, 17 March (London: HM Treasury).

—— (2004c) CAFOD Pope Paul IV Memorial Lecture, 8 December.

—— (2005a) *Budget Statement*, 16 March (London: HM Treasury).

—— (2005b) *G8 and other International Issues*. Evidence given to the House of Commons Treasury Select Committee, 19 July 2005, Session 2005–06. HC 399-I (London: The Stationery Office).

—— (2005c) *Global Europe: Full Employment Europe* (London: HM Treasury).

—— (2006a) Pre-Budget Report statement to the House of Commons, 6 December 2006 (London: HM Treasury).

—— (2006b) Speech at the Lord Mayor's Banquet, Mansion House, 21 June.

—— (2006c) *Moving Britain Forward, Selected Speeches, 1997–2006* (London: Bloomsbury).

—— (2006d) First Donald Dewar Memorial Lecture, Glasgow University, 12 October.

—— (2007a) Speech at the Mansion House, City of London, 20 June.

—— (2007b) Presentation at the Public Service Reform Conference: 'Twenty-first century public services – learning from the front line', London, 27 March.

—— (2007c) Transcript of interview with Andrew Marr for the *Sunday AM* programme, 7 January. Available online: www.bbc.co.uk/1/hi/uk_politics/6241819.stm.

Brown, W. (2000) 'Putting Partnership into Practice in Britain', *British Journal of Industrial Relations*, 38(2): 299–316.

Buller, J. (1999) 'Britain and the European Union' in P. Catterall and V. Preston (eds), *Britain in 1997* (London: Institute of Contemporary British History).

Buller, J. and A. Gamble (2008) 'Britain and the Euro: the Political Economy of Retrenchment' in K. Dyson (ed.), *European States and the Euro: The First Decade* (Oxford: Oxford University Press).

Bulpitt, J. (1986) 'The Discipline of the New Democracy: Mrs Thatcher's Domestic Statecraft', *Political Studies*, 34(1): 19–39.

Business Guardian (2007) 'Banking bonanza – how the profits stack up', *Guardian Unlimited*, 15 April. Available online: www.business.guardian.co.uk/page/0,2018075,00.html.

Butler Report (2004) *Review of Intelligence on Weapons of Mass Destruction. Chairman: The Rt Hon The Lord Butler of Brockwell KG GCB CVO*, HC 898 (London: The Stationery Office).

Cairncross, A. (1985) *Years of Recovery* (London: Methuen).

Callaghan, J. (1987) *Time and Chance* (London: Collins).

Cameron, D. (2005a) 'The Need for Public Service Reform', speech in Portsmouth, 9 September.

—— (2005b) 'Ending the Blair Era', speech at St Peter's Church, London, 10 November.

—— (2006a) 'Meeting the Challenge of Climate Change', speech in Oslo, 21 April.

—— (2006b) 'Fighting Global Poverty', speech in Oxford, 29 June.

—— (2006c) 'Tackling Poverty in Britain Today', speech at the Centre for Social Justice, London, 18 January.

—— (2006d) 'Modern Conservatism', speech at Demos, London, 30 January.

—— (2006e) 'Commercial Responsibility before Profits', speech at the Business in the Community Conference, 9 May.

—— (2007a) 'Security for Our Society; Opportunity in Your Life', speech in Tooting, London, 18 June.

—— (2007b) 'The EU – A New Agenda for the 21st Century', speech to the Movement for European Reform Conference, Brussels, 21 March.

*Campbell, A. (2007) *The Blair Years* (London: Hutchinson).

Campbell, J. (1993) *Edward Heath: A Biography* (London: Jonathan Cape).

Campbell, M. (2006) 'Introduction' in J. Astle, D. Laws, P. Marshall and A. Murray (eds), *Britain After Blair: A Liberal Agenda* (London: Profile Books).

—— (2007) 'My Priorities for a Liberal Britain', speech in London, 8 June.

Catterall, P. and V. Preston (eds) (1999) *Britain in 1997* (London: Institute of Contemporary British History).

Centre for Economic Performance (2005) 'Welfare to Work: The evidence of Labour's New Deal policies' (London: Centre for Economic Performance).

Cerny, P. and M. Evans (2004) 'Globalisation and Public Policy Under New Labour', *Policy Studies*, 25(1): 51–65.

Charlwood, A. (2004) 'The New Generation of Trade Union Leaders and Prospects for Union Revitalization', *British Journal of Industrial Relations*, 42(2): 379–97.

Chennells, L. (1997) 'The Windfall Tax', *Fiscal Studies*, 18(3): 279–91.

Chote, R. and C. Emmerson (2005) *The Public Finances: Election Briefing 2005* (London: Institute for Fiscal Studies).

Church, C. and D. Phinnemore (2006) *Understanding the European Constitution: An Introduction to the EU Constitutional Treaty* (London: Routledge).

Citizens Advice (2007) '2007 starts with 15% more debt problems than 2006', Citizens Advice press release, 16 February.

Clausewitz, C. (1976/1993 [1832]) *On War*, trans. M. Howard and P. Paret (Princeton: Princeton University Press).

Coates, A. (2006) 'Culture, the Enemy and the Moral Restraint of War' in R. Sorabji and D. Rodin (eds), *The Ethics of War: Shared Problems in Different Traditions* (Aldershot: Ashgate).

Coats, D. (2005) 'Labour and the Unions: Murder, Divorce or a Trial Separation', *Renewal*, 13(1): 27–35.

Cohen, E. (2002) *Supreme Command: Soldiers, Statesmen, and Leadership in Wartime* (New York: The Free Press).

Conservative Party (1947) *Verbatim Report of the Proceedings of the 68th Annual Conference, October 2–4 1947* (London: National Union of Conservative and Unionist Associations).

—— (1974a) *Firm Action for a Fair Britain* (London: Conservative Central Office).

—— (1974b) *Putting Britain First: A National Policy from the Conservatives* (London: Conservative Central Office).

Constitution Committee, House of Lords (2006) *Fourteenth Report: Meeting with the Lord Chief Justice*, HL Paper 213, Session 2005–06 (London: The Stationery Office).

—— (2007) *Sixth Report: Relations between the executive, the judiciary and Parliament*, HL Paper 151, Session 2006–07 (London: The Stationery Office).

Cook, R. (1999) 'Pre-Helsinki Council debate', speech to the House of Commons, HC Debates, 1 December.

Coopey, R., S. Fielding and N. Tiratsoo (1993) *The Wilson Governments, 1964–1970* (London: Pinter).

Cowley, P. (2001) 'Don't Panic! Putting those select committee votes into perspective', *Renewal*, 9: 102–5.

—— (2002) *Revolts and Rebellions: Parliamentary Voting Under Blair* (London: Politico's).

*—— (2005) *The Rebels: How Blair Misled His Majority* (London: Politico's).

—— (2007) 'Parliament' in A. Seldon (ed.), *Blair's Britain* (Cambridge: Cambridge University Press).

Cowley, P. and M. Stuart (2003) 'In Place of Strife? The PLP in Government, 1997–2001', *Political Studies*, 51: 315–31.

Cowley, P. and P. Norton, with M. Stuart with M. Bailey (1996) *Blair's Bastards* (Hull: Centre for Legislative Studies).

CPPBB (Commission on Public Policy and British Business) (1997) *Promoting Prosperity: A Business Agenda for Britain* (London: Vintage).

Credit Action (2007) *Debt Facts and Figures: Compiled 1 February 2007* (Lincoln: Credit Action).

—— (2008) *Debt Facts and Figures – Compiled 4th January 2008* (London: Credit Action).

Criddle, B. (1984) 'Candidates' in D. Butler and D. Kavanagh, *The British General Election of 1983* (London: Macmillan).

Croft, J. (2002) *Whitehall and the Human Rights Act 1998: The First Year* (London: Constitution Unit UCL).

*Cronin, J. (2004) *New Labour's Pasts* (London: Pearson Longman).

Crosland, A. (1956/1964) *The Future of Socialism* (London: Cape).

Curtice, J. and B. Seyd (2001) 'Is Devolution Strengthening or Weakening the UK?' in A. Park et al. (eds), *British Social Attitudes, The 18th Report* (London: Sage).

Daalder, I. and M. O'Hanlon (2000) *Winning Ugly: NATO's War to Save Kosovo* (Washington, DC: Brookings Institution Press).

Daily Telegraph (2007) 'Northern Rock in numbers', 20 December.

Davies, J. (2005) 'Local Governance and the Dialectics of Hierarchy, Market and Network', *Policy Studies*, 26(3): 311–35.

Deacon, A. (2002) *Perspectives on Welfare* (Buckingham: Open University Press).

Deighton, A. (2001) 'European Union Policy' in A. Seldon (ed.), *The Blair Effect* (London: Little, Brown & Co.).

Department for Constitutional Affairs (2001) *The House of Lords: Completing the Reform*. Cmnd. 5291 (London: The Stationery Office).

—— (2006) *Review of the Implementation of the Human Rights Act* (London: Department for Constitutional Affairs). www.dca.gov.uk/peoples-rights/human-rights/pdf/full_review.pdf.

Department for Work and Pensions (2006) *A New Deal for Welfare: Empowering People to Work*. Cm. 6730 (London: The Stationery Office).

Diamond, J. (2004) 'Local Regeneration Initiatives and Capacity Building: Whose "capacity" and "building" for what?', *Community Development Journal*, 39(2): 177–89.

Diamond, L. (1975) *Royal Commission on the Distribution of Income and Wealth: Report Number 1*, Cmnd. 6171 (London: HM Stationery Office).

Dilnot, A. and P. Johnson (eds) (1997) *Election Briefing 1997* (London: Institute for Fiscal Studies).

DiNardo, R. and D. Hughes (1995) 'Some Cautionary Thoughts on Information Warfare', *Airpower Journal*, 9(4): 1–10.

*Driver, S. and L. Martell (1998) *New Labour: Politics After Thatcherism* (Cambridge: Polity Press).

Duff, A. (2005) *The Struggle for Europe's Constitution* (London: IB Tauris/Federal Trust).

Dunleavy, P. and G. Jones (1993) 'Leaders, Politics and Institutional Change: The Decline of Prime Ministerial Accountability to the House of Commons, 1868–1990', *British Journal of Political Science*, 23: 267–98.

Dyson, K. (ed.) (2008) *European States and the Euro: The First Decade* (Oxford: Oxford University Press).

Elliott, L. (2007) 'Britain has three times the official number of jobless', *Guardian*, 13 June.

Emmerson, C., C. Frayne and G. Tetlow (2007) 'Challenges for Public Spending' in *The Institute for Fiscal Studies Green Budget January 2007* (London: The Institute for Fiscal Studies).

Englefield, D., J. Seaton and I. White (1995) *Facts About the British Prime Ministers* (London: Mansell).

Eurostat (1999) *The European Union Labour Market Survey* (Luxembourg: Statistical Office of the European Communities).

Evans, M. (1995) *Charter 88: A Successful Challenge to the British Political Tradition?* (Aldershot: Ashgate).

—— (1999) 'The Constitution Under New Labour' in G. Taylor (ed.), *The Impact of New Labour* (London: Macmillan), pp. 71–92.

*—— (2003) *Constitution-making and the Labour Party* (Basingstoke: Palgrave Macmillan).

—— (2004) 'Elite Theory' in C. Hay, M. Lister and D. Marsh (eds), *State Theory: Theories and Issues* (Basingstoke: Palgrave Macmillan).

—— (2006) 'Afghanistan? The good news is that things are nothing like as bad as the media say', *Parliamentary Brief* (December): 10–11.

Fairclough, N. (2000) *New Labour, New Language?* (New York: Routledge).

*Fielding, S. (2002) *The Labour Party: Continuity and Change in the Making of New Labour* (Basingstoke: Palgrave Macmillan).

Finlayson, A. (2003) *Making Sense of New Labour* (London: Lawrence and Wishart).

Foley, M. (1993) *The Rise of the British Presidency* (Manchester: Manchester University Press).

—— (2000) *The British Presidency: Tony Blair and the Politics of Public Leadership* (Manchester: Manchester University Press).

—— (2004) 'Presidential Attribution as an Agency of Prime Ministerial Critique in a Parliamentary Democracy: The Case of Tony Blair', *The British Journal of Politics and International Relations*, 6(3): 292–311.

Foot, M. (1973) *Aneurin Bevan* (London: Davis-Poynter).

Foreign and Commonwealth Office (2001) *European Communities No. 1: Treaty of Nice Amending the Treaty on European Union, the Treaties Establishing the European Communities and Certain Related Acts*. Cm. 5090 (London: The Stationery Office).

—— (2004) *White Paper on the Treaty Establishing a Constitution for Europe*. Cm. 6309 (London: Foreign and Commonwealth Office).

Frayne, C. (2007) 'Public Finances', presentation at the Institute for Fiscal Studies' Post-Budget briefing, 23 March.

Friis, L. and A. Murphy (1999) 'The European Union and Central and Eastern Europe: Governance and Boundaries', *Journal of Common Market Studies*, 37(2): 211–32.

Gamble, A. (2002) 'For' in *In or Out? Labour and the Euro*, Fabian Ideas, 601 (London: Fabian Society).

Gennard, J. (2002) 'Employee Relations Public Policy Developments, 1997–2001: A break with the past?', *Employee Relations*, 24(6): 581–94.

George, S. (1990) *An Awkward Partner* (Oxford: Oxford University Press).

Giddens, A. (1998) *The Third Way: The Renewal of Social Democracy* (Cambridge: Polity Press).

—— (2000) *The Third Way and its Critics* (Cambridge: Polity Press).

—— (2002) *Where Now for New Labour?* (Cambridge: Polity Press).

—— (2006) *Europe in a Global Age* (Cambridge: Polity Press).

*—— (2007) *Over to you, Mr Brown: How Labour Can Win Again* (Cambridge: Polity Press).

Giddens, A. and P. Diamond (2005) *The New Egalitarianism* (Cambridge: Polity Press).

Glyn, A. and S. Wood (2001) 'Economic Policy under New Labour: How Social Democratic is the Blair Government?', *Political Quarterly*, 72(1): 50–66.

*Gould, P. (1998) *The Unfinished Revolution* (London: HarperCollins).

Graham, R. and B. Groom (2000) 'A New Dynamic at Nice', *Financial Times*, 12 December.

Grainger, J. (2005) *Tony Blair and the Ideal Type* (London: Imprint Academic).

Gray, C. (1990) *War, Peace, and Victory: Strategy and Statecraft for the Next Century* (New York: Simon & Schuster).

—— (1999) *Modern Strategy* (Oxford: Oxford University Press).

—— (2003) *Maintaining Effective Deterrence* (Carlisle, PA: Strategic Studies Institute).

—— (2004) *The Sherriff: America's Defence of the New World Order* (Lexington: The University Press of Kentucky).

Gunaratna, R. (2002) *Inside Al Qaeda: Global Network of Terror* (London: Hurst & Co.).

Haas, E. (1970) 'The Study of Regional Integration: Reflections on the Joy and Anguish of Pretheorising', *International Organisation*, 4: 607–46.

Hamann, K. and J. Kelly (2003) 'The Domestic Sources of Differences in Labour Market Policies', *British Journal of Industrial Relations*, 41(4): 639–63.

Hattersley, R. (2005) 'Forget David Blunkett. The resignation we're all waiting for is Tony Blair's', *The Times*, 3 November.

*Hay, C. (1999) *The Political Economy of New Labour: Labouring under False Pretences?* (Manchester: Manchester University Press).

Hay, C., M. Lister and D. Marsh (eds) (2004) *State Theory: Theories and Issues* (Basingstoke: Palgrave Macmillan).

Hayek, F. (1976) *Law, Legislation and Liberty, Vol. II: The Mirage of Social Justice* (London: Kegan Paul).

Heery, E. (2005) 'Trade Unionism under New Labour', The Shirley Lerner Memorial Lecture 2005, 12 May (Manchester: Manchester Industrial Relations Society).

Heffernan, R. (1999) *New Labour and Thatcherism: Political Change in Britain* (New York: St Martin's Press).

*—— (2001) *New Labour and Thatcherism* (Basingstoke: Palgrave Macmillan).

—— (2005) 'Exploring (and Explaining) the British Prime Minister', *British Journal of Politics and International Relations*, 7: 605–20.

Hickson, K. (2007) 'Reply to Stephen Meredith, Mr Crosland's Nightmare? New Labour and Equality in Perspective', *British Journal of Politics and International Relations*, 9: 165–8.

Hills, J. (2004) *Inequality and the State* (Oxford: Oxford University Press).

Hindmoor, A. (2004) *New Labour at the Centre* (Oxford: Oxford University Press).

Hinton, J. (1983) *Labour and Socialism* (Brighton: Wheatsheaf).

HM Government (1969) *In Place of Strife: A Policy For Industrial Relations*, Cmnd. 3888 (London: HM Stationery Office).

HM Revenue and Customs (2007) 'Am I eligible for Child Tax Credit?' http://taxcredits.direct.gov.uk/what_child_eligible.html.

HM Treasury (1997) *Fiscal Policy: Lessons from the Last Economic Cycle* (London: HM Treasury).

—— (2003a) *The Strength to Take the Long-term Decisions for Britain: Seizing the opportunities of the global economy. Pre-Budget Report 2003*. Cm. 6042 (London: The Stationery Office).

—— (2003b) *UK Membership of the Single Currency: An Assessment of the Five Economic Tests*. Cm. 5776 (London: HM Treasury).

—— (2005) *Britain Meeting the Global Challenge: Enterprise, fairness and responsibility: Pre-Budget Report, December 2005*. Cm. 6701 (London: HM Treasury).

—— (2006) *Investing in Britain's Potential: Building our long-term future. Pre-Budget Report 2006*. Cm. 6984 (London: The Stationery Office).

—— (2007a) *Budget 2007. Building Britain's Long-term Future: Prosperity and fairness for families. Economic and Fiscal Strategy Report and Financial Statement and Budget Report.* HC 342 (London: The Stationery Office).

—— (2007b) *Public Expenditure Statistical Analyses 2007.* Cm. 7091 (London: The Stationery Office).

—— (2008) *Statement: Northern Rock,* 21 January (London: HM Treasury).

Hobsbawm, E. (1977) 'Some Reflections on "The Break-up of Britain"', *New Left Review,* 105: 3–24.

Home Office (2006) *Countering International Terrorism: The United Kingdom's Strategy* (London: Home Office). http://security.homeoffice.gov.uk/news-publications/ publication-search/general/Contest-Strategy.

House of Commons Defence Committee (HCDC) (2007) *The Future of the UK's Strategic Nuclear Deterrent: The White Paper.* HC 225-I (London: HMSO). www. publications.parliament.uk/pa/cm200607/cmselect/cmdfence/225/225ii.pdf.

House of Commons Treasury Committee (2007) *The 2006 Pre-Budget Report, Second Report of Session 2006–07.* HC 115 (London: The Stationery Office).

Howell, C. (2001) 'The End of the Relationship between Social Democratic Parties and Trade Unions?', *Studies in Political Economy,* 65: 7–37.

—— (2004) 'Is There a Third Way for Industrial Relations?', *British Journal of Industrial Relations,* 42(1): 1–22.

Howorth, J. (2004) 'Discourse, Ideas and Epistemic Communities in European Security and Defence Policy', *West European Politics,* 27(2): 211–34.

Huber, E. and J. Stephens (2001) *Development and Crisis of the Welfare State* (Chicago: University of Chicago Press).

Hutton, W. (1995) *The State We're In* (London: Cape).

IMF (2006) 'IMF Executive Board Concludes 2005 Article IV Consultation with the United Kingdom', Public Information Notice No.06/24, 3 March (Washington, DC: International Monetary Fund).

—— (2007) *United Kingdom: 2006 Article IV Consultation – Staff Report,* March (Washington, DC: International Monetary Fund).

Institute for Fiscal Studies (2006) *The IFS Green Budget: January 2006* (London: Institute for Fiscal Studies).

—— (2007a) *Public Finance Bulletin,* 20 March (London: Institute for Fiscal Studies).

—— (2007b) *Poverty in the UK* (London: Institute for Fiscal Studies).

—— (2007c) *The IFS Green Budget 2007* (London: Institute for Fiscal Studies).

Ipsos MORI (2007) *Government Delivery Index: Satisfaction with the Chancellor Trends* (London: Ipsos MORI).

Jenkins, S. (2006) *Thatcher & Sons: A Revolution in Three Acts* (London: Allen Lane).

Jones, B. (2004) 'Devolution' in B. Jones, D. Kavanagh, M. Moran and P. Norton (eds), *Politics UK,* 5th edn (London: Pearson Education), pp. 305–25.

Joseph, K. (1976) *Stranded on the Middle Ground* (London: Centre for Policy Studies).

Joseph, K. and J. Sumption (1978) *Equality* (London: John Murray).

Kampfner, J. (2004) *Blair's Wars* (London: Free Press).

*Keegan, W. (2003) *The Prudence of Mr Gordon Brown* (Chichester: John Wiley).

Klein, R. (2005) 'Transforming the NHS' in M. Powell, L. Bauld and K. Clarke, *Social Policy Review 17* (Bristol: The Policy Press).

Labour Party (1937) *Labour's Immediate Programme* (London: Labour Party).
—— (1945) *Let Us Face the Future* (London: Labour Party).
—— (1959) *Labour Party Annual Conference Report* (London: Labour Party).
—— (1963) *Labour Party Annual Conference Report* (London: Labour Party).
—— (1983) *The New Hope for Britain* (London: Labour Party).
—— (1996a) *New Politics, New Britain – Restoring trust in the way we are governed* (London: Labour Party).
—— (1996b) *New Labour, New Life for Britain* (London: Labour Party).
—— (1996c) *New Britain: Labour's Contract for a New Britain* (London: Labour Party).
—— (1997) *New Labour, Because Britain Deserves Better* (London: Labour Party).
—— (2005) *Britain Forward Not Back* (London: Labour Party).
—— (2007) *Financial Statements for the Year Ended 31 December 2006* (London: Labour Party).
Lambeth, B. (2001) *NATO's Air War for Kosovo: A Strategic and Operational Assessment* (Santa Monica: RAND).
Laws, D. (2004) 'Reclaiming Liberalism: A Liberal Agenda for the Liberal Democrats' in P. Marshall and D. Laws (eds), *The Orange Book: Reclaiming Liberalism* (London: Profile Books).
Lawson, N. (1992) *The View from No.11: Memoirs of a Tory Radical* (London: Bantam Press).
Le Grand, J. (2003) *Motivation, Agency and Public Policy: Of Knights and Knaves, Pawns and Queens* (Oxford: Oxford University Press).
*Lee, S. (2007) *Best for Britain? The Politics and Legacy of Gordon Brown* (Oxford: Oneworld).
Leonard, D. and S. Crosland (1999) *Crosland and New Labour* (London: Macmillan Press).
Leopold, J. (2006) 'Trade Unions and the Third Round of Political Fund Review Balloting', *Industrial Relations Journal*, 37(3): 190–208.
*Levitas, R. (1998/2005) *The Inclusive Society? Social Exclusion and New Labour* (Basingstoke: Palgrave Macmillan).
Lister, R. (2004) *Poverty* (Cambridge: Polity Press).
Little, R. and M. Wickham-Jones (eds) (2000) *New Labour's Foreign Policy. A New Moral Crusade?* (Manchester: Manchester University Press).
Lonsdale, D. (2007) 'Strategy: The Challenge of Complexity', *Defence Studies*, 7(1): 42–64.
Ludlam, S. and A. Taylor (2003) 'The Political Representation of the Labour Interest in Britain', *British Journal of Industrial Relations*, 41(4): 727–49.
*Ludlam, S. and M. Smith (eds) (2004) *Governing as New Labour* (Basingstoke: Palgrave Macmillan).
Ludlam, S., M. Bodah and D. Coates (2002) 'Trajectories of Solidarity: Changing union–party linkages in the UK and the USA', *British Journal of Industrial Relations*, 4(2): 222–44.
Luttwak, E. (1987) *Strategy: The Logic of War and Peace* (Cambridge: The Belknap Press).
Macintosh, J. (1978), 'Has Social Democracy Failed in Britain?', *Political Quarterly*, 2(1): 259–70.
*MacIntyre, D. (1999) *Mandelson and New Labour* (London: HarperCollins).

Magnette, P. and K. Nicolaidis (2004) 'The European Convention: Bargaining in the Shadow of Rhetoric', *West European Politics*, 27(3): 381–404.

*Mandelson, P. (2002) *The Blair Revolution Revisited* (London: Politico's).

Marquand, D. (1988) *The Unprincipled Society: New Demands and Old Politics* (London: Fontana).

—— (1991) *The Progressive Dilemma* (London: Heinemann).

—— (2000) 'Democracy in Britain', *Political Quarterly*, 71(3): 268–76.

Marsh, D., D. Richards and M. Smith (2003) 'Unequal Plurality: Towards an asymmetric power model of British politics', *Government and Opposition*, 38(3): 306–32.

Marshall, P. (2006) 'Foreword' in J. Astle, D. Laws, P. Marshall and A. Murray (eds), *Britain After Blair: A Liberal Agenda* (London: Profile Books).

Marshall, P. and D. Laws (eds) (2004) *The Orange Book: Reclaiming Liberalism* (London: Profile Books).

McIlroy, J. (2007) *Defend the link – but make it work for union members! Cash for honours, New Labour and the Trade Unions*, 5 March (London: Union Ideas Network).

McKay, S. (2001) 'Between Flexibility and Regulation: Rights, Equality and Protection at Work', *British Journal of Industrial Relations*, 39(2): 285–303.

McSmith, A. and P. Wintour (1999) 'Straw set for climbdown on refugee laws', *Observer*, 2 May.

Mellows-Facer, A. (2006) *General Election 2005: House of Commons Library Research Paper 05/33* (London: House of Commons Library).

Meredith, S. (2006) 'Mr Crosland's Nightmare? New Labour and Equality in Historical Perspective', *British Journal of Politics and International Relations*, 8(2): 238–55.

Metcalf, D. (2004) 'British Unions: Resurgence or Perdition?', Provocation Series 1 (1). (London: The Work Foundation).

Michie, J. and D. Wilkinson (1994) 'The Growth of Unemployment in the 1980s' in J. Michie and J. Grieve-Smith (eds), *Unemployment in Europe* (London: Academic Press).

Millen, R. and S. Metz (2004) *Insurgency and Counterinsurgency in the 21st Century: Reconceptualizing Threat and Response* (Carlisle, PA: Strategic Studies Institute). www.au.af.mil/au/awc/awcgate/ssi/insurgency21c.pdf.

Minister of Reconstruction (1944) *Employment Policy*. Cmnd. 6527 (London: HM Treasury).

Ministry of Defence (1998) *Strategic Defence Review* (London: Ministry of Defence). www.mod.uk/DefenceInternet/AboutDefence/CorporatePublications/PolicyStr ategyandPlanning/StrategicDefenceReview.htm.

—— (2006) 'The Future of the United Kingdom's Nuclear Deterrent' (London: The Stationery Office). www.mod.uk/DefenceInternet/AboutDefence/ CorporatePublications/PolicyStrategyandPlanning/DefenceWhitePaper2006 Cm6994.htm.

Ministry of Justice (2007) *The Governance of Britain*, Cm. 7170 (London: The Stationery Office).

Minkin, L. (1991) *The Contentious Alliance* (Edinburgh: Edinburgh University Press).

Moore, M. (1995) *Creating Public Value: Strategic Management in Government* (Cambridge: Harvard University Press).

Morgan, K. (1997) *Callaghan: A Life* (Oxford: Oxford University Press).

Morrison, J. (2001) *Reforming Britain: New Labour, New Constitution?* (London: Reuters).

Mullard, M. (1993) *The Politics of Public Expenditure* (London: Routledge).

Mullard, M. and R. Swaray (2006) 'The Politics of Public Expenditure from Thatcher to Blair', *Policy and Politics*, 34(3): 495–515.

Murray, W. and M. Grimsley (1994) 'Introduction: On Strategy' in W. Murray, M. Knox and A. Bernstein (eds), *The Making of Strategy: Rulers, States, and War* (Cambridge: Cambridge University Press).

Murray, W. and R. Scales Jr. (2003) *The Iraq War: A Military History* (Cambridge: Belknap Press).

Nash, D. (2006) 'Recent Industrial Relations Developments in the UK: Continuity and Change under New Labour 1997–2005', *Journal of Industrial Relations*, 48(3): 401–14.

*Naughtie, J. (2001) *The Rivals* (London: Fourth Estate).

Neunreither, K. and A. Weiner (eds) (2000) *European Integration After Amsterdam* (Oxford: Oxford University Press).

Nicol, M. (2006) 'War in Afghanistan: Britain's Vietnam', *Mail on Sunday*, 1 October. www.dailymail.co.uk/pages/live/articles/news/news.html?in_article_id=407830&in_page_id=1770.

Norman, P. (2005) *The Accidental Constitution: The Story of the European Convention* (2nd edn) (Brussels: EuroComment).

Norton, P. (1975) *Dissension in the House of Commons, 1945–1974* (London: Macmillan).

—— (1978) *Conservative Dissidents* (London: Temple Smith).

—— (1987a) 'Prime Ministerial Power: A Framework for Analysis', *Teaching Politics*, 16: 325–45.

—— (1987b) 'Mrs Thatcher and the Conservative Party: Another Institution Handbagged?' in K. Minogue and M. Biddiss (eds), *Thatcherism: Personality and Politics* (London: Macmillan).

—— (1990) '"The Lady's Not for Turning": But What About the Rest of the Party? Mrs Thatcher and the Conservative Party 1979–89', *Parliamentary Affairs*, 43: 41–58.

—— (2000) 'Barons in a Shrinking Kingdom: Senior Ministers in British Government' in R. Rhodes (ed.), *Transforming British Government*, Vol. 2: *Changing Roles and Relationships* (London: Macmillan Press).

—— (2003a) 'Governing Alone', *Parliamentary Affairs*, 56: 543–59.

—— (2003b) 'The Presidentialisation of British Politics', *Government and Opposition*, 38: 274–8.

*—— (2007a) 'Tony Blair and the Constitution', *British Politics*, 2: 269–81.

—— (2007b) 'The Constitution' in A. Seldon (ed.), *Blair's Britain 1997–2007* (Cambridge: Cambridge University Press).

O'Hara, G. and H. Parr (2006) *The Wilson Governments 1964–1970 Reconsidered* (London: Routledge).

Oborne, P. (2004) 'Blair downgraded the Labour whips – and now he is paying the price', *Spectator*, 17 January.

Office for National Statistics (2006) *The Pink Book: 2006 Edition* (London: The Stationery Office).

—— (2007a) *Consumer Price Indices: June 2007* (London: Office for National Statistics).

—— (2007b) *Public Sector Finances June 2007* (London: Office for National Statistics).

—— (2007c) *Business Investment: Revised results – 4th quarter 2006* (London: The Stationery Office).

—— (2007d) *International Comparisons of Productivity, 21 February 2007* (London: The Stationery Office).

—— (2007e) *Balance of Payments 4th Quarter and Annual 2006* (London: The Stationery Office).

—— (2007f) *Balance of Payments 1st Quarter 2007* (London: The Stationery Office).

—— (2007g) *Balance of Payments 3rd Quarter 2007* (London: The Stationery Office).

—— (2007h) *Business Investment: Revised results – 3rd quarter 2007* (London: Office for National Statistics).

—— (2007i) *Public Sector Finances: November 2007* (London: Office for National Statistics).

Office of the Leader of the House of Commons (2007) *The Governance of Britain – The Government's Draft Legislative Programme*, Cm. 7175 (London: The Stationery Office).

Osborne, G. (2007) Speech to the Confederation of British Industry, London, 7 March.

Panitch, L. and C. Leys (2001) *The End of Parliamentary Socialism: From New Left to New Labour* (London: Verso).

*Peston, R. (2005) *Brown's Britain* (London: Short Books).

Peters, R. (2004) 'In Praise of Attrition', *Parameters* (Summer). http://carlisle-www.army.mil/usawc/Parameters/04summer/peters.htm.

Pimlott, B. (1992) *Harold Wilson* (London: HarperCollins).

Plant, R. (1991) 'Criteria for Electoral Systems: The Labour Party and Electoral Reform', *Parliamentary Affairs*, 44(4): 549–57.

*—— (2001) 'Blair and Ideology' in A. Seldon (ed.), *The Blair Effect* (London: Little, Brown & Co.).

PM Press Conference (2005) Prime Minister's Press Conference, 5 August. www.number-10.gov.uk/output/Page8041.asp.

Pollock, A. (2004) *NHS plc: The Privatisation of our Health Care* (London: Verso).

Porter, A. and R. Winnett (2008) 'Northern Rock crisis dents London's reputation', *Daily Telegraph*, 11 January.

Powell, J. (2007) 'Why the West should not fear to intervene', *Observer*, 18 November.

*Powell, M. (1999) *New Labour, New Welfare State? The 'Third Way' in British Social Policy* (Bristol: Policy Press).

Powell, M., L. Bauld and K. Clarke (2005) *Social Policy Review 17* (Bristol: Policy Press)

Power Inquiry (2005) *Power to the People* (London: The Power Inquiry).

*Pym, H. and N. Kochan (1998) *Gordon Brown: The First Year in Power* (London: Bloomsbury).

Radice, G. (2004) *Diaries 1980–2001* (London: Weidenfeld & Nicolson).

Rawls, J. (1999) *The Law of Peoples* (Cambridge: Harvard University Press).

*Rawnsley, A. (2000) *Servants of the People: The Inside Story of New Labour* (London: Hamish Hamilton).

—— (2001) *Servants of the People* (London: Penguin Books).

Record, J. and W. Terrill (2004) *Iraq and Vietnam: Differences, Similarities, and Insights* (Carlisle, PA: Strategic Studies Institute).

Reid, J. (2005) 'Social Democratic Politics in an Age of Consumerism', speech at Paisley University, 27 January. www.labour.org.uk/ac2004news?ux_news_id=socdemoc.

*Rentoul, J. (1996) *Tony Blair* (London: Warner Books).

—— (2001) *Tony Blair: Prime Minister* (London: Little, Brown & Co.).

Richards, S. (1996) 'In search of cracks on tax', *New Statesman*, 26 July.

Riddell, P. (2001) 'Blair as Prime Minister' in A. Seldon (ed.), *The Blair Effect* (London: Little, Brown & Co.).

—— (2004) *Hug Them Close: Blair, Clinton, Bush and the 'Special Relationship'* (London: Politico's).

—— (2005) *The Unfulfilled Prime Minister* (London: Politico's).

—— (2007) 'No, minister – six other mandarins have doubts on Brown', *The Times*, 21 March.

Russell, M. (2000) *Reforming the House of Lords* (Oxford: Oxford University Press).

SCCA (2006) *Seventh Report of the Select Committee on Constitutional Affairs* (London: HMSO).

Seldon, A. (1997) *Major: A Political Life* (London: Weidenfeld and Nicolson).

*—— (ed.) (2001) *The Blair Effect* (London: Little, Brown & Co.).

*—— (2004) *Blair* (London: Free Press).

*—— (ed.) (2007) *Blair's Britain* (Cambridge: Cambridge University Press).

*Seldon, A. and D. Kavanagh (eds) (2005) *The Blair Effect 2001–2005* (Cambridge: Cambridge University Press).

Shaw, E. (2002) 'New Labour – New Democratic Centralism?', *West European Politics*, 25(3): 147–70.

—— (2004) 'What Matters is What Works: The Third Way and the Case of the Private Finance Initiative' in W. Leggett, S. Hale and L. Martell (eds), *The Third Way and Beyond: Criticisms, Futures and Alternatives* (Manchester: Manchester University Press).

*—— (2008) *Losing Labour's Soul? New Labour and the Blair Government 1997–2007* (London: Routledge).

Sherman, J. (2002) 'Jumble of No. 10 policy units is "taxing Whitehall"', *The Times*, 13 March.

Short, C. (2004) *An Honourable Deception?* (London: The Free Press).

Sissons, M. and P. French (1964) *Age of Austerity: 1945–51* (Harmondsworth: Penguin).

Skelcher, C. (2005) 'Jurisdictional Integrity, Polycentrism, and the Design of Democratic Governance', *Governance*, 18(1): 89–110.

Skidelsky, R. (2004) *John Maynard Keynes 1883–1946 Economist, Philosopher, Statesman* (London: Pan Books).

Smith, J. (1993) *A Citizens' Democracy* (London: Charter 88).

—— (2005) 'A Missed Opportunity? New Labour's European Policy 1997–2005', *International Affairs*, 81(4): 703–21.

Smith, P. and G. Morton (2001) 'New Labour's Reform of Britain's Employment Law', *British Journal of Industrial Relations*, 39(1): 119–38.

—— (2006) 'Nine Years of New Labour: Neo-liberalism and Workers' Rights', *British Journal of Industrial Relations*, 44(3): 401–20.

Sorensen, E. and J. Torfing (2005) 'The Democratic Anchorage of Governance Networks', *Scandinavian Political Studies*, 28(3): 195–218.

Stelzer, I. (ed.) (2004) *Neo-Conservatism* (London: Atlantic Books).

*Stephens, P. (2004) *Tony Blair: The Price of Leadership* (London: Politico's).

Stoker, G. (ed.) (2000) *The New Politics of British Local Governance* (Basingstoke: Palgrave Macmillan).

—— (2004) 'Is Regional Government the Answer to the English Question?' in S. Chen and A. Wright (eds), *The English Question* (London: Fabian Society), pp. 72–89.

—— (2005) 'Public Value Management: A New Resolution of the Democracy/ Efficiency Trade-off' (Institute for Political and Economic Government, University of Manchester). www.ipeg.org.uk/Paper%20Series/PVM.pdf.

Straw, J. (2002) Speech by the Foreign Secretary at the Hague, 21 February (London: Foreign and Commonwealth Office).

Stubb, A. (2000) 'Negotiating Flexible Integration in the Amsterdam Treaty' in K. Neunreither and A. Weiner (eds), *European Integration After Amsterdam* (Oxford: Oxford University Press).

Summers, H. Jr. (1982) *On Strategy: A Critical Analysis of the Vietnam War* (Novato: Presidio).

Sylvester, R. (1999) 'Blair told: listen to us or lose', *Independent*, 20 June.

Taylor, G. (ed.) (1999) *The Impact of New Labour* (London: Macmillan).

Taylor, M. (2001) 'Too Early to Say? New Labour's First Term', *Political Quarterly*, 72(1): 5–17.

Taylor, R. (2001a) 'Employment Relations Policy' in A. Seldon (ed.), *The Blair Effect: The Blair Government 1997–2001* (London: Little, Brown & Co.).

—— (2001b) 'The Future of Work–Life Balance', an ESRC Future of Work Programme Seminar Series (Swindon: Economic and Social Research Council).

—— (2005) 'Mr Blair's Business Model – Capital and Labour in Flexible Markets' in A. Seldon and D. Kavanagh (eds), *The Blair Effect 2001–2005* (Cambridge: Cambridge University Press).

Teson, F. (1997) *Humanitarian Intervention: An Enquiry into Law and Morality* (Dobbs Ferry: Transnational Publishers).

Thatcher, M. (1996) *The Keith Joseph Memorial Lecture: Liberty and Limited Government* (London: Centre for Policy Studies).

Theakston, K. and M. Gill (2006) 'Rating 20th-Century British Prime Ministers', *British Journal of Politics and International Relations*, 8(2): 193–213.

Thompson, R. (1966) *Defeating Communist Insurgency: Experiences from Malaya and Vietnam* (London: Macmillan Press).

Towers, B. (1999) 'The Most Lightly Regulated Labour Market', *Industrial Relations Journal*, 30(2): 82–95.

Toynbee, P. (2003) *Hard Work* (London: Bloomsbury).

Treasury Committee (2007) *Uncorrected transcript of Oral Evidence given by Mervyn King, Governor of the Bank of England and Sir John Gieve, Deputy Governor (Financial Stability), Bank of England.* HC56-iv (London: The Stationery Office). Available online: www.publications.parliament.uk/pa/cm/cmtreasury.cm.

Tyrie, A. (2007) *Mr Blair's Poodle* (London: Centre for Policy Studies).

Undy, R. (1999) 'New Labour's "Industrial Relations Settlement": The Third Way?', *British Journal of Industrial Relations*, 37(2): 315–36.

—— (2002) 'New Labour and New Unionism, 1997–2001: But is it the same old story?', *Employee Relations*, 24(6): 638–55.

Vickers, R. (2000) 'Labour's Search for a Third Way in Foreign Policy' in R. Little and M. Wickham-Jones (eds), *New Labour's Foreign Policy. A New Moral Crusade?* (Manchester: Manchester University Press).

Vigor, A. (2005) 'An Anglo-Social Approach to Work', *Public Policy Research*, 12(3): 158–67.

Wallace, W. (2005a) 'The Collapse of British Foreign Policy', *International Affairs*, 82(1): 53–68.

—— (2005b) 'Foreign and Security Policy' in H. Wallace, W. Wallace and M. Pollack (eds), *Policy-Making in the European Union* (5th edn) (Oxford: Oxford University Press).

Walzer, M. (1980) 'The Moral Standing of States: A Response to Four Critics', *Philosophy and Public Affairs*, 9(3): 209–29.

Watt, N. (2007) 'Grim Brown warns of a bleak year for Britain', *Observer*, 30 December.

*White, S. (ed.) (2001) *New Labour: The Progressive Future?* (Basingstoke: Palgrave Macmillan).

The White House (2002) *The National Security Strategy of the United States* (Washington, DC: Office of the President of the United States).

*Wickham-Jones, M. (ed.) (2000) *New Labour's Foreign Policy: A New Moral Crusade?* (Manchester: Manchester University Press).

Williams, P. (1982) *Hugh Gaitskell* (Oxford: Oxford University Press).

*—— (2005) *British Foreign Policy Under New Labour, 1997–2005* (Basingstoke: Palgrave Macmillan).

Wilson, H. (1971) *The Labour Government 1964–70: A Personal Record* (London: Weidenfeld and Nicolson).

Wintour, P. (2008) 'Hain: I take full responsibility for undeclared donations', *Guardian*, 11 January.

Wright, A. (1997) *Who Wins Dares: New Labour – New Politics* (London: Fabian Society).

Wylie, J. (1967) *Military Strategy: A General Theory of Power Control* (Annapolis: Naval Institute Press).

Yonwin, J. (2005) *UK Election Statistics: 1918–2004. House of Commons Library Research Paper 04/61* (London: House of Commons Library).

YouGov (2007) *Sunday Times Survey Results, 20th–27th December 2007* (London: YouGov).

—— (2008) *YouGov Survey Results, 7th–9th January 2008* (London: YouGov).

Zielonka, J. (2004) 'Europe Moves Eastward: Challenges of EU Enlargement', *Journal of Democracy*, 15(1): 22–35.

Index

Compiled by Sue Carlton